FAITH-BASED MARKETING

Faith-Based Marketing

The Guide to Reaching 140 Million Christian Consumers

Greg Stielstra
Bob Hutchins

WILEY

John Wiley & Sons, Inc.

Published by John Wiley & Sons, Inc., Hoboken, New Jersey.
Published simultaneously in Canada.

For general information on our other products and services or for technical support, please contact our Customer Care Department within the United States at (800) 762-2974, outside the United States at (317) 572-3993 or fax (317) 572-4002.

Wiley also publishes its books in a variety of electronic formats. Some content that appears in print may not be available in electronic books. For more information about Wiley products, visit our web site at www.wiley.com.

ISBN: 978-0-470-42210-6

Printed in the United States of America.
10 9 8 7 6 5 4 3 2 1

CONTENTS

ACKNOWLEDGMENTS

This book was possible thanks to the contributions of many people. We would like to thank Lyn Cryderman, a friend and our collaborative writer. Lyn turned our thoughts, ideas, and recordings into this book. He did a superb job and delivered on time. If you need a writer, I recommend him highly.

Others who helped by providing interviews or information include John Frost and Alan Mason of Goodratings, Dick Wells of The People's Church, Ron Forseth and James Long of Outreach Marketing, Wayne Hastings of Thomas Nelson Publishers, Mike Reed of Northwood Church, Paul Martin of Advocace Media, Chuck Wallington of Christian Supply and The Covenant Group, Carl Dunn of Carlton Dunn and Associates, Brad Abare of Church Marketing Sucks, Dr. Larry Poland of Master Media International, Lesley Burbridge-Bates of L.A.B. Media, Ken Ott and Jim McCaslin at Buzzplant. Beth Cathey of Renegade Idea Group, James Edward Hicks III of the U.S. Army, Tom Betts of Cornerstone University and Thecommon.org, Mark Rice of CRC Publications, Brent High of Third Coast Sports, and Chris Collinson of Collinson Publishing also contributed. Thank you to Gary Moore for financial insights and for making connections to key people, Veda Brown from Blackgospelpromo.com and Greg Schlueter.

A special thanks to Ryan Dunham and his team at David C. Cook for help with our ministry leader's survey. We couldn't have done it without them.

We would like to thank our team at Wiley, Richard Narramore our editor, and Deborah Schindlar, Chris Wallace, Ann Kenny, Peter Knapp, and Amy Packard for production, cover designs, editorial assistance, marketing, and PR. We are glad to be working with the world's leading business book publisher.

I (Greg) would like to personally thank my wonderful wife Amy, son Dominic, and daughters Shelby and Darby for their love and support and for loving me even when the pressure of deadlines made me cranky.

I (Bob) would like to personally thank my loving wife Kellie, for being an amazing support and encouragement. And to my children, Riley, Lauren, and Sean, thanks for letting Dad take time away to work on this. You are my inspirations. I also would like to thank the BuzzPlant and Ground Force Network team—Bob Strachan, Andrea Lopez, Jim McCaslin, Ken Ott, Brian Wojcik, Susan Bill, Mike Heath, and Matt Manes. You are all amazing!

Finally, we would like to thank you, the reader, whether you come from business or the faith community for your interest in this topic, for the bridges you will soon build between business and the church, and for the ways your efforts will reconcile those two worlds to their mutual benefit.

INTRODUCTION

In 1975, an organization known as Family of Faith Ministries began printing the "Christian Yellow Pages." It was an effort to help Christians identify and hopefully shop at businesses owned by Christians. They knew that 77 percent of Americans define themselves as Christians and deduced that if they shopped at Christian businesses, those businesses would reap a windfall of sales. With all due respect to Family of Faith Ministries, we think they were only half right. True, Christians represent more than half of all consumers and contribute hundreds of millions of dollars to the economy. But Christians are just like any other person—they are discerning shoppers who put price, value, customer service, and convenience ahead of loyalty to businesses that happen to be owned by Christians.

We think it's great that Christians are marketing to other Christians, but it begs the question: Why aren't *you* marketing to Christians?

Between the two of us, we have nearly 30 years of experience marketing to Christians. We have learned that the 140 million Americans who attend church on a weekly basis are a *hidden* and sometimes mysterious market that promises enormous returns to businesses that develop relationships with them and effectively market their products or services in ways that speak to their needs. In this book, we will help you find them and take the mystery out of working with them.

I (Greg) spent 17 years as a marketing executive for two of the world's largest Christian publishing companies. Not only did one of those companies consistently run a business with double-digit profits, we consistently placed religious books on the *New York Times* Best Seller list, including a book—*The Purpose Driven Life*—that outsold any book published by any company, Christian or secular. Our success, along with a couple of other leading Christian publishing companies, led many of the New York-based general publishers to create divisions that published and sold books specifically for Christians. Seeing how marketing to Christians could increase sales for their companies, publishers in Manhattan began singing "Gimme that old time religion" in the halls of their towering office buildings.

While Greg was working for a Christian company, Bob started Buzzplant, an Internet marketing agency, and began helping companies like Time-Life and General Motors reach the faith-based community. At first, I ran into a sentiment that you might be feeling right now: why should I waste my precious marketing dollars on church folk? But after some startling success stories along the way—including my work with the producers of Mel Gibson's blockbuster movie, *The Passion of the Christ*—several Fortune 500 companies soon got it: Christians are ordinary, normal consumers who need what we produce.

We have divided this book into three sections. The first section, "Meet the Christian Consumer," gives you a basic understanding of who Christians are and what they believe. You might be tempted to skip over this, but if you're not a regular churchgoer, don't. To be a successful marketer to the faith-based community, you need to develop relationships with churches and Christian organizations, and this section will make that much easier for you.

The second section, "How to Market to Christians," is more tactical. It will get into the nitty-gritty of actually promoting your product or service to churches and Christian organizations. The final section, "Key Resources for Marketing to Christians" is the largest collection of resources designed specifically for marketing to Christians that you'll find anywhere. In fact, there was much more information than we could fit in this book so we built a companion web site at www.faithbasedmarketing.com. At the site you'll find lists of Christian retailers; media outlets; marketing organizations; public relations firms; music festivals; and thousands of churches, ministries, and parachurch organizations. Not only does it provide contact information, but we also invited each organization to complete its own profile with information about its mission, interests, needs, and restrictions so that you'll know exactly how best to partner with each group.

Throughout the book we use statistics to explain the size of the Christian market. To avoid confusion you only need to understand two numbers: 77 percent of Americans (approximately 231 million) consider themselves Christian and 40 to 45 percent (approximately 140 million) attend worship services weekly.

We believe that great marketing always produces a win-win. If you follow our advice in this book, your company will make more money from increased sales. But Christian consumers will also win because you will have learned how to meet their needs in ways that respect their beliefs and make their lives better.

In our opinion, that's what marketing is all about.

PART I

MEET THE CHRISTIAN CONSUMER

CHAPTER ONE

THE OVERLOOKED 140 MILLION PERSON MARKET

It's Super Bowl Sunday, and crowds begin to gather. Space by space parking lots fill as attendants direct vehicles to open spots farther and farther from the huge edifice. People stream from their cars and head toward the sidewalks—a confluence of humanity emptying into a sea of men and women pressing toward the entrances.

Pulled irresistibly by their common passion, people all across the country follow a similar ritual. Many attend in person; still others listen on the radio or watch on television or the Internet. In total, more than 140 million men, women, and children take part in this weekend spectacle. They are rich and poor, young and old, black, white, Asian, and Hispanic. They form a collection of consumers whose combined spending power totals more than $5.1 trillion annually!

It was the Holy Grail for marketers, but is not what you think. It was Super Bowl Sunday all right, but this was not the Super Bowl. Kick-off for the big game was still more than eight hours away.

This is the church.

Companies that will spend more than $3 million for a 30-second spot during the Super Bowl are missing an even greater opportunity. Surprisingly, the Super Bowl isn't the biggest marketing opportunity of the year. It's not even the biggest opportunity on Super Bowl Sunday. A prize far more tantalizing arrives *every* Sunday morning for those who know where to find it and how to access its power. If you haven't spent much time in church—or even if you regularly attend your church of choice—you may not think of *church* as a potential target for your marketing efforts, but several recent success stories have awakened many in the business world to the size and scope of the U.S. Christian community.

Fully nine out of ten Americans say they believe in God or a higher power, according to most polls. Despite growing religious diversity, the vast majority of Americans define themselves as Christians. In an NBC/*Wall Street Journal* survey conducted in September 2008 (http://www.online.wsj.com/public/resources/documents/WSJ_NBCPoll_092408.pdf), three-fourths of the respondents identified themselves as Protestants or Catholics. And reliable pollsters such as the Gallup Poll, the Institute for Social Research's World Values, and the National Opinion Research Center report that from 40 to 45 percent of Americans regularly attend church. Not exactly a tiny niche when it comes to marketing, as many large companies have discovered.

Fueled by a church-based campaign, *The Purpose Driven Life*, a book explaining God's five purposes for successful living, sold 30 million copies in three years to become the fastest-selling hardcover in U.S. history—faster than any Harry Potter book, faster than a John Grisham novel, faster even than the Bible, the all-time best-selling book in history. The book's author and publisher set aside conventional marketing wisdom to rely on their vast knowledge of the church and the behavior of Christian consumers, demonstrating an important principle we will discuss in this book: To reach this $5.1 trillion market, you need to understand it. Intimately. And we will show you how to do that.

While *The Purpose Driven Life* is a phenomenal success story, it's not the only one. Mel Gibson's blockbuster movie, *The Passion of the Christ*, grossed over $551 million in its first nine weeks despite the use of obscure foreign languages, English subtitles, harsh criticism, and a comparatively modest marketing budget. Instead of wasting precious marketing dollars on traditional strategies, Gibson and his producers focused their efforts on church leaders and Christian opinion shapers who then became voluntary consumer evangelists to more than half of the U.S. population that regularly attend church. Just one example: 100,000 pastors were e-mailed, asking them to mention the movie in a Sunday sermon; much smarter—and far less expensive—than running trailers on expensive television ads. But you don't just randomly collect e-mail lists and start plugging your product. You need to understand the difference between a dispensational Baptist and a Missouri Synod Lutheran, or you'll do more harm than good. And we can help you with that, too.

Still need convincing that faith-based marketing is more than a niche? Look at the past two presidential elections. In 2004, many pundits credit the Bush campaign for tapping into the power of the nation's Bible-belted red states. And both candidates in 2008 poured millions of dollars into trying to reach the nation's evangelicals, a subset of the total Christian market. And whether you think it was genuine or pandering, both candidates took great pains to explain their own Christian beliefs, further indication that they understood the power of the faith-based community.

On any given Sunday, 44 percent of Americans are in church. Can you name a larger group that demonstrates such a singular behavior so consistently? Okay, nearly nine out of ten workers commute to work by car, which is why radio is such a great way to market to consumers. Have you ever targeted your marketing to Hispanics (14 percent of the population), African Americans (11 percent), or retirees (12 percent)? You should, but what if you could reach a demographic larger than those three combined and do it effectively and economically? You can, but you may need to change the way you think about those "religious people."

Christians are not the tiny lunatic fringe so many once thought. Rather, they form a global network of immense size and power comprised of every country, every social or ethnic group, and every economic stratum. Christians now number 2.3 billion or one out of every three people on the planet. That's nearly as large as China and India combined.

Okay, maybe you're not the marketing director for a Hollywood film company or a multinational, global conglomerate; instead, you own a hardware store in a midsize city. Can you grow your business by focusing some of your marketing efforts on people of faith? Absolutely. Forty-four percent of the people living in your community go to church regularly and take their faith seriously. They need to buy garden tools, snow shovels, and paint, just like anyone else. They can choose from among several retailers to buy those products, but if you could learn how to reach them effectively—if you can develop a relationship with them—they will choose you over your competition. But it takes more than putting a religious symbol in a display ad in your local newspaper. Just like any other affinity group, you need to know who they are, what's important to them, and what their needs are. You also need to know how to communicate with them without offending them.

In November 2007, the home improvement chain, Lowe's, sent out a flier that contained an advertisement for "Family Trees," which looked an awful lot like the trees people decorate in their homes during the Christmas season. Lowes received more than 100,000 e-mails from Christians protesting the removal of the word "Christmas," and Lowe's responded with an apology and a return to calling Christmas trees, well, Christmas trees. "It was not our intention to try and be politically correct or to take the significance of Christ out of Christmas," company spokeswoman Karen Cobb replied. Regardless of their reasons for changing the name of Christmas trees, Lowe's learned an important lesson: if you want to do business with Christians, you need to know what's important to them or you could unintentionally offend them. Had they done some research before selecting a new name for Christmas trees, they would have spared themselves a major public relations blunder.

On a more positive note, consider how many local grocery stores have reached out to churches by offering to donate a percentage of their revenue on a particular day. The church promotes this for several weeks ahead of time (free advertising), and on the appointed day the grocery store has a record number of customers show up (more traffic). Increased sales for the store, greater exposure to new customers, and the church gets a nice check to help send their youth group on a mission trip.

The buying power of Christians is evident in the way teenage Christians purchase music. According to Dan Michaels, vice-president of marketing and promotion for INO Records, a Christian label, it's not unusual for a Christian recording artist to sell into the millions of CDs. One of his own artists, the popular band, Mercy Me, has sold more than four million CDs since they were launched in early 2,000. "Christian parents support their kids' interest in our music because of the positive message it conveys," Michaels explained. "You don't always have that with other genres."

People of faith are the largest niche in your market. Whether you are selling cars or carpet, they represent a significant portion of your overall market. You can hope that your current marketing strategies will reach them, and they might. But your competition will be doing the same thing, so to grow your business, you need an edge. We hope to give you that edge in this book, but first, a few words of caution.

COMMERCIALIZING CHRISTIANITY?

We almost hesitate to describe the size of the faith-based market because it could produce unhelpful responses from two groups.

Businesses might mistakenly see only dollar signs, while Christian consumers might only see businesses seeing dollar signs. In other words, everyone might jump to the conclusion that the sole purpose of this book is to help businesses make a lot of money off of Christians. To be absolutely truthful, if you apply the principles we outline in this book, your business *should* benefit financially, but our overarching purpose isn't to help businesses make more money by *exploiting* Christians because that will only produce short-term gains and long-time resentment. Money is basically the best measure for how well a business conducts itself in every area, from producing a product to marketing it, to selling it to treating its employees fairly, and so on. We want to help your business grow, which means you will make more money, and we feel the best way to do that is to understand and respect the faith-based community. So here's what we would say to both groups who may be either overly optimistic or skeptical about mixing business and faith.

First, to businesses: if you're only interested in exploiting Christians, this book will not be much help. We won't provide you with ways to exploit Christians or anyone else. However, if you are interested in creating long-term, loyal customers who will choose your business over your competition, this book is for you. Our goal is to help you better understand the Christian community—their needs, their aspirations, and the reservations some have about you—so that you make more money. If you have a product or a service that will improve the lives of Christians—one that they will truly value—and you carefully follow the principles we outline, you will increase your chances of partnering with Christians in a manner that will result in long-term financial growth.

And to our fellow Christians who may be suspicious about mixing commerce and faith, our goal is to erase the unfair caricatures you've endured and give the business community a more accurate picture of you, your faith, and your traditions. We believe that if businesses know you better, they can serve you better. If you receive better service from a company, you are more likely to do business with it because your needs are being met. So in the end, both you and the business win, and that is our motivation for writing this book—to build a better relationship between business and believers so that both benefit. If a business truly understands Christians then it will be more likely to accommodate them and less likely to do things that offend. If Christians understand businesses better, they will be able to make more intelligent choices about the products and services they buy.

Marketing to Christians (or Anyone Else)

John B. is an independent insurance agent in a midsize city in Illinois. As competition in his area increased, he began looking for better ways to target his modest advertising budget. Sitting in church one Sunday, he looked around and thought there had to be a way to reach people just like him with information about the various types of insurance he sold. Feeling only mildly guilty for daydreaming about his job during church, he nonetheless made a mental note to call the pastor Monday to see what it would cost to place a banner ad on the church's web site. He was surprised—and a little miffed—to learn that the church had a policy forbidding advertising on its web site. But then he had an idea: "Maybe I could teach a free one-day seminar on insurance." He called the pastor, who loved the idea, and four weeks later John was in a meeting room explaining insurance to 45 couples.

Even though John was active in his church, he didn't fully understand the challenges he would face marketing to his own church. While it is true that the church represents a huge opportunity for successful marketing, ignorance of the church could close that door of opportunity. Many churches are a little leery of mixing business with ministry, even to the point of not allowing any kind of commercial enterprise to access its constituents. There are legitimate reasons for this but before we share them with you, we need to be clear about what we mean when we say marketing.

Many consumers—Christian and otherwise—view marketing as an annoying attempt to trick them into buying something they don't need. Unfortunately, we've met people in the marketing profession who pretty much live down to that description. But as a professional marketer, you know that any attempt to force people to buy something, exploit them, or otherwise get them to do something they don't want to do will ultimately fail. The best example of that occurred when Coca-Cola, normally brilliant marketers, tried to force "New Coke" on their consumers in 1985. After secretly working on a new formula to replace the most popular cola beverage in the world, they rolled out New Coke on April 23 with a massive television and print ad campaign, which was flatly rejected by consumers. Sales of the new beverage plummeted as people began paying up to $30 a case for the *old* coke and hoarding as much as they could get their hands on, fearing it would never again be available. Less than three months later, on July 11, Coca-Cola pulled the plug on its new product, replacing it on store shelves with the old formula, which it dubbed "Classic Coke" to further reassure consumers their favorite cola was back. According to Sam Craig, professor of marketing and international business at the Stern School of Business of New York University, Coca-Cola marketers failed to ask the critical question of its consumers: "Do you *want* a new Coke?"

Successful marketing always begins with the consumer—understanding what she needs or values. To the extent that you will become successful in marketing to Christians, you will need to understand them, know what they are passionate about, respect what they believe and why, and discover what they need to improve their lives. Like Coca-Cola, you might think every Christian organization in the country will love your product, but unless you're willing to make the commitment to fully understand this dynamic consumer group, you run the risk of wasting a lot of your company's time and resources.

Marketing is identifying people with needs and connecting them to the product or service that can satisfy their needs. The more profoundly you meet their need, the more satisfied they'll be; the more satisfied they are, the more people they will tell; the more people they tell, the more product you will sell. But it all begins with people, not product. Christians are more likely to support this approach to marketing because it is almost indistinguishable from ministry; it's essentially the mission of the Christian church—find people in need and meet their needs.

FAITH-BASED SKEPTICISM

Okay, so we're on the same page about the definition of marketing, and you're all set to develop a killer marketing plan to inform this very large audience about your product or service. Don't be surprised if you initially find it difficult to get your foot in the church door. Even if you have a great product that Christians truly value and need, you may still face resistance in trying to do business with churches and Christian organizations, and there are two primary reasons for this.

First, some churches are wary of mixing ministry with commerce because of an important story in the Bible: "Money Changers in the Temple." It's pretty important to many Christians, so you should understand it as well. Here's what happened 2,000 years ago that still influences the way some Christians view commerce in the church: Jesus went to the temple to pray and got angry when he saw the merchants doing business there and literally chased them away. This story has special significance because it is the only record in the entire Bible of Jesus, the "Prince of Peace," becoming angry.

A superficial reading of this story suggests it is wrong to do any kind of business in a religious setting, and as recently as a generation ago, many churches disallowed *any* buying and selling on their premises. Now you could choose to view this separation of church and commerce as strange or even silly, or you can begin to recognize that Christians are highly principled people who respect what they believe to be biblical truth. Which response do you think will lead to a better relationship with faith-based ministries? Good—so let's continue with your first theology lesson.

Think about it. Jesus drove businessmen out of the church, and you're trying to get the church to help you sell RVs to its members. Not the best conditions for a great marketing plan, but don't give up. Most churches that used to prohibit commerce in church now allow it, and here's why. Trustworthy Bible scholars have discovered that the merchants who set up shop in the synagogue were not reputable businessmen, but crooked clerics who deliberately cheated these religious consumers, especially widows and the poor. It was customary then to charge temple goers a temple tax before they could enter to worship and pray. Further, the temple clergy required that tax to be paid in temple currency rather than conventional money, which meant they had to exchange their money for temple currency. Pretty slick scheme, huh? The money changers, who were actually the religious leaders, knew the temple goers had no other way to change their currency and charged grossly inflated rates for their temple money. The real message of this story was a warning against dishonesty and exploitation in a house of worship, especially that which is directed at the most vulnerable.

So what's the big deal and why did we lay some theology on you? Even though most churches will welcome your efforts to do business with them, that Bible story still carries some influence, especially on *how* you interact with them, which we will cover in this first section.

On the practical level, Christians may seem a little resistant to business because church leaders view the protection of their parishioners as part of their role as pastor or shepherd, and they worry that businesses are only interested in exploiting their flocks. Here's where the stereotype of crook comes into play, strengthened by churchgoers' own isolated experiences with unethical businesses. A few years ago in Grand Rapids, Michigan, a businessman began approaching people who attended church, offering an investment opportunity that would produce huge returns. Many good church folk who looked at their inadequate retirement accounts felt this would be a good way to prepare for a better retirement and bought shares in his company. What they didn't know was that this man was using their investment dollars to deliver "returns" to other investors he had approached a few weeks earlier—a classic Ponzi scheme causing hundreds of individuals to lose millions of dollars. It only takes a few experiences like this for churches to build an impenetrable wall between them and any outside business. If church leaders initially seem reluctant to work with you, understand that they are only doing their job as shepherds protecting their flocks and will gradually become more receptive if you are open and honest with them.

CASE STUDY: FAITH NIGHT

The Nashville Sounds minor league baseball team had a hunch they could sell more tickets if they marketed to Christians; they just didn't know how. They had seen the demographics: 3,000 churches within a two-hour drive of Nashville. Their first effort—offer a dollar discount to anyone carrying a church bulletin—fizzled. At best, they sold about 200 extra tickets at these "Faith Nights."

Enter Brent High, former youth pastor and executive director of Third Coast Sports Foundation. The Nashville Sounds hired him in December of 2002 and for the next three months never saw him. That's because he was in his car, crisscrossing middle Tennessee, southern Kentucky, and northern Alabama asking pastors what it would take to get more Christians to the ballpark. They told him: help us reach more people with the gospel, not just put on a show. So Brent went to work, lining up great bands to perform, getting players who were Christians to talk about their faith after the game, and in 2003, sponsored five Faith Nights designed to help churches accomplish what was important to them.

It worked.

In 2002, the average Friday night attendance at Greer Stadium was 4,800. For the five Friday night Faith Nights, attendance nearly doubled, averaging just under 11,000. Attendance at the final Faith Night in August was a standing room only 13,000! Corporate sponsorships for Faith Night that first year produced $11,000. Three years later that number climbed to $84,000. And growing.

(Continued)

Four seasons after his first Faith Night, High and his company were sponsoring 175 events, adding major league baseball (Los Angeles Dodgers, Cincinnati Reds, Colorado Rockies, Atlanta Braves, Minnesota Twins, Texas Rangers, Kansas City Royals, and Washington Nationals), arena football, and hockey, which expanded Faith Nights to 60 different teams.

"Christians are out there in huge numbers," High explained for anyone interested in marketing to them. "They are organized, they have e-mail lists, and they have buses to transport their members. As long as you are sincere and approach them in the right way and respect their beliefs, you will be successful."

INTEGRITY WINS

We've covered a good deal of ground here, from the huge opportunity to demographics to theology, but you may have recognized a common theme: you will not get very far with people of faith if you don't have a relationship with them, and you can't have a relationship with them if you don't get to know them. And as you gain a better understanding of Christians, you will discover that they are very much like any other consumer group. They want you to be honest, to conduct your business with integrity, and to respect their values and beliefs. You don't have to share their beliefs in order to market to them—nor should you try to give the impression you do. Christians will have greater respect for you and be more receptive to your business if you do not try to be something you aren't.

As we will discover in the next chapter, Christians have been easy targets for ridicule, usually based on unfair stereotypes and caricatures. Those stereotypes have not only been a disservice to Christians, they may have given you a completely inaccurate view of the very people you'd like to reach.

One final note: the Christian community is a richly diverse group of people who share a common belief in God (approximately half are Catholics and half are Protestants). You may have a friend who attends church, and from your relationship with that person, you might think you have a pretty good working knowledge of Christianity. Or you may even be a regular attender of a particular church and are already beginning to develop a strategy for marketing your product to "the church."

So just to see how well you know this 140 million person market, take the "Faith-Based Marketing Quiz" on page 13–16. Where else can you learn if you're a saint or the Antichrist?

Remember, our purpose for writing this book is to build a better relationship between business and believers by helping them truly understand each other. It works both ways. While you may not fully understand Christians, they also have misconceptions about you. They may seem like kooks to you, and you may appear to be crooks to them, so now let's take a look at how we earned these labels and what you can do about them.

FAITH-BASED MARKETING QUIZ

How well do you understand the faith community? Could you safely connect to this market or would you commit a fatal misstep? Take this quiz and find out:

1. Who preached the Sermon on the Mount?

   A. Martin Luther King, Jr.
   B. Jesus
   C. Billy Graham
   D. Moses

2. Christians and Muslims worship the same God. *True or False?*

3. If you invited people from a Southern Baptist, Methodist, Missouri Synod Lutheran, and Catholic Church to the same gathering, which church's members are least likely to attend?

   A. Southern Baptist
   B. Methodist
   C. Missouri Synod Lutheran
   D. Catholic Church

4. You are selling guitar amplifiers to church worship bands. Which of the following churches won't even consider buying your product?

   A. Churches of Christ
   B. Assemblies of God
   C. Presbyterian
   D. Reformed Church in America

(Continued)

5. You are hosting an event and plan to invite people from the local Jewish Synagogue, Baptist, Seventh Day Adventist, and Catholic churches. Which of the following days would maximize turnout?

   A. Thursday night
   B. Friday night
   C. Saturday night
   D. Sunday night

6. Which of the following is *not* among the Ten Commandments?

   A. Thou shalt not kill.
   B. Do unto others as you would have them do unto you.
   C. Honor your father and mother.
   D. Do not covet.

7. Evangelical Christians believe that a person who performs good works on earth will go to heaven. True or False?

8. Which of the following groups is *not* recognized as a Christian denomination by most other churches?

   A. Covenant
   B. Church of Jesus Christ of Latter-day Saints
   C. Anglican Communion
   D. Wesleyan Reform Union

9. What is mammon?

   A. Bread that fell from Heaven to feed the Israelites during their exodus from Egypt
   B. Money
   C. A godly mother serving as spiritual head of the household
   D. An idol worshipped by the Philistines

10. If you are planning a campaign for De Beers or Maybelline, which of the following groups should you ignore?

   A. Catholics
   B. United Pentecostal
   C. Assemblies of God
   D. All of the above

Was it tougher than you thought? Look at the answers to see how you did. Give yourself one point for each correct answer and find your score on the chart that follows.

Answers: 1-B, 2-False, 3-C, 4-A, 5-A, 6-B, 7-False, 8-B, 9-B, 10-B

Score	Title	Comment
8–10	Saint	Why did you waste your money on this book?
5–7	Pharisee	Don't get cocky—you know just enough to be dangerous.
3–5	Boycott magnet	Start practicing your apology for the press conference.
0–2	Antichrist	Those protestors on CNN are in front of *your* building!

REVIEWING THE QUIZ

1. Jesus preached the Sermon on the Mount. Its text is recorded in the Bible in the book of Matthew. It is considered the greatest recorded collection of Jesus' words and advice.

2. The God of the Bible is "triune," a single deity comprised of three persons: God the father, God the son (Jesus), and the Holy Spirit. The God of the Koran, by contrast, is not triune. Muslims believe Jesus was merely a prophet, but not God. Neither do Muslims recognize the Holy Spirit. By definition then, Christians and Muslims worship a different God.

3. Don't expect many members of the local Missouri Synod Lutheran Church to attend your event if you also invite other denominations. They are discouraged from attending religious events with people from other denominations.

4. The Church of Christ won't buy any guitar amplifiers. They restrict their worship to singing without any musical accompaniment (a cappella) because this was the style used by the first century church.

5. If you want Jews, Baptists, Catholics, and Seventh Day Adventists to attend your event, hold it on a Thursday night. The Jewish Sabbath runs from Friday to Saturday evening. Seventh Day Adventists worship on Saturday, Baptists on Sunday, and many Catholics attend Saturday evening Mass. Thursday is the only night that won't conflict with someone's worship service or observation of the Sabbath.

(Continued)

6. "Do unto others as you would have them do unto you" is a very good idea, but it is not among the Ten Commandments. It's more a suggestion, coming from the New Testament, known to most people as the Golden Rule.

7. According to evangelical Christians, good works will *not* get you to heaven. It's not like a ledger where if good deeds exceed the bad we enjoy a positive balance that earns admission to eternal paradise. The Bible teaches that everyone has sinned and that Jesus was sent to earth to endure punishment for our sin (the Crucifixion). We only need to accept his free gift of salvation to enjoy eternal life. Right living is simply how we express gratitude toward God for saving us from our sins.

8. Even though "Jesus Christ" is part of their name, many Christians don't consider Mormons to be a Christian denomination because their beliefs differ fundamentally from core Christian tenets.

9. The Bible teaches that man cannot serve both God and mammon (money). An appeal to greed may work with some segments of the population, but be careful not to use it to appeal to Christians.

10. Don't bother promoting jewelry or makeup to United Pentecostals because they will not adorn their bodies with either. You might tell them about your new line of combs and brushes though, because Pentecostal women don't cut their hair.

CHAPTER TWO

LOSE YOUR FAITH

EVERYTHING YOU THINK YOU KNOW ABOUT CHRISTIANS IS WRONG

If you live in Manhattan—or have visited this vibrant city—you have probably seen him on Times Square. He has a long beard and is dressed in shabby clothes, and he's holding a giant placard on a wooden stick: *Sinners Repent!* On the "kook scale," he's a few clicks to the left of the guy who plays the guitar in the middle of the street in cowboy boots and underpants.

Or maybe you were clicking the remote control on your wide screen late one night and stumbled across a television program where a guy with a bad haircut and polyester suit was selling white towels he had blessed that would bring you material wealth if you would just send him $20 plus shipping and handling.

Okay—maybe you missed those, but we're sure you've seen at least one episode of *The Simpsons,* and if you have, you certainly know who Ned Flanders is. He's the Christian neighbor; a dork so out of touch with the real world he doesn't even notice when Homer makes fun of him.

If you haven't thought very seriously about marketing to the faith-based community, who can blame you? If every Christian was like Ned Flanders, there just aren't enough cheesy products to keep them supplied. Then again, if Christians are gullible enough to pay $20 for a 50¢ hand towel…

BEYOND THE STEREOTYPES

One of our goals for this book is to bridge the gap between Christians and the business community that may not exactly be at odds with each other, but clearly don't understand each other. Ironically, you will find many Christians in the business community and vice versa, but the two groups remain distant—even a little skeptical of each other—due primarily to the perceptions of each that we see in the media.

A friend of ours who worked at a large Christian publishing company told me about a dinner he had with some colleagues from the secular publisher who had recently purchased his company: "After introductions and some small talk, I asked them what they thought about their company's purchase of our company. There was a bit of a pause, and you could almost see them working up their courage to be truthful. The first one spoke: 'Well, word spread throughout the building that we'd better clean up our language when you guys came to town.' Another: 'I was surprised when I first saw you and you weren't wearing polyester!' (laughter) Then another: 'I honestly considered taking down the Al Gore poster I had on the wall of my office.' Finally: 'Everyone thought you'd come in here with your Bibles and lecture us about how to live.'"

In other words, they thought our friend was an alien, and to them, he really was. That's because everything they knew about Christians came from the media and popular culture. Pat Robertson personally asks God to send a hurricane away from his ministry headquarters; and suddenly, Christians are those strange people who think God plays with hurricanes for fun. Benny Hinn sells "prayer cloths" on television to people so they can use them to perform miracles; and overnight, Christians become ignorant bumpkins led by snake-oil salesmen. A Baptist church excommunicates a member for voting Democrat; and now, every Christian votes Republican because his pastor tells him to. Members of the media, practically illiterate when it comes to Christianity, are ill equipped to cover this beat, so they jump all over the most spectacular—and admittedly kooky—stories, unwittingly turning stereotype into reality.

The late Jerry Falwell was a favorite target of the press, and he obliged by occasionally making some ridiculous statements. Perhaps his biggest blunder was publicly suggesting that one of the characters in the popular children's television program, *Teletubbies*, was gay. Predictably, the press had a heyday with this, as they did whenever he made similar outlandish statements. As they should. Public figures are fair game both when they do something commendable or when they embarrass themselves. But what is *not* fair is to only report on those indiscretions, helping to create an unbalanced and inaccurate picture of that person. You may not have liked his politics, but Jerry Falwell was a visionary man of God who built a world-class university; led a dynamic church that improved the lives of thousands; quietly reached out to unwed mothers, the homeless, and the starving, and formed an organization, Moral Majority, that gave a voice in politics to many Christians who felt ignored. As a college student, he sought and received permission from the administration to use an empty classroom for *four hours a day* just to pray, but profiles of him in newspapers and on television never reported that fact about him. Despite his legacy as a godly leader who counseled heads of state and used his organization's resources to help the helpless, you probably think of him as just another religious kook because the media tended to focus only on his controversial statements.

The authors have gone to church all our lives, and in our professional lives we've hung around all kinds of Christians. Were there some kooks along the way? You bet. But Greg also went to a big public university and saw his share of students staggering back to the dorm after a night of some serious drinking; but it wouldn't be fair to say all college students are binge drinkers, just as it isn't accurate to let that weird guy at church who wore a bolo tie and thick glasses represent the rest of us.

The media's fascination with the bizarre and beguiling works both ways. Thanks to front-page stories about overpaid CEOs of failed banks being rewarded with megamillion dollar golden parachutes, it's not difficult to see why so many people have a jaded view of business. Our work has us rubbing shoulders with executives in some of the biggest companies in the United States; and yes, we've run into a few shady characters but the vast majority of these people are hard working, compassionate, and honest people whose everyday lives in business and their communities do not make front-page news.

Largely, due to incomplete and inaccurate media coverage, Christians are viewed as slightly weird, fanatical, isolated, unsophisticated, culturally deficient, mean spirited, and most important, small. So from a commercial perspective, why bother to target this insignificant group of wackos?

Business, on the other hand, is often presented as greedy, ethically corrupt, driven only by profit, materialistic, and run by a pack of white collar criminals. From the pew and the pulpit, the world of business is a necessary evil landscape to be traveled with caution.

Christians are kooks, and businesspeople are crooks. This offers a convenient dichotomy that gives permission to each group to ignore the other, or at least to hold each other at arm's length. But like most dichotomies, it's false and prevents both groups from experiencing the benefits of a healthy relationship. By allowing the media to act as the liaison between them, neither group has bothered to find out what's true about the other.

ANATOMY OF A KOOK

If Christians make up 77 percent of the U.S. population, then either more than half the population are bona fide weirdos or somehow we have a failure to communicate. Actually, members of the media communicate quite effectively, and they are probably the biggest reason why the faith community is regarded so negatively. Here's how fairly ordinary, decent, sensible people have been turned into an unsophisticated, marginalized minority.

First, and most important, the news media doesn't understand people of faith and has done very little to increase its knowledge of churchgoers. For example, consider the media's experience with evangelicals, a subset of those 140 million church folks. According to Larry Poland of Master Media, his company's research found that only 2 to 3 percent of the people who work in media are evangelical Christians. That compares with about 26 percent of the general population who are evangelicals. He added, "Most media don't have *any* evangelical friends, don't read evangelical publications, and have never been to church." So, for more than half of the nation's regular churchgoers, members of the media are basically ignorant. They just don't know evangelicals or their world, they have no idea what constitutes a news story from that very large community, and yet they report what they determine is *news* about evangelicals.

The same could be said of the media's understanding of Catholics and other subsets of the overall Christian population.

Imagine sending a reporter who has never seen a football game and knows nothing about the sport to cover the Super Bowl. As the quarterback dropped back to pass, we'd probably get a report on what the cheerleaders were wearing, and that's exactly what happens when members of the media attempt to cover Christian ministries. Instead of reporters practically living with their assigned beats, as in sports, business, and political reporting, members of the media spend little time in church, know very few of the leaders and key organizations in the Christian community, which contributes to incomplete and inaccurate reporting.

Another reason you might think Christians are a small handful of kooks is the media's focus on the shocking, the tragic, the unusual, and the bizarre, and here we defend the media somewhat. Many people criticize the media for only reporting bad news. Actually, the role of media is to report news, and much of what happens in any community just isn't news. For example, every day more than 1,200 passenger jets take off and land safely at Chicago's O'Hare International Airport. If you picked up a *Chicago Tribune* after one of those days of successful take offs and landings, you won't see a headline screaming, "Planes Land Safely at O'Hare!" But let just one make a tragic mistake, and headlines all over the world will cover it. Does that mean members of the news media are only interested in bad news? Not necessarily. A plane landing safely is not news because it happens all the time. A plane crash is news because it happens so rarely.

Because Christians are ordinary people going about their lives like any other citizen, they do not generate much news. Hundreds of thousands of pastors and church leaders demonstrate exemplary behavior week after week, year after year, but you seldom see news stories extolling the virtues of U.S. religious leaders. But when one of those leaders is caught stealing from the offering, it makes the front page (as it should). On the one hand, it's comforting not to see many news stories about Christians because it confirms what we believe about people of faith: They're pretty ordinary—real salt-of-the-earth-type people. But the effect of this type of coverage, coupled with media ignorance of the church, results in the public developing a warped perception of Christians.

As if these two factors haven't distorted your view of the faith-based community, another media tendency creates a perfect storm for misinformation—magnifying erroneous coverage. It works like this: All news media can be divided into reporters—people who actually cover a story— and repeaters, and there are precious few reporters. The rest of the media cover the original coverage, accepting it as accurate and passing it on to the rest of the world. So if you have a reporter covering a Christian ministry, and he or she knows little about Christian faith and practice, the likelihood of error is increased—and then those errors are happily repeated by other journalists covering the coverage.

In 2004, the company Greg worked for was about to release an updated translation of the Bible that, among other things, corrected some faulty scholarship regarding references to gender. We spent hundreds of thousands of dollars in a campaign to help educate media and consumers about the features of this new translation. Despite the fact that changes in references to gender amounted to less than 3 percent of the overall updating, a careless reporter inaccurately used the words "gender neutral" rather than "gender accurate" to describe the translation. I'm sure he thought he was being fair and politically correct, but he was dead wrong in his description, and after his story released, practically every other media outlet repeated the error. And because the original reporter had no idea that various conservative denominations are wary of anything that appears to be tampering with the biblical view of gender, he could never have imagined how his choice of words would create a gigantic controversy and cost our company millions of dollars in lost sales and efforts to correct his inaccurate story. He used the only language he knew to describe a product that was foreign to him, and his fellow journalists simply repeated his mistake into millions of households across the nation.

WHAT YOU NEED TO KNOW

You don't need to know all the ins and outs of every Christian denomination to successfully develop relationships with them. But one thing is certain. If you have based your opinion of the Christian community on the common misperceptions and stereotypes generated by the media, you will never receive a fair hearing. While the following list is not exhaustive, it covers some of the more prevalent caricatures of Christians and will begin to help you gain a better understanding of this market.

- *All Christians in the United States are white.* While it is true that the majority of Christians in the United States are white, the demographics of Christianity fairly closely reflect the culture at large. In fact, the percentages of Christians within the African American and Hispanic communities are larger than the percentage of Christians within the white community.
- *All Christians are politically conservative.* Not necessarily. Among evangelicals, who comprise slightly more than half of all Christians in the United States, the majority are Republicans, though that has changed slightly in recent years. But when you include all Christians, roughly half are conservative and half are liberal.
- *Christians are uneducated.* Big mistake to assume that. Christians of all persuasions in the United States have been passionate about education. The majority of private colleges and universities in the United States were started by Christian denominations or organizations, and in many cities, the highest achieving elementary and

secondary schools are Christian schools. Most pastors in the United States hold a master's degree; many also have earned a doctorate.

- *Christians are isolated or cultic.* With 44 percent of Americans attending church regularly, it's a safe bet that if you work at a General Motors plant, almost half your fellow workers are Christians. If you're strolling through a shopping mall in Dallas, you're probably surrounded by Christians who are buying shoes, cameras, and perfume. If you attend a football game at Lambeau Field, probably everyone in the stadium is a Christian because Packers fans obviously have a special relationship with the Almighty. Our point: If you want to become better acquainted with the faith-based community, get to know your neighbor because chances are, he's a Christian. We're everywhere!

- *Christians are cheap.* There's an apocryphal story about a waitress in a hotel that hosted a Christian convention who declared, "I never make much money in tips when the Christians are in town." Like most apocryphal stories, there's probably an element of truth in it, but Christians are like most consumers. They buy virtually every product that any other consumer buys, and like many consumers, they try to be frugal. It would be a mistake, however, to ignore this market because you think they're cheap. Frugal or not, they spend approximately $5.1 trillion annually.

- *Christians are gullible.* Some businesses make the mistake of thinking Christians are an easy mark. Just put a cross on your product, and it will sell. That might work in the short run for a small percentage of Christians, but we wouldn't recommend it as your marketing plan. Churches are huge consumers of everything from electronic equipment to furniture to cleaning supplies to health insurance for their employees. When they make these purchases, they know they are spending the hard-earned money of their parishioners, so they ask questions, compare products, and seek counsel from professionals in their congregations. They will likely be your most discerning customers, which means the more professional you are, the better chance you have of earning their business.

- *Christians are fanatics.* Sometimes the press will report on a story like the one where a family refused to allow their seriously ill daughter to be treated by a physician because they believed God would heal her. We would agree that this type of behavior, extremely rare among Christians, borders on the fanatical. But again, these kinds of stories lead people to the false conclusion that all Christians are fanatics.

CASE STUDY: CHURCHES ARE BIG BUSINESS

A midwestern church with a weekly attendance of 2,920, with another 3,500 watching its Sunday services online has an annual operating budget of $5.3 million to run a 115,000-square-foot facility encompassing nine buildings with 84 rooms that accommodate eight weekly services and 151 different classes trampled by 375,000 pairs of feet every year. Maintaining this ministry requires:

- Paid staff of 35: 18 full-time and 17 part-time employees
- $1,225 per day for utilities
- $500 per day for cleaning
- $350 per day for maintenance, repair, and replacement
- $64,000 per year in insurance
- $37,000 per year for security
- 75+ computers, 3 servers, and 20 printers
- 5 copiers making 700,000 copies per year

RETHINKING THE CHRISTIAN CONSUMER

Businesses target their products to all sorts of consumer groups such as women, teenagers, outdoor enthusiasts, African-Americans, music buffs, jazz music buffs, jazz played on primitive instruments music buffs, jazz played on primitive instruments from the Ivory Coast music buffs—but they have generally ignored one of the largest consumer groups in the nation: the 140 million people who regularly go to church. So businesses miss a great opportunity to present their products to a vibrant new audience, and Christians—including the thousands of nonprofit Christian organizations—are unaware of products and services that could make their lives—and organizations—better.

So as you read this book, we'd like to ask you to set your stereotypes aside, not so much for the sake of Christians, but for your potential success as a business. We don't blame you for being a little nervous about marketing your products to Christians if you think they're just a tiny segment of the population who act strange. They aren't, and in the next chapter, we'll peel back the layers to show you who Christians really are and how you can get to know them even better.

CHAPTER THREE

MEET THE *REAL* CHRISTIAN CONSUMER

THEY ARE NO DIFFERENT. THEY ARE SO DIFFERENT.

A friend of mine (Greg), who is an executive with one of the major Christian music labels, was in New York City recently to make a presentation to the top marketing person at one of the largest cellular phone companies. If I mentioned the name, you would recognize it immediately, but I don't want to embarrass the marketing executive or the company. My friend was there to secure a deal to provide this company with ringtones from his top artists. And for good reason. According to Jupiter Research, ringtone revenue in 2003 was $91 million, and by 2009, it is projected to grow to $724 million. The ringtone business is huge and almost entirely made up of profits, so both the cell phone company and my friend's music label stood to benefit from this meeting. As my buddy tells it, he thought he had delivered a winning presentation but when he wrapped it up, the marketing guy just laughed.

"Christians don't have cell phones!" he scoffed.

Here's a very smart executive being given an opportunity to add significantly to his bottom line, but instead, he blows it because he actually believes that Christians are these backwoods, unsophisticated, technological Luddites who apparently still use rotary phones! Yet this story illustrates the huge gulf separating the Christian community from the business community, so in this chapter we'll do our best to describe who Christians are, what they believe, how they are very much like you, and how they are different. Knowing the truth will make your job marketing to Christians easier and more productive.

WOULD JESUS USE AN iPOD?

If a guy as smart as the cell phone company executive believes Christians are in the Stone Age when it comes to technology, he's probably not alone. Your own company could be missing huge opportunities because you have this image of people who don't use computers, have never heard of Al Gore's famous invention, and therefore, can't be reached by e-mail or sent to a web site to learn about your product. Not only is this a tiny niche, according to this view of Christians, but they still order their clothes from the Sears catalog! Why bother?

Just for the record, we decided to do a little sanity check regarding the whole cell phone issue. In an online survey we conducted for other reasons, we added this question at the end: Do you own a cell phone? This survey only went to self-professed evangelical Christians, and 98 percent of them answered that they did, indeed, own a cell phone—the exact same percentage as the general population. Okay, as marketing guys we do a lot of research, but maybe the sample was too small or we skewed it somehow. So just to be safe, we consulted one of the premier researchers of the Christian community, George Barna of Barna Research, and as a result of several studies his organization conducted on Christians and their use of technology, he concluded that the percentage of Christians who regularly use technology is statistically identical to the percentage of those in the general population. In other words, faith plays no significant role in whether a person uses technology. Except in one category. The percentage of Christians who access spiritual content through *podcasts* is more than double the percentage of the general population. If it's something they are passionate about, Christians will aggressively use technology to learn more about it. That last sentence is a good one to file away for your future marketing efforts.

Christians buy and use computers, modems, printers, scanners, wireless routers, iPods, BlackBerries, and fax machines. They search the web using Google; purchase books and other products on Amazon, eBay, and Craigslist; download and print coupons; and book their own hotels and flights. They click on banner ads, open e-mail targeted to them, connect with like-minded people on Facebook and MySpace, read blogs, listen to podcasts, and watch videos on YouTube.

So if Christians aren't the backwoods Neanderthals you thought they were, who are they really?

WHAT DO WE MEAN WHEN WE SAY CHRISTIAN?

Describing Christians is like describing ice cream—there are many different flavors. When we refer to Christians, we include all of the following groups:

Catholics: The largest Christian denomination in the world, as well as in the United States. Their clergy are usually called priests. Going to church is called "going to Mass." Liturgical, or formal, worship style. Demographically diverse with strong representation in immigrant communities (Polish, Italian, Hispanic).

Orthodox: Very small in number in the United States, and similar to Catholics. Primarily an immigrant church: Greek Orthodox, Russian Orthodox, and so on.

Mainline Protestants: Methodist, Presbyterian, Lutheran, Episcopalian, and United Churches of Christ. Nearly every city and town in the United States will have at least one of these churches. Generally considered liberal in their theology and politics. Emphasis on social outreach, ministry to the poor, justice issues.

Evangelical: Generally smaller denominations and independent churches that focus on introducing others to faith. Most Southern Baptists, the largest Protestant denomination, consider themselves Evangelicals. Think Billy Graham.

Fundamentalist: Most churches with the word "Baptist" in their name are fundamentalist. Conservative theologically and politically. Strong emphasis on traditional family values and morally upright behavior.

Charismatic/Pentecostal: Characterized by their enthusiastic worship style and belief in supernatural healing. Generally the most ethnically diverse among Protestant churches in the United States. Most Christian television has its roots deep in this movement. A dynamic and fast-growing segment of U.S. Christianity.

(Continued)

Seeker or Mega Church: Very large churches (up to 100,000 members in a single church) that deliberately avoid traditional forms of church in order to attract people who do not attend church or have been turned off by it. Informal worship style characterized by upbeat music, use of the arts and visual media, and short, practical sermons. Think Rick Warren and Joel Osteen.

African American Church: Formed of necessity by segregation. Distinguished by lively worship style, upbeat music, powerful and entertaining preaching, and strong family values. Primarily urban with a strong tradition of community involvement.

Emerging Church: Relatively new movement focusing on 20- to 30-year-old demographic. Nontraditional, often meeting in converted warehouses and urban buildings furnished with couches instead of pews and blending traditions from many of the above churches. Strong emphasis on socially responsible living and rejection of materialism.

Parachurch organizations: In addition to the different churches, a very large and robust group of nonprofit organizations work alongside churches in a variety of ways. Ranging from relief organizations such as Catholic Relief Services and World Vision, to youth organizations like Youth Specialties and Young Life, to organizations devoted to family values such as Focus on the Family.

Ordinary People Just Like You

Because people of faith really do try to live up to the ethical teachings of the New Testament, the rest of the population tends to view Christians as "holier than thou" or too good to be true. Which has always puzzled us because even those who claim no religious belief certainly attempt to live morally upright lives, yet no one thinks of them as being strange or out of touch. The reality is that we're all human, and Christians live pretty much the way everyone else in the United States lives, a fact that has been verified by nearly every study comparing the lifestyles of Christians to the rest of the population.

For example, because the church teaches the virtues of marriage and frowns on divorce, you might think that the divorce rate among Christians would be significantly lower than that of people without religious beliefs. Regretably, it isn't. Again, according to pollster George Barna who has made a career of studying Christians, the percentage of Christians who have experienced a divorce is practically identical to the percentage of the population at large—approximately 33 percent for both groups. That's not something we're particularly proud of, but it shows that Christians struggle with many of the same things that challenge the rest of the population.

In a related Barna study of lifestyle choices for Christians and non-Christians, the two groups tended to exhibit more similarity than difference in their choices. For example, when it comes to reaching out to help the disadvantaged, both groups had similar percentages of their populations who volunteered to help the poor. Also, both groups had roughly the same numbers of people who exercised regularly. In evaluating fifteen moral behaviors, Christians are statistically indistinguishable from non-Christians on most of the behaviors studied. When it comes to boycotting products, gambling, and purchasing lottery tickets, both groups were identical. Even in areas where you would normally think there was a big difference between the behavior of Christians and non-Christians, the difference wasn't all that great. For example, 39 percent of the nonchurched acknowledged smoking a cigarette or cigar during the previous week, compared to 28 percent of the churched population (so much for the "we don't smoke and we don't chew" refrain attributed to Christians). Fifteen percent of the non-churched reported drinking enough alcohol to be deemed legally intoxicated during the previous week compared to 6 percent of the churched. Both groups had identical percentages when it came to attending a twelve-step or recovery group. While both groups use the Internet equally, Christians (2 percent) tend to pirate music less than non-Christians (9 percent).

Conventional wisdom suggests that Christians overwhelmingly vote Republican, and while it is true that evangelicals—a subset of U.S. Christianity—tend to vote Republican, Barna's research found that among *all* Christians, 37 percent would vote Democrat compared to 38 percent who would vote Republican. And even among evangelicals, the Republican label is becoming less reliable as younger evangelicals are less likely to follow their parents into the Republican Party. According to the Pew Forum on Religion and Public Life, in 2008, slightly younger evangelicals identified themselves as either independent or Democrat compared to Republican. This could explain why so many politicians in both parties seem to *get religion* during election years.

So, if you think of the typical Christian as married with an intact family who never visits a casino or has a glass of wine and always votes Republican, you're going to need to change your thinking if you want to truly understand this market. Christians shop at the same stores, visit the same web sites, buy the same products, see the same movies, read the same books, vacation at the same theme parks, drive the same cars, use the same credit cards, and struggle with the same issues as anyone else in the United States. In fact, given that nearly half the American population is Christian, it is statistically impossible for such a large segment of our nation to deviate from the norm, which is just another way to say that Christians are pretty normal, despite what you may have read or heard about them.

Because Christians are no different, in many respects, from the population at large, it is impossible to believe they are invisible to businesses and to other customers. It's one thing to know there are Christians in your store—on an average day almost half your customers could be Christians. But knowing they are there is not necessarily going to keep them there, nor is it going to make them feel any particularly loyalty to your business. We'll get into strategies and tactics later on, but for now we'd like to introduce you to a psychological concept known as homophily, which means "love of same." It's a fancy way of saying "birds of a feather flock together." We naturally congregate with people who share our passions, interests, and beliefs. A Christian will be more attracted to a business if he or she believes other Christians are there, and you can help facilitate that and thus increase loyalty from the Christian market. And one of the ways to do that is to stock products that will appeal specifically to Christians.

The retail giant Wal-Mart has done that as well as anyone. If you visit their book section, in addition to the normal bestsellers that would attract any book lover, you will find books from Christian publishers written by authors who are popular among Christians as well as a selection of Bibles. In their music section, you will find a selection of Christian contemporary music. They even have Christian toys! Here's what that says to Christians:

- Wow! They know about me!
- Must be other Christians shop here.

- It feels so good to be around others like me.
- I think I'll come back.

By meeting the specific needs of Christians, you will make them feel better about your store. And while they are in the store, in addition to buying those distinctly Christian products, they will buy soap and perfume and kitchen utensils. In other words, you will have developed incredible customer loyalty, helping Christians make a choice between your store and your competition. By the way, you don't have to be an international retail giant to do that. If your business has any type of waiting lounge or reception area, adding a Christian magazine to the stack of *Time* and *Good Housekeeping* will send the same message.

CASE STUDY: THE OVERLOOKED CHRISTIAN CONVENTION MARKET

According to Chris Collinson, founder and CEO of Collinson Publishing, faith-based organizations conduct thousands of meetings each year where they need the services of hotels and convention facilities. But the convention business is missing an opportunity by not actively marketing to them.

Collinson started a magazine, *Rejuvenate*, to try and bring the convention industry and faith-based organizations together.

"The faith-based convention business is huge but largely invisible to hotels and city convention bureaus," Collinson maintains. "There are literally thousands of faith-based groups who plan meetings that require travel, hotel, and meeting facilities—one organization we work with, the United Methodist Board of Discipleship, holds one thousand meetings a year. But only about one in ten of the salespeople for convention facilities understand the potential of this market."

Collinson's advice to any business desiring to work with faith-based organizations? "Get to know them better. Understand their needs. We find so many of these hotels offering packages that do not meet the specific needs of faith-based organizations, but the hotels that do, get their business."

YET SO DIFFERENT

In terms of behavior, then—where they live, what they wear, how they vote, what they eat—Christians are pretty much like anyone else. For the marketer, that's pretty good news because it means you don't have to look very hard to find them and whatever your product or service, they probably need it. Where they *are* different, however, is in what they believe. In fact, belief may be the *only* thing that distinguishes Christians from the rest of the population, so here's where it might get a little confusing because we're going to try to tell you what Christians believe.

But first, why does it matter? If you were trying to get more customers to visit your web site, why would you need to know what Christians believe? Because the more you know about your customer, the better you can serve him. Traditionally, marketers have focused on demographics (gender, race, income, and so on) and behavioral variables (loyalty to a product, frequency of purchases, etc.) Increasingly, we have all been looking closely at psychographics (interests, values, and attitudes) to help us know our customers, or potential customers, even better. When it comes to demographics and behavioral variables, Christians look pretty much like anyone else. But in terms of psychographics, their beliefs are different. It's what makes them tick, so to speak. Knowing what Christians believe increases your knowledge of this huge consumer group, allowing you to serve them better.

Entire books have been written about Christian belief, but for our purposes the best way to understand what Christians believe is to look at a document known as the Apostle's Creed. In the simplest of terms, this is a short summary of what every Christian believes—Catholic and Protestant. If it doesn't make sense to you, don't worry. We'll unpack it for you after you read it.

> *I believe in God, the Father Almighty,*
>   Creator of heaven and earth.
>
> *I believe in Jesus Christ, his only Son, our Lord,*
>   Who was conceived by the Holy Spirit,
>   Born of the Virgin Mary,
>   Suffered under Pontius Pilate,
>   Was crucified, died, and buried;
>   He descended into hell.
>   On the third day he rose again;
>   He ascended into heaven,
>   Is seated at the right hand of the Father,
>   And will come again to judge the living and the dead.

I believe in the Holy Spirit,
    The holy catholic church,
    The communion of the saints,
    The forgiveness of sins,
    The resurrection of the body
    And the life everlasting. Amen.

Okay, Christians believe in God. You probably already knew that. They believe he is all knowing and all powerful and that he is the only God. They respect other religions, but they do not believe the deities of other religions—be it Buddha, Allah, or one of the many gods of Hinduism—are the same as God.

Not only do Christians *believe* in God, they believe he created everything. The earth. The universe. People. Everything. They may disagree over whether he did it in seven days or over a period of billions of years, but they all acknowledge that he is the creative force behind everything.

Christians also believe in Jesus, not only as a historical figure (even atheists acknowledge his existence), but also as the Son of God. This is what separates Christians from the two other major religions that believe in a singular deity: Jews, who believe in Jehovah/ God, and Muslims, who believe in Allah. Both acknowledge that a man named Jesus existed, but only Christians believe that he was the Son of God.

Now here's where it becomes a little spooky for some. Christians believe that God, through his spirit, impregnated a virgin named Mary. This event is sometimes called the Immaculate Conception, and it resulted in what is referred to by Christians as the Virgin Birth. This is a very big deal for Christians and requires a great deal of faith, a word that you will hear a lot if you hang around them. Faith is the ability to believe something that cannot be proven. Sort of like Cubs fans believing they will win the World Series.

Historians support the next part of the Apostle's Creed—that Jesus was killed under the order of a Roman magistrate named Pontius Pilate and that his death was agonizingly cruel, as you may have discovered if you saw Mel Gibson's *The Passion of the Christ,* a historically accurate depiction of what really happened. The chosen method of execution was to nail his body to a cross, place the cross in the ground, and let him hang until he suffocated. Again, historians record that a small group of Jesus's followers prepared his body for burial after he died and then placed him in a tomb. Have you ever heard of Good Friday? It is the Friday before Easter and it commemorates the day Jesus died.

Why would anyone use the adjective good to describe the anniversary of such a horrible event? We'll get to that.

In this creed, which describes what all Christians believe, after Jesus died he went to hell. Literally. The reason for that—indeed the reason Jesus was killed—is that Christians believe he became a substitute for every human being. That is, he took the punishment that I (Greg) deserve because even though I'm a pretty good person, the truth is, I'm not sinless (and trust me, Bob's no better). I'd list all the reasons why we should be punished, but our wives will probably read this book. But in all seriousness, Christians believe that we're all sinners who deserve to go to hell, but Jesus did it for us. That's why we call it "Good" Friday—we don't have to fear punishment for our wrongdoings because Jesus took it for us.

Easter Sunday is easily the most sacred and revered holiday for Christians and that's because it commemorates the next statement in this Creed. Christians believe that three days after Jesus was buried, he came back to life. They call this the Resurrection, and again, though evidence abounds it's one of those things that can't be proven so it requires a big dose of faith.

If returning from the dead is hard to believe, the next statement may be even harder. After Jesus came back to life and revealed himself to his closest followers (who recorded this in the Bible), he literally ascended into the air to live in a place called heaven, sitting right next to God, his father. These events confirm another significant aspect of what Christians believe—Jesus was both a human and God.

Up to this point, God is really two entities: God and Jesus, his son. But the next part of the Creed describes something that all Christians believe: the Trinity. That is, God is really three gods in one: God the father, Jesus his Son, and now, the Holy Spirit, or more accurately, the very spirit of God. Think of it this way. God and Jesus are a gazillion miles away up in heaven, so they send their spirit back to earth to guide us and give us the power to live godly lives. You might hear a Christian say something like this: "I wasn't sure if I should take that job so I prayed about it and felt that God wanted me to turn it down." Christians believe God guides and directs them here on earth through his Holy Spirit.

Now the next part of this Creed could be confusing (as if the previous parts weren't). When Christians affirm the "catholic" church, they are not referring to the Roman Catholic denomination. In this case, catholic means universal, and so Christians believe that whatever their denomination—Baptist, Methodist, Roman Catholic—they are all part of the same big family of Christians.

Are you still with us?

Maybe the most important part of this Creed is where it talks of forgiveness. You've probably seen the bumper sticker: "Not perfect, just forgiven." It might surprise you to learn that most Christians don't think that highly of themselves. For a lot of reasons, we come off as pretty high minded and righteous. But the truth is, Christians believe that they are sinners—that's right, really bad people—and that the only way out is to be forgiven, and that's what Jesus offered through his death. In effect, when he went to his death he was saying, "You're forgiven. I'm taking your punishment, so pick yourself off the floor and go out and act like decent people." Pretty good deal, when you think of it. Feeling lower than a snake's belly for cheating on your wife? "Forget about it," Jesus says. "I already took what you deserved, so get back in the game and behave yourself. I'm giving you a second (and third, and fourth, and fifth) chance." That's what Christians believe, and they have a term for it: salvation. It literally means you are saved from the punishment you should receive for your sins.

Now here's the payoff. Christians believe that human life goes on forever. Did you see the part earlier in the Creed talking about "judging the living and the dead." Christians believe that those who reject Jesus' offer of forgiveness will be separated eternally from God. That's the hell thing. But those who accept it will be rewarded by an eternal existence with God in heaven. No one knows what heaven is or what it would be like to live there forever, but the Bible assures us that it will be perfect.

CASE STUDY: FAITH-BASED MARKETING CIRCA 1950

Before churches were air conditioned, sitting in church on a hot summer Sunday could get pretty uncomfortable. A very savvy marketer saw that as an opportunity for his business, a funeral home. He had a bunch of "hand fans" made up—basically a piece of poster board stapled to an oversized Popsicle stick. But on the face of the fan, he had the classic portrait of Jesus printed on both sides. Then on the wooden handle, he had the name and address of his business stamped on it (see Figure 3.1). The idea spread like wildfire so that in the 1950s, almost every church had hundreds of fans waiting for the parishioners when they took their places in the pews.

(Continued)

Figure 3.1
Faith-Based Marketing Circa 1950

Note: Heritage Advertising is a Christian-based company that offers many styles and designs in Church Hand Fans. See them at http://yardsigns.org or http://hand-fans.biz, or e-mail them at TenCommandmentSigns@yahoo.com.

Here's what he did right. First, he found a need and met it: a simple, inexpensive solution to make worship—important to Christians—more comfortable. Second, he knew how important Jesus was to Christians. Instead of using that valuable space to shout his message—"Ten percent discount to everyone who brings this fan to our funeral home!"—he turned an unremarkable object into something that reminded Christians of their love for Jesus. Finally, he understated his commercial interest by putting his company's name in an unobtrusive place on the fan. Had he not known what is important to Christians, he might never have come up with the idea in the first place, or he might have executed it in a manner that offended Christians. But he took the time to get to know the Christian community in his city—maybe even visited a church on a hot summer day—and developed a simple marketing plan to reach them. There were several funeral homes in his city. Which one do you think church folks chose when they lost a family member?

ORDINARY PEOPLE WITH EXTRAORDINARY BELIEFS

We'll be the first to admit that for those with almost no understanding of Christianity, that Creed took a toll on your "incredulous index." Three gods in one. A virgin getting pregnant without sleeping with a guy. Dead man rising. Heaven and hell. So here's what we would like to suggest for anyone who might be whistling that *Twilight Zone* tune.

As you develop strategies to grow your business, tape this number to your computer monitor: 230 million. That's how many people in the United States believe what we have just described. They are not kooks or fanatics. They are doctors and lawyers and university professors and mechanics and nurses and carpenters. They live next door to you, go to PTA meetings, coach your daughter's softball team, and look for bargains.

Here's another number: $5.1 trillion. That's how much money Christians spend each year. They spend it on the same things the rest of the population buys, but they are deeply committed to their faith, and their beliefs influence how they behave, even what they buy. You certainly don't have to agree with these beliefs to successfully market to Christians, but knowing how dearly they hold these beliefs and respecting them will enable you to develop relationships and communicate your message to them to your benefit and theirs.

We're pretty sure you're itching to get tactical, and we're almost there. But first we've got just a few tips to keep you from putting your foot in your mouth when you make your first call to a church.

CHAPTER FOUR

DARNED IF YOU DO,
DARNED IF YOU DON'T

COMMON MISTAKES MARKETERS MAKE

Sid Baxter owned a small electronics business in Topeka, Kansas. While visiting a church where a friend's daughter had a special part in a musical, he had a brainstorm as he sat in the huge auditorium. Unlike the little country church he attended as a youngster, this one featured a huge video screen at the front of the room, with several smaller monitors hanging from the walls. Giant speakers flanked the stage delivering awesome sound controlled by two men at a soundboard the size of a motor home. Each singer wore a wireless headset, and the band was wired with state-of-the-art microphones to amplify its sound.

"Maybe I better start trying to sell my stuff to churches," he thought. "This church alone would be a $400,000 payday for me!"

So he made a mental note to get an appointment with whoever ran the church. Two weeks later, he found himself in the well-appointed office of a man whose title was Executive Pastor.

"Well, we've had this system for eight years, and we *have* been thinking of upgrading it. What would you propose we do to improve our overall audio and video system," the pastor inquired.

"First off, you've got room to move up to high def projection," Sid began. "Just imagine how that cute blonde singer would look in 1080 resolution on such a big screen! And to support that visual impact, I'd recommend going to line array speakers—in fact, imagine true surround sound with fully integrated speakers coming at your people from all four corners of the room. You probably want to go with a 64-channel board to accommodate all your input needs. Of course, I'd want to upgrade all your mics, bring in a boom-mounted camera, and replace your two AG-HVX200As with a couple of AG-HPX500s. All told, you'd have the absolute best audio and video system in the county—maybe in the state!"

The pastor was intrigued. He thought of their major productions—Fourth of July, Christmas, Easter. The Christian rock concerts they provided for the teens several times a year. "Maybe we could even rent the auditorium out to local high schools," he thought to himself. "What a great way to reach the community."

"So, your company has done installations like that?" the pastor asked.

"Oh hell yes, pardon my French," Sid replied. Sure it was a little white lie, but he'd always wanted to get into these higher-end gigs—the margins were so much better and besides, he had confidence his crew could learn on the job.

"Tell you what," the pastor continued. "I've heard enough to make a decision. I'll get back to you in two weeks."

Sid was practically skipping as he headed to his car. "I think I'm getting religion," he laughed to himself, imagining his business growing from the dozens of very large churches in the city.

You may conclude from this fictional account that Sid did everything right. Actually, he did everything wrong, and in his excitement he didn't realize that "I'll get back to you" meant "You're toast!" We'll explain why because we want to help you avoid making the common mistakes businesses make when they try to work with Christians. But first, just a word to reinforce what we tried to establish in the first chapter: The Christian market is much bigger than you think.

In Sid's story, we're looking at just one church. If you were dragged off to church as a youngster, it was probably a small building with a few rows of pews on the main floor. If they had a sound system, it was probably a Dukane amplifier sitting on a little table at the back of the church with a wire running up to the pulpit into a ribbon microphone. A couple of speakers in small wooden boxes hung on the wall on each side of the platform. In the basement—the fellowship hall—you'd find a tiny kitchen with a Kenmore range, a donated refrigerator, and a couple of cabinets built by one of the men in the church. That was about it.

Today's new churches—many called *mega churches*—buy sound systems costing thousands of dollars. They buy acres of carpets and select seating configurations that cause local furniture suppliers to salivate at the prospective sale. They equip state of the art kitchens with appliances you'd find in a five-star restaurant and regularly prepare banquets that require the buying of large quantities of food and beverages. They furnish suites of offices with desks, furniture, computers, file cabinets, telephones, and bookshelves. With paid staffs of anywhere from a half dozen to as many as fifty, they purchase health insurance, life insurance, 401(k) plans, and other benefits for their employees. Classrooms for hundreds of kids who attend Sunday school need reams of construction paper, scissors, glue, crayons, and other school supplies. Many need audio and video production studios to record and turn their services into DVDs that they sell in fully equipped bookstores (which need cash registers, display shelves, merchandising resources, and so on). To maintain these sprawling buildings, they purchase cleaning supplies (or contract with professional cleaning companies), paint, hardware, and tools. Their campuses are professionally landscaped. If they are in northern climates they contract with snow removal services, and every few years they resurface their massive parking lots. And that's just one church! (See "Churches Are Big Business," page 24.)

In other words, whatever your business, you probably sell something a church can use, and if you market to them effectively, you will indeed grow your business.

Sid was right to get jazzed about the prospect of getting the contract for the church's new sound system, but he went about it all wrong, and in this chapter we want to help you avoid the most common mistakes marketers make with Christians.

WATCH YOUR LANGUAGE

It may seem silly to you, but Sid made his first mistake when he let a mild expletive slip. Christians are a little sensitive about profanity. While it's true that Christians are normal people, much like everyone else, and that some may occasionally break out with a hell or a damn, they generally try to avoid profanity and especially don't like to hear it in church. The pastor let it pass, but you can bet he made a mental note of it. Obviously, he would never refuse to do business with someone just because he swore, but in any initial meeting with a client, you're being sized up. Remember, great marketing involves developing a relationship with your client, not just selling a product. Your goal should be to make your potential client feel comfortable with you, and an innocent slip of the tongue will raise a yellow flag. Not a good way to start a relationship.

We've noticed a troubling trend among major advertisers to use bleeped-out expletives to draw attention to their products. For example, in recent Passat ads, passengers surviving a crash blurt out, "Holy …!" It trails off before the banned word as the announcer says, "Safe Happens." Writing in *USA Today*, Theresa Howard cites Dodge, Comcast, and Volkswagen for flirting with language limits. She quotes Suzanne Powers, chief strategy officer for agency TBWA/Chiat/Day: "The bleep is unexpected. It's an interesting way to disrupt the viewer and do something out of the ordinary."

Yes, it's out of the ordinary, but then again so are most auto accidents, and we try to avoid those. We don't deny that advertising needs to stand out from the background noise of our lives and that the unexpected can accomplish that, but to what end? You can get my attention at a dinner party either by shouting cuss words over the crowd *or* by whispering my name. Relevance is more powerful than the unexpected. If you get my attention with the unexpected, I will return to whatever I was doing when I see it lacks relevance. However once relevance secures my attention, it also attracts me. Have agencies learned nothing from Google? It rose to search engine dominance—and now pay-per-click advertising—by ranking search results by their relevance. When marketing to Christians, your goal is to show them how your product relates to their needs. Trust us, you won't get very far using profane or vulgar language.

One of the reasons we walked you through the Apostle's Creed in the previous chapter was to help you understand what is important to Christians. Not only is God very important to Christians, but also his various names and especially the way they are used. So while a hell or a damn might be mildly offensive to Christians, profanity that uses God's name could easily be a deal breaker. Whether it's the very common and seemingly benign exclamation "Omigod" or an earthy "goddam," Christians will get their hackles up when they hear it and be inclined to give their business to someone else. Out of respect for their beliefs, never use God or Jesus as an expletive. A funny story about Sharon might help you remember how serious an offense this is.

Sharon was a young woman who had recently become a Christian. A delightful and talented sales executive, she had an impressive work record with two Fortune 500 companies. She left the corporate world to work for a large Protestant denomination, but she took with her a bit too much salty language. One of her favorite expletives was the word "Jesus," as in "Jesus, that was a boring meeting." The first time she did that, she recounts, she noticed the people around her got real quiet and exchanged looks between themselves. After about the third time, one of her coworkers pulled her into her cubicle and gently said, "Um, Sharon, I know you don't mean any harm, but when you say Jesus the way you do, it's really offensive to us." Sharon was mortified, and got it right away. As a new Christian, she treasured her relationship with Jesus and understood his sacrifice on her behalf, but old habits die hard. She vowed to herself that she would watch her language and eventually came up with a *save* whenever the word slipped out. Her colleagues smiled when they heard her use the word the next time: "Jesus...is wonderful!"

Using the wrong language can put a quick end to your relationship with Christians and Christian organizations. Our friend Andy Sernovitz, the founding president of the word-of-mouth marketing association, was scheduled for an interview on a large Christian radio network until that network discovered his blog was titled *Damn, I Wish I'd Thought of That*, after which they promptly cancelled his appearance.

All this to say that when it comes to working with Christians and faith-based organizations, language matters. We actually believe this is good advice when working with any business, because, remember, a good percentage of the people in those businesses are Christians. You will have a much better chance developing a great relationship with Christians if you leave your profanity at the door.

KEEP YOUR CLOTHES ON

A former CEO of a major publishing company—a talented leader with phenomenal marketing instincts—used to say, "What stops the eye starts the sale." And nothing stops the eye like a curvy blonde in a bikini. Marketers of everything from beer to Beemers have used this seemingly innocuous technique to draw attention to their product. And not just the national advertisers. A local furniture store in a midsize city padded its mattress line with a television spot showing an attractive woman in a modest negligee. Harmless, perhaps, but not the approach if you're targeting Christians. Sid's comment about the "cute blonde" was yet another mistake he made in trying to market his company, and here's why.

First, Christians aren't prudes. We don't know of any Christian guys who look the other way when the Victoria's Secret ad tries to sell underwear. Some of us have even tried the chicken wings at a national restaurant chain that uses an owl as its logo—just to try the wings, not to look at the owls. When it comes to the Old Milwaukee Swedish Bikini Team or Alicia Silverstone baring it all for a PETA commercial, we're as vulnerable as the next guy.

And yet, using sexual images or innuendo to market to Christians will ultimately backfire because people of faith believe such efforts encourage them to disobey at least two strong warnings in the Bible: lust and unfaithfulness. That's not to say Christians never lust or are unfaithful to their spouses—remember, we're just like everyone else. But overt efforts to use sexual imagery to attract attention could actually cause Christians to avoid your product because they do not want to support anything that runs counter to their beliefs. To Christians, women are to be treated with respect, not as objects. Christian men are taught to avoid putting themselves in the path of temptation, and Christian women will not appreciate efforts to turn their husband's attention away from them.

In practical terms, our advice is to avoid the temptation to use provocative images to attract attention to your product. It will indeed attract attention, but not the attention you want. If you use images in a brochure or commercial, show married men and women together, enjoying each other's company. Respect the Christian's belief that even though their marriage may be as difficult as anyone else's, it's a covenant they made before God. They will not be comfortable with anything that tempts them to break that covenant, and we'll return to that restaurant chain as a great example.

Because of the advertising—even the name—used by Hooters, my (Greg's) wife has always believed that these places were innappropriate, so obviously, she would never step inside one, nor would she be pleased if I gave them my business. And trust me, I'm not going to try to change her mind by saying, "No Amy, these are just normal restaurants where the waitresses wear really tight hot pants and accentuate their breasts by wearing extremely tight T-shirts." Now I realize that Hooters isn't out to corner the Christian market, but any business that overtly uses sex can expect the same lack of support from Christians as Hooters is getting from us.

WHAT KINDS OF MARKETING MAKE CHRISTIANS NERVOUS

Christians in the United States increasingly feel at odds with contemporary culture. According to a Pew Research Center survey, 40 percent of Americans affiliated with a particular religion feel a "conflict between being a devout religious person and living in a modern society." Those numbers rose to 49 percent among evangelicals and 46 percent among African American churches. Forty-two percent say they feel "threatened by Hollywood."

According to Scott Shuford, CEO of FrontGate Media, a firm that works with companies trying to reach devout Christians, "I do believe that many are as offended by and reject the OMG and OMFG *Gossip Girl* ads or an Abercrombie & Fitch catalog as they are by anything else in culture that specifically offends them." In other words, advertising that depends on the raunch factor will surely offend Christians, and even if they buy your product marketed that way, they won't feel good about your company. "Parents have to make a choice as to what is more important: pleasing their kids' taste and sensibilities, or satisfying God's standards as defined in the Bible," pollster George Barna explains. "When the decision is made to keep their children happy, Christian parents are often left with a pit in their stomachs."

APPEAL TO NEED, NOT GREED

Jim Clark is the only person in history to take three companies from start up to market valuations in excess of one billion dollars: Silicon Graphics, Netscape, and Healtheon Web MD. He told journalist Michael Lewis that once his after-tax wealth eclipsed a billion dollars, he would retire. When Clark's wealth exceeded four billion, and he continued working, Lewis reminded him of his pledge. "I thought you were going to retire," Lewis said. To which Clark replied, "I will, once I pass Larry Ellison." Ellison, the founder and CEO of Oracle, was worth about ten billion dollars at the time. The two moguls had invested their money differently, and Lewis quickly calculated that Clark would surpass Ellison in about eight months. "What then," Lewis asked. "Will you want to have more money than Bill Gates?" Clark denied such a lofty ambition initially but came clean about an hour later. "Just for a little while," he confessed, "I'd like to have the most."

Sid's third mistake was appealing to the pastor's vanity—to have the biggest and best sound system in the city. Too many marketers want you to believe a lie: What you have determines your value. The horrible consequence of this line of thinking is that, as long as someone else has more than you do, you are worth less. And no one wants to be worth less.

Christians calculate their worth another way. They believe their value is determined by what their creator was willing to give in exchange for them, and God gave his only Son to spare them the consequences of their sins, as we learned in the previous chapter. Therefore, each person's worth is immeasurable regardless of the size of their home or their church's sound system. Does this mean Christians don't need nice homes or cars or large screen televisions? Of course not. But it is important for you to understand that most Christians try to avoid the temptation to believe that those kinds of things give them status or a sense of superiority over a neighbor who doesn't have name brand designer clothes.

Marketing to Christians by attempting to get them to chase after stuff for the sake of prestige is really tempting them with a form of idolatry and will turn them off. It just won't work. You will be far more successful marketing to Christians if you seek to meet their needs rather than play to the human desire for more. Number Ten of the Ten Commandments warns Christians about the dangers of keeping up with the Joneses. If Christians are commanded not to covet, then marketers would be wise to not lead Christians into that sin.

BE REAL

In our profession as marketers, we face a huge temptation: lying. If we're trying to market a great mousetrap and we know there are dozens of competing mousetraps, we want to make sure consumers know why ours is better. Does it catch mice? Yes. Is it safe? Yes. Easy to use? Yes. If it breaks, will you replace it? Yes. Will it make my coffee in the morning? Um, sure! Okay, maybe you're never tempted to tell such a whopper, but in our efforts to market our products, it's easy to stretch the truth a little, as Sid did when he assured the pastor his company had experience installing such a massive audio/video system. And here's how he probably justified his little white lie:

> Our guys are really talented, and although we've never actually done a job this big, we've done some pretty big jobs, and I'm completely confident they'll do a super installation. The church will be happy. I'll be happy. No need to raise any red flags right now. In a few weeks, we will have shown the pastor that we were the right company for the job, and he'll never know I was playing him.

While we believe it's just good business to practice integrity with any consumer, it is especially important that you conduct yourself ethically when working with Christians. In Chapter 1, we outlined reasons why Christians and faith-based organizations are a little skeptical of business, and one of those spoke to the suspicion that businesses are all about exploiting people—selling them what they don't need, tricking them into making unwise investments. Nothing galvanizes that skepticism more than dropping your guard when it comes to integrity. And what's insidious about breaches of integrity is that they are often easily rationalized. No one ever wakes up and declares, "I'm going to mislead my customers today." Instead, in our sincere efforts to serve our consumers—to meet their needs—we sometimes take a good story and make it better than it really is.

It would be unfair and untrue to suggest Christians value integrity more than non-Christians. But because the Bible offers so many warnings against untruthfulness, integrity holds a high position in their hierarchy of values. They revere people and businesses that maintain high standards of integrity, and they avoid those that don't. Before watchdogs investigated Christian ministries to make sure they weren't fleecing their followers, the famous preacher, Billy Graham, instituted rigid rules for the handling of money, appeals for donations, and the conduct of everyone who worked on his team. Sadly, a handful of other television evangelists succumbed to the temptations that come with receiving huge amounts of money. Even though he is in the twilight of his career, Billy Graham's organization still receives generous support from Christians all over the globe, while those who were duplicitous saw their support plummet and eventually had to shut down their organizations. Christians will never do business with anyone who has a reputation for dishonesty.

In practical terms, integrity is best demonstrated in your brand. Integrity means "wholeness" or "completeness." Everything is in harmony. Therefore, everything your company does must support your brand. On one hand, if your brand is to provide trustworthy investment counseling and one of your employees violates that trust by advising an elderly couple to invest in a high-risk fund, your brand is compromised. On the other hand, every time you deliver on your brand, you ensure customer loyalty because people prefer to do business with trustworthy merchants.

In our opinion, one of the best U.S. companies in terms of integrity is the outdoor clothing and equipment giant, L.L. Bean. Founded in 1912 as a mail order retailer, it sold one product: a waterproof boot called the Maine Hunting Shoe or "Bean Boot." But in its first year of business, it faced a huge crisis. Fully 90 percent of the boots it shipped were defective. To get his new company off the ground, founder Leon Bean had offered a full money-back guarantee on his boots. Returning the revenue on 90 percent of his first shipment threatened to sink his business, but he made good on it. The result? High-level consumer trust that continues to this day, establishing L.L. Bean not only as a financially successful company, but one known for its stellar customer service.

Integrity doesn't just happen. It's an ongoing, deliberate effort to be what you say you are in every aspect of your business. You should periodically test yourself to ensure that you're walking the talk. Here's one way to do that:

1. *Decide what your business stands for.* Write it down.
2. *Make it public.* Tell every employee. Tell every customer. This creates an expectation you must live up to. It helps hold you accountable.
3. *Test every aspect of your company against this standard.* Make sure your products, your policies, your practices all support your position. Are you whole, or do you have conflicts?
4. *Get an outside opinion.* Few businesses will admit their shortcomings and even honest businesses are too close to the forest to see the trees, so get an outside opinion. Ask your customers. Tell them, this is what we stand for and then ask them to identify areas where the business isn't living up to that goal. Don't just ask for a critique, but also ask for help. Your customers will gladly tell you what you could do to improve, and many of their ideas will be good. Take a look at www.comcastmustdie.com. This site illustrates what happens when a company is "disintegrated." Bob Garfield, the ad critic for *Ad Age* magazine, started the site as a way to improve the service he was getting from the company. It caught on, and now many dissatisfied Comcast customers use it

to vent. Astoundingly, Comcast reads the complaints to identify customers with problems so it can help them. After declaring victory over Comcast, Garfield launched www.customercircus.net where, "other infamously arrogant corporations will be subjected to power of aggregated rage."

As for the consumer's willingness to help, www.mystarbucksidea .com is a great example of an integrated company inviting its customers to participate in building its business and its brand.

5. *Make sure your ads match your ads.* Are you saying the same thing with all of your advertising? From the sign on your building to the way you answer the phone, create a common expectation among your customers and then meet or exceed it.

6. *Make sure your ads match reality.* Now that all of your advertising promises the same thing, make sure that every part of your company delivers on that promise. If it does, then you're whole.

UNHOLY MARKETING PARTNERSHIPS

If you don't understand the subtle differences within the Christian community, you could make a fatal mistake. What one Christian denomination embraces, another may reject. Take a close look at the picture I snapped while on a business trip (Figure 4.1, page 49). Yep, Samuel Adams beer is sponsoring a Catholic Church's Oktoberfest. Catholics may enjoy a cold one in the church basement over a good game of bingo, but Sam Adams would be run out of town were it to try this same approach with, say, the Nazarene church down the street. The faith-based community is large, well financed, and influential, but always do your homework before you develop your marketing strategy.

TIME TO GET TACTICAL

In these first four chapters, we have tried to help you better understand the Christian community and the challenges you may face as you begin to market to them. We hope we have whetted your appetite while at the same time helped you develop a healthy respect for people of faith. Our guess is that you're already developing new marketing plans

Figure 4.1
Unholy Marketing Partnerships

to reach this robust market, so in the next section we will describe the nuts and bolts of how you market specifically to Christians. To get ready for that, here are five questions to answer:

1. What is (are) my product(s) or service(s)?
2. Why would a church or Christian organization need this product or service?
3. Why would an individual Christian need my product?
4. Who are my top two competitors that provide this product or service?
5. Am I satisfied with the way I am reaching Christians or Christian organizations with information about my product?

PART II

HOW TO MARKET TO CHRISTIANS

CHAPTER FIVE

MEET AND GREET

HOW TO GET TO KNOW YOUR AUDIENCE

If you were a marketer for Colgate toothpaste in 1962 and wanted to convince women their teeth would be whiter if they used your product, you advertised on the popular NBC television program, *Queen for a Day*, and watched sales climb overnight. In fact, if you ran that ad on all three networks, you could reach 80 percent of all women in the United States! Today, if you want to reach women with information about your product, you've got some choices to make. How old is she? Is she a stay-at-home mom or does she work outside the home? What are her hobbies? What's her household income? Is she a Republican or Democrat? Married or divorced? White, Hispanic, or African American? Once that's settled, you've got to chose from more than 400 television channels, 18,000 national magazines, AM radio, FM radio, digital radio, satellite radio, Internet radio, *and* billions of web pages cataloged by Google.

To be an effective marketer, you can no longer interact with your customer from a distance. Mass marketing strategies, which gained prominence in the 1920s with the advent of commercial radio, allowed businesses to interact with the broadest, largest audiences for the lowest cost. It worked in the 1960s, but with the proliferation of new media channels and the diverse media habits of consumers, mass-market strategies focusing on a single medium are no longer effective. In fact, according to the *Los Angeles Times*, 2008 marked the first time online advertising spending surpassed television, radio, and movie advertising spending combined (http://latimesblogs.latimes.com/technology/2008/07/spending-on-onl.html). Now, you need to develop a closer relationship with consumers in order to market to them. If you're interested in marketing to people of faith, that's great news because the church, unlike any other market segment, makes it easy to develop those relationships, and in this chapter we show you how.

THEY DON'T HAVE LEPROSY

In ancient times and in primitive cultures, people who had leprosy were quarantined in isolated leper colonies, and everyone else did their best to stay away. Sometimes, that's how marketers treat the faith community. Imagine being a journalist assigned to cover business in China and trying to do it from your office in Los Angeles. Sounds crazy, but that's how many businesses relate to churches—they'd like to sell them office equipment, but they've never spent any time in churches.

You can't market effectively to Christians by keeping your distance. You can't communicate with them remotely, safely insulated from them. You need to get up close and personal, meet them, read what they read, watch what they watch, listen to what they listen to—all in an effort to better understand them and develop a relationship with them. Like any subculture, the Christian community has its own language, customs, celebrities, and peculiarities, and the more you understand this subculture, the better you will be able to serve them. Remember Sid the salesman in the previous chapter? One visit to a church, and he thought he could grow his business with them, but when he pitched his product, he revealed how little he knew his customer and why they should probably stick with their current supplier.

We know what you're thinking: "This is just a ploy to get me to go to church."

You caught us! How'd you know that we get a free pencil for every guest we bring to church? Seriously, visiting a church now and then is a good idea if you want to market to Christians, but we've got a better idea. We've developed a simple process that is guaranteed to give you the best understanding of the faith-based audience you want to reach in your geographical region.

In the following pages, we're going to show you how to get to know churches. The faith-based community includes hundreds of other organizations, including parachurch organizations (see sidebar page 55), Christian schools, Christian colleges, home school organizations, and Christian media, and you can use the same process we describe here to become better acquainted with those organizations.

WHAT'S A PARACHURCH?

In addition to the approximately 350,000 churches in the United States, several thousand "parachurch organizations" offer yet another opportunity to reach people of faith. The term parachurch uses the Greek prefix para which means beside or alongside, which is what a parachurch organization does—they work alongside the church providing services or other ministries to help it fulfill its mission.

For example, most churches want to help solve problems of world hunger and poverty but as individual churches they do not have the infrastructure to do that. So parachurch organizations such as World Vision, Catholic Charities, World Relief, Samaritan's Purse, and Feed the Hungry were formed to partner with churches on these massive problems.

Many parachurch organizations have a huge national, even global reach with multi-million dollar budgets and thousands of paid employees. They are largely non-profit and communicate regularly with their donors through magazines and newsletters. For example, the Billy Graham Evangelistic Association has offices in eight countries around the world and distributes 6.7 million copies of its official magazine, Decision (by comparison, *U.S. News and World Report* distributes 1.8 million copies).

Parachurch organizations also operate locally, supporting churches in your city or region with homeless shelters, marriage and family counseling, youth programs, adoption services, pregnancy counseling, prison ministry, health clinics, etc. The best place to begin learning about the parachurch organizations in your area is to look under "Social Service and Welfare Organizations" in your Yellow Pages. Look for organizations using words like "ministries" or the name of a church (Lutheran, Catholic, and so on) You may also contact your local United Way and ask for a list of affiliated organizations that are faith-based. Finally, as you develop relationships with area pastors, ask them which local parachurch ministries they support.

FIND FAITH-BASED BUSINESS OPPORTUNITIES

For some, this may be pretty basic, but it's the best way to *get closer* to the faith-based market: build a database of information about the Christian community in your area. Once you know the landscape, you can develop strategies for marketing to it. So, let's start with your computer.

Open the popular search engine, Google, and in the search box, type the word "churches," and then in parentheses type in your city and state. When you click enter, the first thing you'll see is a map with some virtual pushpins stuck in it under the heading "Local business results for churches" (your city and state). Below the map you'll see the usual listing of results for your search—in my case, Google lists more than 600,000 entries for my city. If you were to scroll through those pages, you'd soon discover that not every entry is a church. For example, you might find a listing of "hotels near Christ Church," or "sermons from First Presbyterian." For now, ignore those pages and look for the link just below the map that says, "more results near (your city)." This will take you to several pages that list individual churches, and on each page you will also have an updated map. And if you click on the map, you will get a larger version with controls to zoom in and take a closer look at the neighborhood.

Now, even when you click on "more results in your city," you may find thousands of entries. That's because Google's definition of local may be much broader than your needs. However, the first several pages will list the churches closest to you as well as the larger churches in your area. In most areas, if you focus on those first 10 to 12 pages, you will have a fairly comprehensive list of significant churches to target for your business. You can always add to that list as time permits. If you took the time to scroll through the entire list, however, you would begin to grasp the sheer volume of churches in your area, all potential customers for your product or service.

With just a few clicks, then, you have gained access to a wealth of information for building a church database. Click on any of the churches listed, and you will find everything from contact information, names of the senior pastor, and key staff to special programs and types of services the church offers. In other words, you can learn a lot about the churches in your area without actually attending them. But the important thing is to capture this information in a database.* Your database can be as simple as a spreadsheet, Microsoft Access, or even Outlook. An even better tool would be one of the many customer relationship management (CRM) softwares, such as ACT! Whatever system you use, make sure you gather as much pertinent information as

---

*For a comprehensive database of church and parachurch organizations visit www.faithbased marketing.com.

possible—names, telephone and fax numbers, web site URLs, e-mail addresses—and use a notes section to record anything of particular interest to your business or product.

As a marketer, you know that one of the biggest challenges in communicating with businesses is knowing who to contact. Nothing is more frustrating than sending a company brochure or an introductory letter to a person who does not have the authority to make decisions regarding purchases. This can get a little tricky with churches, so what you want to look for is a complete list of church staff. Then try to identify at least three specific positions: senior pastor, executive pastor (or in some cases, business manager), and administrative assistant/church secretary. For larger churches, the executive pastor is the person who oversees the operational side of the church and is usually the best person to contact for your business purposes. Smaller and medium-size churches may not have an executive pastor, and often, the senior pastor wears so many hats that contacting him or her might not get a timely response. You would probably be better off making the church secretary or administrative assistant your contact person. Most larger churches list all paid staff, and depending on your business, you may want to contact a specific staff member. For example, if you are marketing cleaning supplies and the church puts its custodian on its web site, he's the one you would contact. So your first task when you open a church's web site is to identify key staff members.

Don't rush this process. Spend enough time on each church's web site to allow you to click on every page. In addition to hard data, you will discover a wealth of anecdotal information—things like a photo of the church indicating the size of the building/physical plant, special programs and services offered to their congregants, how often and when they meet, when they undertake expansion projects or new building plans, and photographs of key staff that you will someday meet face-to-face.

AVOID LONG DISTANCE MARKETING

Christians are relational, and until they get to know you, you're barely a distant relative. If you want to be taken seriously, meet personally with the pastor or leader of any church or Christian

(Continued)

organization you want to reach. Even if the pastor or executive director isn't the one who makes the day-to-day decisions on products or services, he or she is the person who influences everyone else on staff. They are the gatekeepers, and you're standing outside the gate.

When Brent High was hired by a baseball team to market to Christians (see sidebar, page 11), he spent his first three months on the job driving to churches and meeting face-to-face with pastors. He knew it would be more difficult getting to first base, so to speak, by making phone calls, sending e-mails, or even sending elaborate packages in the mail to describe his vision for getting Christians to buy tickets to ball games. It was more effective face-to-face.

So what did Brent do when he got a meeting with a pastor? "I simply asked them what was most important to them as a church and how could I help them with that," High explained.

If you can show the pastor how your product or service can help the church do a better job of being the church, the gate will be swung wide open for you.

CONNECT THE DOTS

As you study these web sites, begin thinking creatively about how your business could grow by meeting the specific needs of each church. For example, let's say you own a fabric store in your city, one of three stores competing for market share. And as you spend some time on a church's web site you discover that they feature drama—short plays every Sunday and major productions on various holidays. (This is very common in larger churches, and we're not talking the old bathrobe Christmas plays of years past.) You might consider contacting the person responsible for these dramas and offer to host a free Saturday morning workshop on costume making. Something that simple could make your business the go-to store for that church's purchases of fabric, sewing machines, and other products—and the volunteers who attend your workshop could become new customers. Or you might just decide to donate fabric for the next big pageant at that church in exchange for a credit in the program that will be read by several thousand local consumers. All this from spending 15 minutes on a web site.

We spent some time on just one church's web site in our area, and here's what we found. The church:

- Has a fleet of vans to provide transportation for the elderly and others who can't drive to church (tire, vehicle maintenance, fuel, new vans).
- Builds houses each year with Habitat for Humanity, an organization that provides houses to the poor (lumber, tools, hardware).
- Runs a free health clinic (medical supplies, pharmaceuticals).
- Provides free meals to the elderly (groceries and cooking utensils).
- Runs a camp for underprivileged children (recreational equipment, bedding, towels and linens, craft supplies, groceries).
- Transports the homeless to the church, feeds them, gives them a new set of clothes and shoes, lets them take a shower, and takes them back to the inner city with a sack lunch (clothing, groceries, toiletries).
- Provides Christmas gifts to children in the city whose parents have fallen on hard times (toys, clothing, wrapping paper).
- Has a wedding administrator (contact person for everything from florists, photographers and videographers, wedding dress shops and tuxedo rentals, receptions halls, caterers, DJs, and so on).
- Runs a preschool (teaching supplies, crafts, toys, furniture).

At just one church, we found more than a dozen specific community outreach programs that required the regular purchase of products. That should tell you two things: One, churches are not greedy, but generous; and two, churches purchase thousands of dollars of supplies just for their outreach programs. A savvy local business will look for ways to partner with this church even if it means offering your products or services at a discount because the volume will be high and the relationship will be long term. The positive impact you have on that church extends to all the volunteers who work with those outreach programs and eventually to the entire congregation thanks to word-of-mouth. That's great public relations for your business.

But there's more. The web site we visited continued to list all the programs the church offered. For example, we noticed that they have an extensive music program with choirs and ensembles, even a hand bell choir. So where's the connection if your business isn't music? Let's say you're the marketing director for a shopping mall. Music groups love to perform, and shoppers always appreciate a free concert, especially around the holidays. Invite their music groups to perform in your mall, and it's a win-win-win. Shoppers will appreciate this extra benefit, the music groups appreciate the opportunity to perform, *and* parents and family members will show up at your mall to support their musicians. One of the goals in marketing is increased traffic, and you just did that by visiting a web site.

Our brief visit to that web site also told us that the church is planning a major volunteer workday to spruce up the church—painting, cleaning, brush clearing, and so on. If you sell paint, tools, or cleaning supplies, you just discovered a great way to develop a relationship with that church. Call them and offer a discount and free delivery if they order their supplies from you, and if nothing else, they will be impressed that you know so much about their church and want to help them. If you sell pizzas, why not call and offer free pizzas to feed the volunteers and become the ongoing source for all those teen pizza parties churches sponsor?

In addition to these opportunities, we found at least a dozen other connections between a local business and this church, and we spent a total of about 10 minutes on this site. And that's just one church in our city. So just by browsing a web site, you will begin to see how your business can partner with a church to serve their needs and grow your business, which is why we recommend that you begin your faith-based marketing program on the Internet.

This phase of your market research gives you a basic understanding of the church landscape in your area or region. Capture as much of this information in your database as you can because it will be instrumental in developing and implementing your marketing strategies. You will have phone and fax numbers, e-mail addresses, and postal addresses to use in sending marketing materials. You will have the names of the senior pastor and other key staffers. You will know which churches are closest to your business. And you will begin to get ideas for how your business could serve the needs of each church. Just a start for marketing your products or services to churches, but a good start.

GO TO CHURCH

Okay, we lied. We really are trying to get you to go to church. But it's not what you think. Whether you go to church or not is your business, but a personal visit to the church is *good* for your business. Remember, great marketing is about developing relationships. Depending on your time or the size of your marketing department, you may not be able to visit every church in your area, but you should at least try to visit several of the larger churches closest to your business. Using your Internet research, visit the ones that need your products or services. If your business is national in scope, consider giving this assignment to local franchise operators or your field salespeople.

Don't worry if you're not a Christian. If you're that reporter covering China, you don't have to be Chinese to do your job, but you do have to go to China.

We recommend that you start by identifying a dozen churches that you will commit to visiting in the coming year. Check their web sites to see when they hold their services, and plan your visit for a Sunday morning because typically this is when they are in full operation with the largest number of people in attendance (many larger, contemporary churches also have a Saturday night service that will be unlike any memories you have of church). Make a schedule for the year and get these visits on your planner and then show up. Park in the parking lot, join the crowd heading for the front doors, shake hands with the greeter at the door, and don't worry about fitting in. You will.

Once inside, make sure you grab a *bulletin* (see sample in Figure 5.1 on page 62). First, the bulletin will tell you what will be happening during the service, so when everyone stands to sing, you'll be ready for it. But the bulletin also gives announcements about activities and programs that will be happening during the week—another research tool for you to use to learn more about the church and its needs, so make sure you take it with you when you leave. As you head into the auditorium (sometimes referred to as a sanctuary), take in your surroundings. As the old rhyme says, "Here's the church, here's the steeple, open the doors, and see all the people." Chances are you will see a few people you know which should put you at ease, and you'll also see that people who attend church are pretty normal. If you haven't been to church in a while, you may notice that "Sunday-go-to-meeting" dress has become more casual. Feel free to sit wherever you like, but don't be surprised if an usher offers to help you find a seat. Also, don't be surprised if as you sit down, a perfect stranger extends his hand and greets you. Christians are very friendly; they love to see new people visit their church and make those new people feel welcome. If your visit takes you to a Catholic church, you will notice that most people kneel or bow briefly toward the front of the church before they take their seat. It's a custom, not a rule; so don't feel you have to do it too, because there will be others who don't.

Figure 5.1
Church Bulletin

ACT OF PRAISE　　　　　　　　　　　　Rock of Ages

GOD OFFERS THE WORD TO US

FIRST READING　　　　　　　　　　Isaiah 60:1-6 (OT, P. 649)

CHILDREN'S MESSAGE　　　　　　　　　Kristin Clark-Banks
*(Parents of children **2 years-Pre-K** may escort their children to **Children's**
Church in Room 117 downstairs following the Children's Message)*

GOSPEL　　　　　　　　　　　　Matthew 2:1-12 (NT, P. 1)

SERMON　　　　　　　　　　　　　Rev. Tom Gildemeister

WE OFFER OUR RESPONSE TO GOD

RESPONSE　　　　　　　　　　　　　　Jon Calvin, pianist
*As the response is played, you are invited to
reflect on what God is saying to you through the music
and the Word, read and proclaimed.*

PRAYERS OF THE PEOPLE

INVITATION

CONFESSION and PARDON

> **Merciful God,**
> **we confess that we have not loved you with our whole heart.**
> **We have failed to be an obedient church.**
> **We have not done your will,**
> **we have broken your law,**
> **we have rebelled against your love,**
> **we have not loved your neighbors,**
> **and we have not heard the cry of the needy.**
> **Forgive us, we pray.**
>
> **Free us for joyful obedience,**
> **through Jesus Christ our Lord. Amen.**

All may offer prayers of confession in silence.

Hear the good news:
　　Christ died for us while we were yet sinners;
　　that proves God's love toward us.
In the name of Jesus Christ, you are forgiven!

In the name of Jesus Christ, you are forgiven!
Glory to God. Amen.

Once the service begins, the best advice we can give you is "go with the flow." Every church does things slightly differently, so just do what everyone else does. Catholic churches are known for standing, sitting, and kneeling seemingly without warning, so stay alert and do your best. There will be group singing of hymns or other music that may be unfamiliar to you, and if you don't feel like singing, don't. No one's keeping score. Most services allow a brief time for people to greet each other. The pastor or worship leader will say something like, "Let's take a moment to greet each other." Or if it's a more formal church, they will announce that it's time for "the passing of the peace." Basically, it's a time where people will turn toward one another, shake hands, and exchange a greeting. Churches also collect an "offering," where small containers are passed down the rows for people to deposit money—that's really how the church is funded. But again, don't feel obligated to participate. In fact, in many churches, prior to the offering a pastor will explain to visitors that the offering is for regular attendees—visitors are not expected to give. Listen to the announcements and the sermon because they will help you understand what the church views as important and how they go about supporting it with their various programs.

After the service, make it a point to meet the senior pastor. He or she will usually be at the back of the auditorium greeting people as they leave. Introduce yourself and the business you represent, and mention that this is your first visit to the church. Just be truthful: "I wanted to learn more about your church to see if there are ways my business can help you with your ministries." That's an honest statement and won't be construed as crassly commercial. It would also be appropriate to tell the pastor you'd like to buy him lunch in order to get to know him better. Like any other business client, pastors are accustomed to doing business over lunch and will appreciate the gesture.

The pastor may invite you to wait around for a personal tour of the building, but even if he doesn't, tour the place on your own to get a better idea about the scope of its operation. Most churches will have an entire section devoted to education—Sunday School and other forms of religious education—so make sure you visit that area. In the lobby or *narthex* you may find a rack of literature or an information booth with all sorts of printed information. Look specifically for anything aimed at visitors and take it with you, because it will provide even more information that will help you better understand this church.

Whatever you do, do not say or do anything that could be construed as trying to drum up business. Remember the story of Jesus chasing money changers out of the temple? Any overt attempts to sell or market as you visit the church will seem inappropriate or even offensive to most pastors. The purpose of your trip is to meet the members and leadership of the church so you can get to know them better. Relationships first, business later.

CHURCH ETIQUETTE

Believe it or not, visiting a church will be one of your easiest and most enjoyable research projects. Church members love welcoming visitors and go out of their way to make you feel at home. Here are some tips to help you avoid accidentally sticking your foot in your mouth:

Dress code: Office casual will ensure that you'll blend in at most churches.

Arrival: Check the times of services and arrive a little early. Once the service begins, they will still seat you, but you'll feel like the guy who steps over everyone 10 minutes into the movie.

Singing: Christians love to sing, and depending on the church, you will either sing hymns from a hymnbook found in a rack on the seat in front of you or a giant video screen at the front of the church. If the songs are unfamiliar, just listen and take it all in.

Prayer: There will be a point in the service where a pastor will pray aloud as everyone else listens, usually with their heads bowed. Out of respect, you should do the same, but if you sneak a peek, you won't be the only one.

Bibles: In many churches, people will carry Bibles with them and read along silently as the pastor reads aloud. If you don't have a Bible, don't worry. Most churches have Bibles at each seat for those who don't have them, but it's perfectly okay to just listen. Don't be surprised if the person next to you reaches over to let you read along in her Bible. Remember, Christians are friendly!

Communion: You may be visiting on a Sunday when the church performs a special service known as communion (Catholic churches and other traditional churches do this every Sunday). Because churches have differing practices as to who should participate, we suggest you simply observe and not join in. Don't worry, you won't be the only one.

Baptisms: Some churches "baptize" new Christians during the service. This could involve sprinkling some water over the head of the person or dunking them completely underwater in a pool designed for that purpose. It's often a very moving event, certainly a sacred time for the church. It's a public sign, taught by the Bible, of a person's desire to become a Christian.

CONTINUE YOUR EDUCATION

Okay, you went to church (better than you expected, right?), experienced a Sunday-morning service, toured the facility, met the pastor, and left with a handful of additional information. You've gotten a glimpse of just how big the church is, how the people who attend are like any other consumer your business serves, and what it is that 140 million people do every Sunday morning. Was it worth it? Look at it this way. Between your Internet browsing and the visit to the church, you have gleaned an impressive amount of market research for your business. You have a better feel for the needs of this church and probably came away with a handful of specific ideas for how to market your products or services to that church. Not a bad return on your investment of 75 minutes. But don't stop there.

The following Monday, send a letter or e-mail to the pastor (you already have that contact information in your database) thanking him or her for the church's hospitality and mentioning anything that impressed you (the sermon, the music, the architecture, etc.). Then end by reiterating your invitation to meet with the pastor over lunch or coffee, specifically asking if he would be available anytime in the next week or two. That's it. No hard sell. No special offers or specific ideas. Just a note of appreciation and support, and an invitation.

With the visit fresh on your mind and your e-mail on its way, pull out the bulletin and any other printed information you obtained, and continue with your market research. Wearing your marketer's hat, look at the upcoming activities listed in the bulletin. For example, in one of the bulletins we picked up from a local church, we learned that they would be holding a fund-raising golf tournament in four weeks to benefit their outreach to the homeless. This presents a great opportunity for a local business to increase its exposure and develop a relationship with the church by offering to sponsor one of the holes in the tournament or to contribute a gift certificate for one of the many door prizes such tournaments offer.

In another church bulletin from our area, we learned that the church sponsors a retreat for engaged couples. Perfect for a real estate company to put together a packet of information for each couple, including listings of starter homes and rental units. If you attempted to do this cold, you'd probably get a polite "no thank-you," but once you establish a relationship with the church, they will be more likely to see this is a great bonus for their retreat. This same church advertised a need for lunch bags for an outing it was planning for a youth event. If you're in the restaurant business, what better way to gain exposure than to donate lunch bags with your logo on it? And just from reading this church bulletin, we learned that the church is encouraging its members to stock up on gifts for the Angel Tree program (Angel Tree is a nationwide effort sponsored by Prison Fellowship to provide Christmas gifts for children who have a parent in prison). The notice actually asked members to "watch for sales on gift items." They're practically advertising for you—a follow-up call to the head of that church's Angel Tree program with a special discount to everyone who brings in that bulletin could generate new business for your store.

We visited another church and picked up a magazine published by the church's denominational organization. One of the articles offered practical advice for churches in the market for a new sound system. It specifically warned against buying a prepackaged system, opting instead for a system designed for the unique needs of the church. Valuable information if you owned an electronics store and were about to approach that church with a prepackaged system. That same magazine encouraged its churches to become more intentional about increasing racial and ethnic diversity. If you represent a minority-owned business, you just received a wide open door to help that church do what its denominational leaders want to see them do.

You get the idea. Two days ago, you knew nothing about the church you visited. Now you have some specific ideas about how you can market your business to that church. Oh, by the way, church bulletins often publish the attendance numbers from the previous week's service. One of the churches we visited reported 4,600 in attendance. So we're not talking small here. How often can you reach that many people at little or no cost? And that's just one church.

THE "NO MYSTERY" MARKET

No other organizations provide such clear information concerning their beliefs, their values, or how to reach them. Most audience segments are a mystery to marketers, forcing them to invest tens or even hundreds of thousands of dollars researching those groups in order to learn what their beliefs are, what's important to them, and how they behave. Not so with the church. In one of the booklets we picked up for visitors, the church actually published this statement: "If you have read this far, then you know why we exist (their purpose), what we value (their values) and how we live those values through the priority of our essential ministries (their behavior)." While most groups keep this information quiet, forcing you to ferret it out through your research, churches offer this information freely, publishing it every week in the material you pick up from their web sites and your visits. That's a gold mine.

They also take the mystery out of this market by segmenting their audience for you. Most marketers spend lots of money trying to identify media channels to help them reach young people, singles, newly married people, or people over sixty. But churches automatically segment their entire congregation into groups just like that so they can build specific ministries to serve those segments. Churches literally minister to people "from the cradle to the grave," designing specific programs, resources, and experiences for both age-group segments and lifestyle or behavioral segments. Looking over a church bulletin from one of the churches we visited, we learned that there were programs for teens, young teens, college students, preschoolers, senior citizens, grade schoolers, young parents, and so on. But they also offered programming and resources for "nearly weds," people who have been divorced, women interested in diet and fitness, expectant parents, and so on. They also offered three Bible studies in Spanish. All of this provided valuable information about the ethnic makeup of this church.

Earlier in this chapter, we told you that with the advent of segmented marketing, businesses can no longer market to *everyone*, but must target their efforts to specific groups based on age, gender, ethnicity, and behaviors. You can spend thousands of dollars in market research in your city to find those audiences, or you can develop relationships with churches that already do this for you. If you've followed our directions in this chapter, you now have the beginnings of a powerful database to help you match your products or services with the needs of a sizable share of your market. In other words, you're ready to do some faith-based marketing.

CHAPTER SIX

SERVE, DON'T SELL

BUILDING YOUR BRAND

Here's a little-known secret about many Christians. They feel a little persecuted, picked on by the media, made fun of in movies and on television. It's not a major complex or anything, just this feeling that "you better be careful about letting anyone know you're a Christian because they'll think you're weird."

Why are we telling you this? Because people who feel like outsiders really treasure their friends and allies, and we believe it's possible for your business to become a friend to Christians. In fact, the best way to market to Christians is to think "serve" rather than "sell." This is important—maybe the most important point we make in this book because we're talking about a mindset, an attitude, and that's something you can't fake. If you approach it as a gimmick, it won't work, but if you truly see yourself as an ally to the Christian consumer and look for ways to serve or help them, we guarantee success.

If this sounds far-fetched to you, think of your favorite place to get your hair cut or your car serviced. Why do you keep going back? Certainly because they've earned your trust by giving you a decent haircut or oil change. But we're ready to bet there are other decent barbers and mechanics near you who will do just as good a job and maybe even for less money. You go back to these businesses because somehow they've convinced you they are more than just a business. They're on your side—they care about you. The barber probably learned the names of your kids and asked about them. The mechanic warned you against buying a car that he knew had some major problems. Both genuinely went out of their way to serve your best needs when it came to haircuts and auto repair. They didn't give you free haircuts or special discounts, but because they took a special interest in what was important to you, they cared about the very things you care about.

The quickest way to close a sale is not to ask for the sale but rather to show your commitment to these people by helping them accomplish the good they're trying to accomplish through the efforts of their church. What you win by doing this is their respect and their loyalty. You demonstrate that you have their best interests in mind, and because Christians often feel that the rest of the culture is against them, you become an ally. Not only do they give you their business because they trust you, but they tell all their friends about your business as well.

Case Study on Serving

The best way for us to explain what we mean by "serve, don't sell" is to tell you about Chuck Walllington, the owner of a Christian bookstore, Christian Supply, Inc. in Spartanburg, South Carolina. You probably have never heard of Christian Supply, but it is the largest family-owned Christian retail operation in the world. If you know anything about retail, you know that independent stores fight to compete with the big chains, but Chuck's independent bookstore continues to prosper and grow. With an inventory turn rate of 4.1, Christian Supply is well ahead of his counterparts in Christian retailing. This number is even more commendable because of the store's large size (35,000 square feet), which makes good inventory turns and sales per square foot challenging. Christian Supply's average sales per square foot is an impressive $217. All this success makes Chuck a pretty reliable source on how to market to the faith community. In addition to thousands of individual customers who walk into his store every day, Christian Supply services more than 70,000 church accounts!

From the day he and his family went into business, they believed that if they could develop an intimate connection with their community, they would be successful. So one of the first things they did to serve the churches in their community was to sponsor a conference for all the church choir directors in their area. For a nominal fee, they could attend a world-class event featuring 70 workshops to help them improve their skills, enjoy a concert featuring well-known religious musicians, hear inspirational speakers, and receive *$600 worth of choral music for their church music libraries—free!* This event, which they've been doing now for 29 years, draws more than 1,500 choir directors from area churches. When those choir directors need to buy new music for their choirs, where do you think they call to place the order?

"When we started this conference," Chuck told us:

> Our goal was not to sell music but to provide a retreat for the music staff of a church, to impact their lives. This isn't a formula or a gimmick where you say, "if we do this for them our business will grow by x percent." If your only interest is in selling, Christians will see through it from a hundred miles away. They won't support phonies. But if they know you truly care about them and want to help them, you won't have to sell your product. They'll come to you asking for it. Caring for a customer is more important than any gimmick or discount.

Chuck also sponsors something he calls the Winter Book Ministry Project where he features one book for three weeks (late January through Valentine's Day), selling it at half-price, but also making it available free to anyone who wants it and can't afford it even at half-price. (Incidentally, when he sells it at half-price, he's losing money because he usually has to pay between 53 and 54 percent to the publisher). You might think he's just dumping a slow-moving product, but he specifically chooses a current, popular book that contains a positive message that will nurture the spiritual health and growth of the community. Last year, they sold at half-price or gave away 3,500 copies during the three weeks, but then sold 12,000 throughout the rest of the year, a huge volume for a single title in any store.

"But we really don't do it to sell books," Chuck explains. "We believe books change lives, and by selecting one book each year to make available and affordable to as many people as we can, we are serving our community—making it better. That's really why we do it, not to sell more books."

What Chuck is describing is really the Golden Rule, which traces its origins to the Bible. Do something for others, and they will return the favor. Ironically, a recent tragedy at Christian Supply is further proof that if you adopt a "serve, don't sell" mindset, your customers become your friends. In early 2008, Chuck discovered a trusted friend and employee had been embezzling from the company. Because the case was still being investigated when we interviewed Chuck, he couldn't get too specific, but indicated it was in the high six-figure range—enough to potentially force him out of business. Thinking his vendors were being paid, Chuck later discovered the employee cooked the books to make it look like the bills were being paid while pocketing that money on the sly. It was devastating, but when word got out that Christian Supply might shut down, all those years of serving his customers paid off in a way that still causes Chuck to shake his head in disbelief.

A local businessman and regular customer walked in the day after the news broke and offered to loan me some money to keep the store open. I politely declined, telling him I would never be able to live with myself if I couldn't pay him back or keep up with the terms of the loan. He came back with his wife later that day and handed me an envelope and told me to open it after he left. Inside was a check for $250,000 and his "terms": 0 percent interest, to be paid back as God blesses you.

Individual customers would come in and purchase gift cards for $50 and $100, and after they purchased them, they would cut them up right in front of us to demonstrate this was a donation. It was like buying books but not taking them off the shelves. Vendors called to say they were writing off the bad debts that were a result of my employee's embezzling. A gift company we do business with sent a skid of product—$10,000 worth—at no charge to help us get back on our feet. We received literally hundreds of such offers.

The point we're making here is that when you adopt an attitude of service—of looking first to meet your customers' needs, not just to sell them a product—they will reward you with their loyalty. That doesn't mean just being nice and hoping for the best. Christian Supply has one of the most detailed, targeted, and strategic marketing plans seen in their industry, and their plan focuses on a well-defined core customer, utilizing the Internet to reach those customers, which now number more than 50,000. This from a relatively small, independent bookstore in a midsize city. But because those customers and churches believe that Christian Supply is more interested in serving them than selling to them, they are fiercely loyal.

SERVING TO SELL: THE PRINCIPLES

The "serve, not sell" philosophy of marketing is not a gimmick or a tactic, but a different way of looking at your customers. Most marketing seeks to attract attention and then deliver information about a service or product. This approach is different. It requires you to become an ally to your customers and is based on three principles:

First, *discover* what the church, organization, or individual is trying to accomplish. For organizations and churches, you can discover what they are trying to accomplish by spending time on their web sites along with follow-up face-to-face visits. This will also help you learn what is important to individuals, because most Christians have the same goals and interests as their churches. Know the church, and you'll know a lot about individual Christians.

Second, *help* them accomplish their objectives by complementing or multiplying their efforts with your business, product, or service. Here's where you may need to do what we sometimes call "soul searching," because this has to be sincere. Your main objective is to serve them. Don't serve because you expect or require sales to follow. Serve to serve, and then watch sales increase as a natural—rather than required—result.

Finally, *position* your business to benefit, but don't require it. In other words, never demand a response, but plan for it. For example, if you discover that a church is trying to provide a free thanksgiving dinner to the homeless and you have decided your coffee shop will provide free coffee and tea for the event because you want the church to give these men and women the very best experience possible, don't make it a condition that the pastor asks everyone in her church to stop in for coffee on the way to church every Sunday. But be prepared because when Christians learn of your support, they will want to give you their business.

The pushier you are—the more *commercial* the manner in which you try to help—the more suspicion you will create. But a consistent, "no-strings attached" approach to helping the church or organization accomplish something that's important to them will create long-term loyal, and, yes, profitable customers.

SERVE, DON'T SELL—HOW TO DO IT

Ready to give it a try? In order to show you how to increase your sales by serving first, we're going to create a fictitious church based on our research of dozens of churches in our city. We will identify actual programs that we discovered at these churches, but for the sake of convenience, we'll place them inside the walls of a single, fictitious church: Springville Community Church. (Remember, in addition to churches, you will also find other religious organizations in your community, and the tactics we describe here will work with those as well).

This particular church sits at a busy intersection in a suburb of a major Southern city where it conducts a Saturday evening service and two Sunday morning services that attract a total of 4,500 men, women, and children. By spending time on their web site, reading their church bulletin and other printed materials, we discovered the following activities were extremely important to this church and have suggested a specific marketing strategy for each activity based on the philosophy of "serve, not sell."

By the way, although these are actual events and activities from churches in our area, they are fairly typical of the types of things churches do. We'll be offering some marketing ideas for each activity to help you see the difference between serving and selling. We may not cover your type of business; so as you read through these samples, begin thinking about how your business could serve. The best way to do that is to ask yourself these questions: "How can my business help them accomplish this activity? How can I help them make it better?"

Golf Tournament

Springville Community Church sponsors an annual "Graceworks Golf Tournament" to benefit a local charity, and a number of churches participate, sending their golfers to the tournament where they pay a fairly high entry fee, which goes to the local charity. How could a business "serve" this charity event? Look at the purpose of the tournament—a local charity. That's what's important to the church. Determine how your business can help them. If you're not sure, contact the tournament director, introduce yourself and your business, and ask how you can help. After he comes to, he might suggest that you sponsor a hole (basically a donation in exchange for exposure). Or place a poster in your business and solicit donations from your own customers. In other words, look for ways to stand alongside that church to help them accomplish their goal of supporting a local charity.

Let's say you own a golf course, but not the one where the tournament is being played. Lost opportunity? Not at all. You can still help the church accomplish its mission by inviting them to send their golfers to your course to prepare for the tournament, and in exchange, you will make a donation to the charity. What will happen? The pastor or tournament director will encourage everyone who plans to play in the tournament to go to your golf course to practice because it will benefit a cause the church believes in. While you're at it, hold a pretournament sale in your pro shop, with proceeds going to the charity.

Be creative. Suppose you own a tax preparation business. Whenever someone enters a charity golf tournament, he or she makes a charitable donation through the entry fee. Good time to contact participating churches and offer to provide a free miniseminar on charitable giving and taxes. You may end up giving this 20-minute presentation to adult Sunday-school classes in dozens of churches throughout your community.

Virtually any business could help a church that sponsors a golf tournament, if only by making a donation. But do it to help, not just to attract attention to your business and sell stuff.

New and Expectant Parent Dinner

Springville Community Church offers a nice evening to new and expectant parents with a dinner, special speakers, and music. This tells you that the church is interested in young parents and wants to help them learn more about parenting. The new parents have an infant and need child-care services. The church likely has a nursery, but it's always a pain finding qualified volunteer staff in the middle of the week. So if you own a day-care center, why not contact the church and offer to send your trained child-care workers to the church to staff the nursery for their "New and Expectant Parent Dinner"? Your focus was on serving the needs of the church, and you didn't sell a thing, except a lot of goodwill and the possibility of future business.

CEO Fellowship

This is a monthly luncheon at the church for CEOs of businesses from all over the city. They gather to learn how to live out their faith in their workday world. If you represent the regional business magazine in this area, call the church and offer to give them your mailing list of CEOs or company presidents so that they might increase their attendance. Also, ask how many free copies of your magazine they would like as a bonus for everyone who attends the CEO Fellowship. Don't ask for anything in exchange—just say you want to help build the event. Small investment for building a relationship of trust with the church that will most likely provide you with new subscribers and potential advertising.

Church Bulletin Outreach

All churches publish a bulletin—a printed program explaining the order of the Sunday service and containing announcements for the coming week. All churches want to grow—bring in new people. For the most part, they would frown on using the bulletin to advertise, so don't call and offer to place an ad in their bulletin. However, if you represent a restaurant near the church, tell the pastor you will give a discount for Sunday brunch to every party that comes with a copy of that bulletin. I can almost guarantee the pastor will encourage his regular worshipers to invite friends to come to church, using the bulletin and your business as an incentive. This would also work for any business offering a product or service that people regularly need.

Members' Recipe Cookbook

Springville Community Church announced plans to publish a cook-book featuring the signature recipes of its members. They gather the recipes, collect them in a book, and then sell the books to raise money for a ministry of the church. It's a lengthy and involved process requiring tons of volunteer hours and printing costs so high that the margins produce little profit for funding the ministry.

If you represented a local printing company, you might consider offering your services for free or at a significant discount in order to help the church raise more money for ministry. Churches spend thousands of dollars creating printed materials, so this could begin a long-term relationship between your business and the church.

But what if you own a web-design business, or your business is large enough to have a fairly sophisticated web team? You could serve the church by offering to create a web site allowing members to submit their recipes online, and then your creative staff could design and develop the cookbook for the church and give it to them on a CD, which the church could copy and sell to its members who probably would prefer looking up recipes on their laptops instead of cluttering up their bookshelves. Better yet, make the web site password accessible and let the church sell passwords so members can go directly to the web site. It's cheaper than a CD, so the church makes more money for ministry. Either way, unit costs would be a lot less, producing more money for the church's ministry. Don't charge them, and don't try to sell anything to them. The next time they need the services of a web designer or whatever your business sells, they will call you.

Church Photographic Directory

Our church also creates a photo directory every few years, and in their bulletin we discovered they put out a call for help in designing the cover of the directory. Graphic design studios or advertising agencies could offer to design the cover in exchange for credit in the directory. Again, churches often need such services, but now you not only have served the church and thus positioned yourself for more business, but you gained exposure to the 2,000 families in the directory that also may need your services someday.

Homeless Lunch Program

This church gives a free sack lunch to homeless men and women once a week. It has issued a plea on its web site for lunch bags and hand sanitizer. Okay, you just discovered that this church values helping the homeless. Anything you do that can help them with this ministry will endear your business to them. If your business uses paper or plastic bags with your logo on them, you could easily donate the bags, include hand sanitizer as a gift, and then throw in several hundred coupons for your business. We can assure you they will be distributed throughout the church, along with appreciation to your business for helping them with their homeless ministry.

Grocers can offer free food, clothing stores can offer a free pair of socks or gloves to go in each lunch bag, restaurants can donate plastic spoons and forks or paper cups with their logo—all with coupons the church can give to its members. Again, serve, but don't attempt to sell. With your actions, you are saying, "We believe in your ministry to the homeless and we want to help."

AIDS Walk

Springville Community Church holds a walk each year to raise awareness about AIDS and raise money to fight and treat the disease. Actually, this is a common type of fund-raiser that many churches sponsor, and they offer great opportunities for your business to serve. Any business could contact a bottled water supplier and have special labels applied to hundreds of water bottles that volunteers distribute to the walkers/runners. Any business could contact the church and ask for pledge forms for its employees to be able to pledge their financial support for the event. More specifically, if you own a shoe store, you could offer a discount on walking or running shoes to anyone participating in the event, with the difference between the discount price and full retail price going to the event. This is a "two-fer" because the church not only gets additional funding from you, but the great pricing might attract more participants for the walk.

Use your imagination. Radio stations could offer their sound equipment and an on-air personality to emcee the event. Health clinics could offer free blood pressure testing and first-aid services. Professional photographers could offer to cover the event, giving the church a photo album commemorating the event. Restaurants could offer free meals as prizes for those who raised the most money. Imagine helping to turn their event into the biggest fund-raising walk in the county. That's what we mean by "serve."

Angel Tree

This church (and thousands around the country) sponsors Angel Tree, which provides Christmas gifts to children with a parent in prison. Sponsored by Prison Fellowship, families in the church adopt a boy or girl, learn his or her age and interests, then go Christmas shopping for that child. So if you represent any business that sells anything kids would like to get for Christmas, you can serve this church and actually sell at the same time. Anything from having a special "Angel Tree Shopping Night" at your store, to e-mailing the church with a coupon they can print and distribute to as many people as they need, offering significant discounts on your products. If you sell gift wrap, invite anyone who has an Angel Tree gift to come to your store and have it professionally gift wrapped. All of these efforts will attract new customers to your store because you are helping the church members accomplish something that is important to them.

Church Members in the Military

We noticed in our church's bulletin that a number of the members are serving in the military, and members were encouraged to pray for them. This helped us discover that the church cares deeply about its members serving in harm's way. So how can your business serve this church so that they might eventually send their business your way? Soldiers overseas love care packages, and perhaps your business could donate products that they might appreciate (toiletries, books, magazines, candy, and so on). If you're in the retail business, you could create a bulletin board with large blank letters for people to write a note of encouragement to soldiers whose names the church provides, and after they are written, the church can mail them. Do you sell phone cards? Consider giving each church family with a son or daughter overseas one free international phone card. You have just told the church you care in a way that is appropriate and helpful.

Silent Auction Fund-Raiser

You've all seen them—churches and other organizations raise money by placing items on several tables with a place where people can record their bids. An auction without the noisy auctioneer. We recommend you support these fund-raisers, but do it with coupons or gift cards. This way, the value is very clear to the bidder, and the name of your business is prominent. But best of all, the coupon drives traffic to your business—potential new and long-term customers for you because you chose to serve, not sell. The more coupons or gift cards you donate (which you can afford by offering them in smaller amounts), the more customers you will gain.

Church Sport Ministry

Our church provides several opportunities for its members to join sports teams, telling us that recreation and fitness is important to the church. If you own a sporting goods company, don't try to sell the teams bats and balls or uniforms. That's selling, not serving. Instead, offer to host an evening for all the church's sports teams and present a program on the care and prevention of sports injuries. Serve soft drinks and snacks. Have people from your staff demonstrate proper training exercises for the different sports. Give everyone who attends a coupon or free product. Invite teams to send their action photos to your web site. In other words, create a partnership with this church's sports ministry, and the sales will follow.

Youth Group Mission Trips

Springville Community Church, and thousands like it, plans trips for its teenagers to theme parks and other attractions, and often the church will send its youth groups to a place where members can help those less fortunate. Regardless of where it travels, the group needs to raise money for the trip, and here's where you come in. Suppose you own a car wash and wanted to help. *Selling* would be going to the pastor and telling him if he promotes your car wash in church, you will donate money to the youth group. Trust us, the pastor won't bite. But if you called the pastor and said, "I want to help your kids pay for their trip, and will let them use my automated car wash next Saturday from 8:00 AM to 5:00 PM. After my expenses, every penny of profit will go to the youth group," the pastor will make sure every family—and their friends and neighbors—create a traffic jam at your car wash. Why? Because your offer invested in the lives of kids more than it tried to generate sales. Because this church values its teens, you became an ally. Distribute coupons for discounts on future visits to the customers that come that day, and you'll ensure future business.

Church Coffee Hour

The church also provides free coffee for its members after the morning worship service. If you own a bakery, call the pastor and say, "We would like to help you give your members more than coffee after your service. Would it be okay if we came over with freshly baked pastries next Sunday?" We don't know any pastor who would turn down free donuts for his parishioners, so have your employees in their white aprons with your company name on the front deliver and distribute donuts at that church. No strings attached. No attempts to sell donuts the rest of the year.

How the Government Can Help You Market to Churches

As a for-profit business, you know how much money the IRS drains from your earnings every year. You also know that marketing expenses for your business are tax deductible, but did you know that donations to churches or religious organization are also deductible? More than 90 percent of small businesses in the United States donate to charity. Not only does it aid the community, but it's also a great way to increase your visibility.

If you donate money, goods, or services to an approved charitable organization, they may be deducted on your company's income tax return (if the organization does not operate under a federally approved designation, such as 501(c)(3), it is probably not as legitimate as it seems). Always pay by check when you make a financial contribution and ask for a receipt from the organization.

Generally speaking, a gift of property may be deducted in the amount of its fair market value (FMV)—what a consumer would be willing to pay for the item. So if you donated 10 pizzas that normally cost $15 to a church youth group, you could deduct $150 on your return. Limitations do exist on the overall amount you can deduct for gifts of property, so always consult your tax account to determine the best way to make such gifts.

State and local tax laws may vary, so it is always a good idea to consult with a tax accountant to determine the best way to donate to churches and religious organizations.

SERVING MADE EASY

We began this chapter with a story of how one small business created phenomenal customer loyalty (and increased sales) by serving area churches. We'd like to close with an example of how a much larger retailer found a way to serve churches in a way that has generated hundreds of thousands of dollars for churches and driven high volumes of customers into its stores.

Meijer, Inc. is a regional grocery/mega store chain with 180 stores in five midwestern states. Recognizing the challenge churches and other nonprofits face in raising funds to sustain their organizations, it initiated the "Meijer Rewards" program. Essentially, when churches register, whenever its members shop at the store, one percent of their total shopping bill goes back to the church. They produce marketing materials for the church to promote the program to its members and create an account, allowing the church to track the money it receives from its members' shopping trips. Every month, the church receives a check from Meijer based on the purchases made that month by everyone from the church who shopped there.

Churches value the program not just because they receive additional money, but because they don't have to ask their members to do anything different from what they normally do every week: shop for groceries and other supplies for their families. They view the megastore as a friend and have no problem recommending the store to parishioners. And Meijer gains an advantage in the competitive grocery market because it reached out to serve the church, not just to sell to it.

This is a great example of creatively finding ways to partner with churches. Meijer saw a need and set about finding a way to help churches meet that need. If churches believe you care about their ministry, they will reward you with loyalty and increased business. But it always starts with serving the needs of your consumers, not trying to sell them products or services they may not need.

Regardless of the size of your business, you can use the "serve, don't sell" philosophy to develop unprecedented customer loyalty. Churches and other religious organizations may resist overt attempts to market your products or services to their members, but they will become your best consumer evangelists if you find ways to serve them. On their web sites and in their printed materials, they provide you with all the information you need to determine what's important to them, what they are trying to accomplish, and what they might need to reach those important ministry goals. Once you connect your company with what the organization is passionate about, that organization will do your marketing for you.

CHAPTER SEVEN

WORD-OF-MOUTH

When you're in the market for a new car, which of the following influences your decision the most: stylishly produced television advertising, full-page ads in your local newspaper, special promotions mailed directly to your home, or a trusted friend who recently bought a new car and can't stop talking about it?

All of these forms of communication, along with your own research, play into your final decision, but if you're like most consumers, nothing closes the deal like the recommendation of a friend—what's called word-of-mouth. Word-of-mouth is without question the most potent form of advertising today. The term is in vogue these days, leading many to think of it as a new phenomenon, but in reality, word-of-mouth has been around since the beginning of commerce. It's just that with so many communications technologies at our disposal that escalate the effect of word-of-mouth, it is suddenly more visible. It is also more important to consumers now than ever before because of the incredible proliferation of choices—it serves as a filter for conflicting messages from advertisers.

A friend of ours was shopping for a new cell phone and became frustrated by all the models and plans available. This was a few months after Apple's new iPhone was introduced and because of all the hype and almost nonstop advertising, he had pretty much made up his mind to buy one. That is until he talked to a friend of his who had tried the iPhone, but switched to Palm because he seldom used all the cool features of the iPhone. Based on that one recommendation, he bought a Palm. With all the information sent to him in the mail by all the cell phone companies, he had somehow never even heard about (or remembered) the Palm phone. Three sentences from a trusted friend won out over millions of dollars of very creative and compelling advertising.

We're not making this word-of-mouth thing up. Reliable research has provided hard data supporting the superiority of word-of-mouth to influence consumer behavior. In 2005, BIGresearch, a consumer behavior market intelligence company, surveyed 15,000 consumers on the influence various media play in their purchase decisions. Here's their top ten ranking (http://brandautopsy.typepad.com/brandautopsy/2006/01/the_influential.html):

1. Word-of-mouth
2. Television
3. Coupons
4. Newspaper inserts
5. Editorial (reading articles)
6. Direct mail
7. Magazines
8. In-store promotion
9. Cable television
10. Online advertising

According to a study by the Keller Fay Group, word-of-mouth is the biggest factor in business-to-business purchase decisions. Fully half of the executives surveyed said that they are highly likely to buy a product or service based on word-of-mouth, and 49 percent pass on what they've learned to others (www.kellerfay.com/news/Executive percent20WOM percent20Release percent20FINAL.pdf). Further, they claim that word-of-mouth has twice the influence of advertising, direct mail, or press coverage (www.marketingservicestalk.com/news/jac/jac101.html).

A recent article from the Word-of-mouth Marketing Association reported that 59 percent of college students pick word-of-mouth as their preferred method for learning about new products and services. According to the Edelman Trust Barometer 2007, word-of-mouth is two times more important than advertising or editorial in influencing opinions. Word-of-mouth is one-and-a-half times more valuable in marketing than it was 25 years ago. The giant consumer researcher, Nielsen, claims that the number-one form of advertising is a personal recommendation from another consumer; number three is another consumer's opinion posted online, which is yet another form of word-of-mouth. And finally, researchers have identified the most trusted spokesperson for a brand in all of Europe, North America, and Latin America: "a person like me." Savvy marketers understand this because, according to PQMedia, word-of-mouth spending was expected to hit $1.3 billion in 2008, an increase of 33 percent over the previous year (http://www.pqmedia.com/about-press-20071115-wommf.html).

In other words, people tend to trust the word of another over words and information communicated through other forms of advertising, and this is where the church comes in. Word-of-mouth, though incredibly effective in society at large, is even more effective within the context of the church. Few segments of society provide such a vast audience of "people like me"—140 million people who have the same beliefs and, because of those shared beliefs, trust each other. Some of the biggest word-of-mouth campaigns in history have taken place within the church environment.

A Warning about Word-of-Mouth

Like any effective marketing tool, word-of-mouth can be abused. With access to consumers more available than during any other time in history, the opportunity to deceive increases. Unethical marketers often will try anything to gain access to consumers. But those practices eventually backfire in the marketplace, and they will permanently end your relationship with the faith-based community.

We recommend you abide by the Word-of-Mouth Marketing Association's (WOMMA) ethics guidelines:

- *Honesty of relationships:* You say who you are speaking for.
- *Honesty of opinion:* You say what you believe.
- *Honesty of identity:* You never obscure your identity.

You can find a more complete treatment of these guidelines by visiting www.womma.org/ethics/.

Faith-Based Word-of-Mouth

You may think you already know the formula for making a best-selling book: Take a book on a generally popular secular topic written by a well-known author and launch it with loads of national advertising and public relations (PR)—presto, a best seller. I (Greg) spent most of my marketing career in publishing and watched how this was done with

Hillary Clinton's book, *Living History*. She was perhaps the best-known woman in the United States, the book was on a generally popular topic, and it arrived amid a flurry of national advertising and publicity. It was an instant *New York Times* best seller, selling more than 200,000 copies per month for three months—an incredible performance—leading *USA Today* to name her the best-selling nonfiction author in the United States that year. Except they were wrong!

In the same time period that Mrs. Clinton's book was selling 200,000 copies a month, a little-known Baptist preacher wrote a book on a seemingly narrow religious topic that didn't get any national advertising or PR for 18 months following its release, and yet it sold *one million copies a month* during that same three-month period and then went on to sell a million copies a month for 18 consecutive months! In three years, it sold 30 million copies, making it the fastest-selling hardcover book in history.

How did *The Purpose Driven Life,* by now-famous pastor and author, Rick Warren, outsell every other book in the United States? You can learn the full story in my (Greg's) first book, *PyroMarketing*, but the answer is word-of-mouth. Warren had written a book for pastors 10 years previous called *The Purpose-Driven Church*, which began a close relationship between him and church leaders across the United States. He followed that up by offering resources online for pastors at a web site created especially for them: www.pastors.com. The majority of churches in the United States have congregations of around 100, and the pastor is often the only paid employee, overwhelmed with all the responsibilities of leading a church. Warren came alongside them as a friend—a partner in ministry—offering them sermon outlines and other resources to help them become successful. They loved it, and the list eventually grew to 85,000 pastors who looked to Warren as a trusted ally. When he wrote his second book, he decided to launch it with the help of those pastors, offering the $20 book for $7 if they would conduct a 40-day campaign in their churches. He sent a single e-mail to his list and 1,200 churches agreed to participate. The campaign consisted of asking the pastor to preach six sermons based on the six sections of the book. Each member would also buy the $20 book for just $7 and commit to reading a chapter a day for 40 days. Finally, small groups in each church met in homes to discuss the book during this 40-day campaign. Members of participating churches immediately bought 400,000 copies, though at barely a breakeven price for the publisher.

Nearly everyone in the publishing food chain thought this plan would be disastrous. The publisher, who had projected first-year sales (at full retail price) of 100,000, feared that by virtually giving away the book, they would lose money and exhaust market demand. Retailers wondered why any consumer would come into their stores to buy a $20 book when they could get it through their church for $7 (or sometimes free, as churches bought the book and gave one to each member). But within two months those 400,000 "consumer evangelists," through their recommendations to friends and coworkers, drove sales to two million copies. By selling the book at cost, Warren enabled an army of 400,000 people to become familiar with the book, experience its benefits, and then tell all their friends about it. And once the snowball began, it kept building and, as they say, the rest is publishing history.

You might think Warren had an advantage because he was an "insider"—a leader in the church, but someone as offbeat and with as colorful a history in Hollywood as Mel Gibson pulled off a similar marketing triumph, using the same word-of-mouth tactics, on his film, *The Passion of the Christ*. After investing his own money to produce the film because no studio would get behind it, Gibson had little left over to market the film. So already, he was at a huge disadvantage because without the backing of a major studio, getting widespread distribution is almost impossible. The normal procedure for turning a movie into a hit is to find a distributor who will pour between $20 and $40 million into marketing the film through television, web sites, and other traditional marketing venues targeting moviegoers; but Gibson, a Catholic Christian, after investing over $20 million to make the film, was looking for a more economical way to market it. So he asked himself, "Who would be most likely to want to see a movie about the suffering, death, and resurrection of Jesus Christ?" He decided, wisely, that pastors—especially evangelical pastors—would be most interested because it was basically the story they had been trying to tell their own congregations for years. So rather than investing in a big advertising campaign to moviegoers, he began inviting pastors from all over the United States to private screenings of the film, even before it was complete. They would have an intimate experience with the film, see how it remained true to the biblical story they treasured so much, and begin to imagine its effect on their congregations and on those who had never heard the story before. Initially, he showed it to fairly small groups of pastors—10 to 12 at a time. But as word began to spread about the film, the pastors who had seen it got excited about it and began telling other pastors about it. The screening audiences grew until the month prior to the film's release, when he showed it to groups of 5,000 pastors at a time! Remember, pastors have an enormous influence over their congregations, so already he had developed a sizable force of word-of-mouth marketers.

One of those final screenings was at Willow Creek Community Church in South Barrington, Illinois—one of the largest churches in the United States. At the end of the film, the pastor of Willow Creek, Bill Hybels, took the stage and after several moments of silence he turned to Gibson, who joined him on the platform, and spoke for every one of the 5,000 pastors in the auditorium: "All right, what do you need us to do?" They had experienced the power of the film and were *volunteering* to help him promote it. Pastors all over the United States urged their congregations to see the movie, with many churches providing free bus transportation to theaters. It's safe to say that the huge success of the film came solely from this ingenious word-of-mouth campaign.

Admittedly, those two examples had a lot going for them: a popular pastor and a well-known movie star. Can the little guy benefit from faith-based word-of-mouth marketing? In other words, could someone like you use word-of-mouth in the faith community to turn your product into a best seller? Absolutely! In early 2007, an unknown author by the name of William P. Young worked with two freelance editors, Wayne Jacobsen and Brad Cummings, to write a fictional story called *The Shack*. Unable to find a publisher, they decided to publish it themselves, printing a small quantity of paperbacks and selling them out of Cummings' garage, and introduced it to the Christian community through a series of podcasts. Generally, self-publishing is seldom successful—if you sell a couple thousand books, you're lucky. But the powerful content of the book inspired readers to begin telling their friends about it, and it soon caught the attention of the giant retail chain, Barnes & Noble, who agreed to carry it in their stores. As sales began to climb, the online retailer Amazon went out on a limb and ordered *one* copy. But the buzz continued, leading the publishing giant, Hachette, to seek a deal with the authors. Even as they were working out the agreement, the book hit the number-one spot on the *New York Times* Best Seller list as a self-published book.

At that point, these unknown authors with no national platform had spent just $250 on marketing.

Why Word-of-Mouth Works

It's not that word-of-mouth is something new, but the reason it works so well is tied closely to the declining influence of mass media. In the last century, marketers could rely on the mass media to get their message out to huge numbers of people. With only three television networks and a handful of national magazines, you could communicate directly with the masses by purchasing advertising in those vehicles. Furthermore, marketers faced a huge demand for a limited supply of products (maybe three or four brands of laundry detergent, a handful of electronics brands, and so on). World War II contributed by creating the perfect storm for successful marketing. During the war, women began working in factories and purchased "war bonds" to support the war. When the men came home, we now had two-income families with healthy savings accounts, producing a robust economy where if you wanted to sell a refrigerator, you placed an ad in *Life* magazine, made sure your warehouse was full, and you didn't worry too much about competition because besides Kelvinator and Kenmore, there weren't too many brands to choose from. During this period, brands spoke directly to consumers. They had a monopoly on communication, so much so that everything a person knew about a brand came directly from advertising. If you think we're exaggerating, find someone over 50 and give them this little quiz:

1. Finish this tag line: "Winston tastes good..."
2. What goes "plop, plop, fizz, fizz?"
3. If you used a product where "a little dab will do ya?" what was the product?
4. Which bar of soap is 99 percent pure?
5. Finish the words to this song: "See the United States in your..."

(Find the answers at www.faithbasedmarketing.com.)

Life was good for marketers in a mass-media-influenced society.

Consider how things have changed. In 2003 alone, there were more than 26,000 new food and household products introduced, including 115 new deodorants, 187 new breakfast cereals, and 303 brand new women's perfumes. We still have high consumer demand—that hasn't changed. While major companies still employ mass marketing techniques, the proliferation of media has created the opportunity to target specific audiences more effectively, but not the harder-to-reach large audiences that it once could. Those six national magazines in 1900 have grown to 18,000. We have hundreds of television channels, and the once-dominant AM radio competes with FM, satellite, digital, and online streaming audio over personal computers and cell phones. And of course, marketers can go directly to consumers via the billions of web pages cataloged by Google. But this proliferation of advertising has not improved its effectiveness. In fact, the opposite is true. Consumers inundated by more than 3,000 advertising messages each day long to escape it. A Yankelovich survey conducted in 2003 found that one-third of Americans would accept a lower standard of living if it meant they could live in a society free of advertising. Advertisers have tried to compensate for that resistance by bludgeoning us with more and more advertising, which has only made consumers more reliant on word-of-mouth. In a confusing marketplace with all of these conflicting advertising messages, we no longer know what to trust, so we have stopped listening to mass media and begun trusting each other. With dozens of investment companies claiming they will give you the best returns on your 401(k), you ask one of your friends over coffee which company he uses to manage his retirement account.

One final change worth noting. On October 30, 1938, at 8 P.M., an estimated six million Americans tuned in to the Orson Welles radio broadcast of "The War of the Worlds." Fully two million people believed the science fiction broadcast and thought that aliens were actually landing in peoples' backyards and incinerating them with ray guns. Why? In 1938, 80 percent of Americans had a radio, but only 35 percent had a telephone. This meant that nearly everyone could hear the broadcast, but very few could actually corroborate its validity. During most of the last century, people were well connected to mass media but poorly connected to each other. If I watched a television program in 1958, there's a good chance I could talk about it with my neighbor next door because he very likely saw it too, as our media choices were limited. However, if I wanted to talk about it with my friends scattered throughout the county, I could write them a letter or wait a few weeks until I saw them, but I probably wouldn't call them on the phone because unless they lived in my neighborhood, the call was long distance and cost two dollars a minute. In other words, except for a handful of people on my street, I was not very well connected with others. When we are well connected to media but poorly connected to each other, *we tend to organize by proximity into communities of convenience.*

Compare that with today, especially since 2000. Social networks including MySpace, Facebook, LinkedIn, Friendster, Orkut, Bebo,

and others now number 580 million users (http://www.comscore.
com/press/release.asp?press=2396) and are growing at a rate of
between 9 and 66 percent a year depending on the region. In 2004,
blogs numbered two million, but Technorati, the blog search engine,
now counts more than 133 million (http://technorati.com/blogging/
state-of-the-blogosphere/), with 120,000 new blogs created every day
(http://technorati.com/weblog/2007/04/328.html) producing about
17 new blog posts per second. In 1994, 340,000 people in the United
States had cell phones; today that number has climbed to 229 million
(http://www.ctia.org/advocacy/research/index.cfm/AID/10377); we now
have more cell phones than landlines. Last year you and I sent 1 *tril-
lion* text messages according to World Cellular Data Metrics, a practice that is growing annually at a rate of 154 percent (mostly due to
Greg's 14-year-old daughter). We have unlimited minutes, e-mail, voice
mail, Skype (the video conferencing service), even a service that allows
us to let people know what we are doing minute-by-minute (Twitter).
Our point is this: We are in the midst of an unprecedented explosion
of interpersonal connectivity that makes word-of-mouth more powerful
than it has ever been. It has never been easier for us to connect with
each other. And because of that, we can now do what we have always
wanted to do, and that is to *organize by affinity into communities of interest.*

One of those affinities or passions around which people organize is
Christianity and the faith they have in common with other people. So
while the actual church building on the corner has always and will continue for some time to be a place where like-minded people connect, now
Christians can connect and converse with other Christians, from their
church and across the globe, around their common faith. Sort of the corner church on steroids. In fact, the book, *The Shack*, referred to earlier,
actually got its start as a podcast described as "an ever-expanding conversation among those thinking outside the box of organized religion."

A Simple, Foolproof Word-of-Mouth Model

In the next few chapters, we're going to show you how to market to
Christians through various media—the Internet, radio, print, and so
on. But first we want to give you a model to use with all of those media:
PyroMarketing. It's a simple process that anyone can follow.

Remember what you learned about fire in high school science? You
need four things to start and encourage a fire: fuel, heat, oxygen, and

the heat that results from chemical reaction. There's a lot of energy stored in the fuel's molecules, but there's also a very strong bond that keeps those molecules from breaking down easily. If you apply heat to the fuel, you will excite those molecules, and if you can excite them beyond their ignition temperature, then the bonds will break, releasing the electrons from the fuel, which will rush to join the oxygen in the surrounding air. At that point, you have a fire. The output of that fire is light, and loads of heat that excite surrounding fuel, causing your fire to spread.

In the PyroMarketing model, marketing to consumers is like trying to start a fire. There's money in their wallets, but also a very strong bond between them and their money. They won't give it up easily. Marketing is the heat—it supplies the activating energy that can get them excited about a new product or service. If it pushes them past their ignition point, the bond with their money breaks, at which point they exchange it for what we call the oxygen of PyroMarketing, or Oh!2 This refers not just to the product or service, but to an exceptional service or an outstanding product. The output of this process is the consumer's reaction expressed as word-of-mouth that causes our fire to grow or die, depending on the consumer's satisfaction.

When consumers are thrilled by their purchase, their temperature increases and the fire spreads. If they are dissatisfied, the temperature cools and the fire goes out.

So how do you start a huge marketing fire and keep it going?

PyroMarketing starts with oxygen, or Oh!2—a remarkable product or service. This is critical to your success in marketing to the church. The air we breathe is 22 percent oxygen, enough to start and sustain a growing fire. If the oxygen content dips to 18 percent, combustion weakens and the fire struggles. Let it slip below 15 percent, and the fire may go out. Don't expect a wildfire if you have a "15 percent product." PyroMarketing won't work with lousy products, but if you have a truly great product or service, PyroMarketing is the fastest and most economical way to market it successfully. Mel Gibson never would have gotten such huge support from the church if he had made a substandard or even average movie. But because Christians found it so spectacular, they actually volunteered to market it for him.

If you have a product that appeals to Christians, then your first task is to *gather the driest tinder*. This means focusing all of your marketing efforts on the particular Christians most likely to buy, benefit from, and become enthusiastic customer evangelists for your product or service.

This is critical to successful word of mouth. When it comes to spreading the word, not all customers are created equal. Not only are some more likely to buy, they are also more likely to tell others. It's not that they are more connected or influential. Their effectiveness at spreading word-of-mouth is a function of their personal passion, interest, or need for the particular product you are selling.

Perhaps you've heard the expression, "hunger is the best cook." It means that the degree of a person's satisfaction depends on the quality of the food, but also the depth of their need. The hungrier they are, the better the food will taste. If they're starving, then a peanut-butter-and-jelly sandwich will taste like French cuisine.

Advertising is better at communicating than it is at coercing. If you find the people who are naturally inclined toward your product, you won't have to do much convincing. People with a high interest or a deep need have a low ignition temperature. They are ready to buy, and the slightest heat from your advertising is enough to set them ablaze. What's more, their deep need makes them more likely to be pleased with their purchase and to tell other people as a result. Rick Warren could have tried to market his book to everyone in the United States; but instead, he started with 1,200 pastors with whom he had been serving for a decade. Once they experienced his book, they spread the fire for him to the people in their congregations, who told their friends and neighbors outside the church. Great word-of-mouth is the closest thing to free advertising you'll ever get.

The second step in the PyroMarketing process is to *touch it with the match.* This means giving people an experience with your product or service. If you want people to laugh, don't tell them you're funny, tell them a joke. Experience is the shortcut to product understanding and the quickest, most believable way to plant a brand impression in a consumer's mind. It generates far more heat than mere advertising and has the power to ignite even the mildly interested.

Experience was key to the success of *The Purpose Driven Life* and *The Passion of the Christ.* Both Rick Warren and Mel Gibson touched the driest tinder with the match.

Rick Warren created the "40 Days of Purpose" campaign. It asked pastors to preach six sermons based on the book's content on consecutive Sundays, it required every church member to read a chapter from the book each day for 40 days, and it also divided churches into small groups of eight or ten people that met once a week in each other's homes to discuss the book's content and implication for their lives.

Mel Gibson didn't send a postcard to pastors announcing his movie; instead he invited them to watch the whole thing during private screenings. He gave them the deepest, most complete experience he could with his film, and the result was instant and powerful. Convinced of the power of the film to change lives, pastors began evangelizing for it with their congregations.

The third step in PyroMarketing is to *fan the flames.* This means giving your customers tools that help them spread your message to their social network, and it's never been easier than it is today. If your company has a sales force, then you probably train and equip it to more effectively take your company's message to its prospective customers. You should. But you also need to realize that your satisfied customers represent an unpaid sales and marketing force that you should also equip. After all, if they're going to spread your message without compensation, shouldn't you at least give them tools that make that process easier and more effective?

Rick Warren gave pastors a turnkey program that helped them introduce his book to their church. Mel Gibson, with the help of Outreach Marketing, provided pastors with an array of tools that made it easier to share the movie with the people in their congregation. He gave them copies of the movie trailer they could play during the service. He provided movie flyers that fit inside church bulletins. He created micro-web sites and Internet ad banners for churches to add to their existing web sites. One company even created a television ad for the film that churches could customize with their own logo before running—at their own expense—on local television stations.

Without these tools, pastors would, no doubt, have told their congregations about *The Purpose Driven Life* and *The Passion of the Christ.* But the tools Warren and Gibson provided made it possible for those pastors to tell more people more quickly and reach farther than they could have without those tools.

Someday, you'll want to start another fire, and it will be a lot easier if you follow the fourth and final step in the PyroMarketing process: *Save the coals.* In PyroMarketing, that means holding on to the names and contact information of everyone who responded to your marketing so that you can go back to them again quickly and affordably while using your new marketing budget to expand your reach and enlarge your market. PyroMarketing is like buying a house—it's a long-term investment. Each campaign is a payment building equity for the future.

In a nutshell, that's PyroMarketing: a potent mix of great product and strategically placed marketing resources targeted to those who will spread the fire for you. Perhaps the most important component of this model is finding the driest tinder—the people most likely to become customer evangelists for you. The "fire" from word-of-mouth spreads fastest among people who are similar, who believe and act alike.

CASE STUDY: BUILDING WORD-OF-MOUTH

When my (Bob's) company, Ground Force Network, was asked to help market the novel, *Skin,* by Ted Dekker, we recruited a "street team" from our database of passionate volunteers (coals we had saved from previous campaigns), as well as the author's fan community. Our goal was to equip this team to increase online traffic to a series of YouTube videos (fan the flames and touch it with a match) that highlighted the book and drove visitors to an online contest and order page for the book. Winners of the contest would find their names used in the novel, further building anticipation for the book's release.

We created a special *Skin*-branded web site to manage this campaign, allowing people to sign up and participate in everything from opting to receive tips for spreading the word to clicking on links to the YouTube videos and contest. We also created a special button on the main web site where members could send the HTML e-mail about the book to their friends (fan the flames and touch it with a match). Street team members sent this e-mail to hundreds of individuals who responded with an amazingly high 69 percent open rate because it came directly from a peer.

Throughout the campaign, we drove members to for-your-eyes-only episodes from the novel hosted on YouTube and encouraged them to circulate the episodes to their friends. These episodes were viewed a total of 38,198 times during the short campaign.

The novel became a *New York Times* best seller.

Ground Force Network is an innovative word-of-mouth marketing company focusing on the faith-based market.

www.groundforcenetwork.com

No market segment delivers like-minded people as the church does. No market segment offers you built-in communications vehicles to help you reach them.

We've covered a lot of territory in this chapter, so here's a quick review:

- Word-of-mouth is the best form of promotion and advertising.
- Word-of-mouth works best in the church.
- Word-of-mouth works because people are resistant to traditional advertising and confused by overwhelming choice and must rely on like-minded people to filter those messages.
- PyroMarketing is the best model for starting and encouraging word-of-mouth in any setting, but especially in the church.

In the next four chapters, we will show you how to reach Christians using print, radio, online, and direct marketing. As you read, consider everything in the context of the PyroMarketing model so that the fire you start with traditional marketing methods can grow from word-of-mouth, giving you the highest return on your limited marketing dollars.

CHAPTER EIGHT

RADIO STRATEGIES

Steve H. couldn't figure out why his radio advertising wasn't delivering a better response from church folks in his city. As the owner of a tax preparation business, he had developed a special service to help people who donated money to nonprofits better understand the tax benefits. He began running 30-second spots right after January 1 specifically targeted to people who gave money to their church. He offered a free consultation to any client who brought a church bulletin into his office and offered to give 10 percent of his fee to the client's church. But the ads just weren't pulling in the customers. "Maybe this faith-based marketing thing isn't so hot after all," he thought as he dialed the station's account rep to cancel his ads.

Steve did a great job of finding a way to serve the needs of the local faith-based community, doing enough homework to learn that Christians are generous; they donate as much as 10 percent of their income to their churches and other Christian organizations. He knew that they, like everyone else, appreciate a bargain, and he truly believed his tax advice could save them a lot of money. Finally, he knew that Christians appreciate those who support their churches and other organizations. So why didn't his good efforts pay off?

The account rep at the station he chose to work with showed him impressive numbers from the quarterly rate book—the most listened-to station in town. Knowing that 77 percent of Americans claim to be Christians, he reasoned that picking the station with the most listeners would reach the highest number of Christians. What Steve *didn't* know is that Christians have their own radio stations and listen to them, well, religiously. The Christian radio station in his city probably didn't do as well in the ratings—didn't deliver as many listeners as the bigger station. But if he wanted to reach Christians, he wouldn't find a more concentrated audience than Christian radio. Virtually everyone who listens to Christian radio is a Christian, making it a powerful medium for marketing to people of faith.

WELCOME TO CHRISTIAN RADIO

Radio is still one of the most cost-effective ways to reach large numbers of people in a given city or region. Eighty percent of Americans listen to radio every day. Advertisers receive upwards of two hours a day of captive listening from commuters in larger cities. Radio delivers larger target audiences at lower costs compared to television, magazines, and newspapers. But if you're targeting Christians, don't assume that the station with the highest Arbitron ratings will give you the results you want.

We can almost guarantee that wherever you do business, you will find a Christian radio station influencing the faith-based community in your city or region. With more than 2,500 Christian radio stations and 34 Christian radio networks in the United States, people of faith can listen to music that reflects their values and beliefs, hear popular preachers deliver inspiring sermons, tune in to talk shows that address their unique concerns, *and* discover which businesses support their faith.

First, the basics, Christian radio, like its secular counterpart, is divided into commercial and noncommercial stations. Unlike secular radio, the majority of Christian radio stations are noncommercial or listener-supported. For advertisers, that means your message cannot include any call to action—you can describe the pizza at Joe's Café, but you can't invite listeners to go to Joe's to buy pizza. But don't let that keep you from promoting your product or service on Christian radio. More on that later.

Christian radio is a "values and lifestyles" format—a lot like country radio stations. In other words, it is segmented by a shared ideology, not a demographic. That's why for any given station, the age demographic could be 25 to 75. People listen because of what they believe, not because of their age or income.

Christian radio offers three basic formats: *preaching and teaching, music,* and *a hybrid* of both. Check the reference section of this book for a listing of Christian radio stations by format and visit www.faithbasedmarketing.com for an extensive listing of stations.

Preaching and teaching, the largest format, is similar to television—30-minute programs featuring popular preachers and Christian leaders, with commercials or donor announcements in between. Audience age is 60 plus all the way up to 75, and the only Christian radio format that skews male.

Music stations come in all genres, from southern gospel to Christian hip-hop, but the largest two are inspirational (softer, slower music with a

50- to 60-year-old audience) and adult contemporary (more mainstream, contemporary music with a 35-plus-year-old, largely female, audience). Some Christian radio stations will combine preaching and teaching (often in the morning) with music later in the day to cater to a younger audience.

One of the more exciting developments in Christian radio is stations that want to engage a much younger demographic: Generation Y, or people between the ages of 16 to 25. We mention this for two reasons. First, traditionally this is a lucrative market for advertisers. And second, while most Christian radio stations may seem protective of their listeners and therefore stay away from some products, stations that cater to this demographic tend to engage culture more. In other words, you might find more openness to your business at a station targeting younger listeners.

Here's an interesting fact we learned from our friend, Alan Mason. Alan and his business partner, John Frost, are consultants to Christian radio stations and know more about the medium than just about anyone. Alan told us that Christian radio boasts the highest percentage of people who listen to one station and one station only. For the advertiser, that's huge. Your message isn't competing with hundreds of messages from other stations, and if you buy multiple spots during the day, they are heard enough times by listeners to make a huge impact. If high frequency is part of your strategy, you'll achieve it more quickly and affordably with Christian radio.

Finally, audiences for Christian radio have grown dramatically. Between 2002 and 2006, it was the fastest-growing format in all of radio. In recent years, the rate of growth has leveled somewhat, but it still adds new listeners every year. One of Alan's top clients, EMF Broadcasting, creates programming for a network of Christian radio stations with an audience of more than four million listeners, and they have accomplished this through listener recommendations. "It's all been word of mouth," Alan told us, which underscores the communal nature of Christian radio—a new station opens in a city, and the Christian grapevine goes to work!

If you've never heard of Christian radio or have only known about it from a call sign and the designation "religious" in your Arbitron book, contact one of the pastors with whom you are developing a relationship and ask him or her where to find the local Christian radio station. Then tune in and listen for a few days. We think you'll be surprised at both the production quality and entertainment value of the content.

And if you've *heard* of Christian radio but think of it as too small or insignificant for your marketing efforts, think Procter & Gamble.

For several years, rumors have spread throughout some segments of the Christian community that Procter & Gamble's logo was a secret satanic symbol, suggesting that the giant company promoted Satan worship. You would think a company as large as Procter & Gamble—the world's biggest advertiser—might just ignore something like this, but they didn't (which further underscores the size and importance of Christian consumers). They contracted with Salem Radio Reps, an agency that places ads on Christian radio nationwide, and asked Mike Reed, their account executive at the time, to create a series of ads that hit the issue head on. Instead, Mike suggested they simply advertise their products without mentioning the controversy. Why? Mike knew that Christians place enormous trust in the Christian radio stations. The relative few who might be worried that Procter & Gamble was peddling Satan instead of soap would call the station manager to complain, but once the station manager debunked the rumor, the caller would be satisfied (and probably tell all her friends the rumor wasn't true). In other words, let the trusted station defend the beleaguered corporation. It worked. A spokesman for Procter & Gamble later claimed that "the medium Christians trust the most is Christian radio."

CASE STUDY: PURPOSE-DRIVEN RADIO

One of my (Greg's) strategies for marketing the book, *The Purpose Driven Life*, was to use radio. But instead of just buying spots promoting the book, we decided to let people experience the book by using content from the book itself to produce a series of 90-second spots—known in radio as a "short-form radio program"—and included a 30-second window the station could sell to advertisers. We timed it to coincide with the "40 Days of Purpose" campaign running in local churches to let the station benefit from the wildfire of interest that was building in their communities. More than 600 stations picked up the program, ran it at no cost to my marketing budget, and many created additional revenue by selling the 30-second window as an advertisement.

Why You Should Use Christian Radio

Christians listen to Christian radio not only because it represents what they like, but also who they are. That creates a level of loyalty not seen in secular radio. According to Alan Mason, Christian radio generates the most loyalty of any radio format: 46 percent of listeners become fans. Country stations, the next highest in terms of loyalty, turn 36 percent of their listeners into fans. As a potential advertiser, you need to understand why Christian radio produces such loyalty. In a word: trust.

Christian radio is an oasis on a loud and chaotic radio dial that often serves up troubling messages. It's not unusual for a Christian radio station to be played in a home all day long, and for the car radio to be tuned to that same station. Unlike traditional radio, Christian radio stations are able to appeal to the entire family. They often sponsor rock concerts with Christian rock bands that they play during hours when teens tune in. But they also sponsor marriage seminars and singles retreats and offer programming for a wide range of interests and age groups. Families, especially parents, view Christian radio as an ally, helping them and their children negotiate the difficult moral and ethical issues facing them every day.

Christian radio also serves as a tacit endorsement for your product or service when you advertise. That's because the station's management filters every message. When you buy airtime on a secular radio station, they really don't care what you say or what you're selling. As long as your product is legal and you don't use foul language, you're on. Station managers of Christian radio stations believe they have a responsibility to make sure whatever goes over the airwaves under their call sign must support the biblical values and tastes of Christians. At a Christian radio station in Seattle, the program director goes on the air every month to talk about the businesses they turned down for advertising because the product or message was inappropriate for a Christian audience. Unless you're a head shop selling bongs or the local strip club, this isn't a problem for most businesses.

If you advertise your custom framing shop on secular radio, you're just another framing shop; advertise on Christian radio, and you have the tacit blessing and approval of a trusted gatekeeper. Companies spend thousands of dollars building trust in a brand; Christian radio short-circuits that process, providing immediate brand recognition and trust, measured in real dollars. Again, our friend Alan recounted holding focus groups for a station in Portland, Oregon, where people said they would buy from any advertiser they heard on that station because it was owned by a Christian. That's not a guaranteed response to an ad, but pretty close. If you have a presence on Christian radio, you in essence become a part of the family. Because you support *their* station, you are seen as trusted allies.

BENEFITS OF CHRISTIAN RADIO

Paul Martin is the cofounder and president of Advocace Media, an agency that connects national advertisers with listener-supported Christian radio. He lists three primary benefits for advertising on Christian radio:

1. *Reach and engagement:* No other medium delivers as many committed Christians as Christian radio. They listen longer—often it's the only radio station they listen to—and depend on the station for information about family-friendly entertainment, events, and products.

2. *Limited competition:* The average commercial station runs 12 to 16 minutes of commercials per hour, but a listener-supported Christian station runs only 2 minutes. Seldom will your ad compete with a similar business in a given time slot, giving your product or service exclusivity for the listener.

3. *Cost efficiency:* Christian radio is an advertising bargain. Cost per thousand for advertising on commercial radio averages between $22 and $25; that drops to a $5 to $7 cost per thousand for Christian radio. And remember, you're getting an extremely loyal and committed audience.

Another huge advantage of Christian radio, according to Martin, is that you have several additional opportunities to communicate your message to listeners, because the station goes to them frequently through their web site, e-mail blasts, direct mail, and in many cases, monthly newsletters. Because they depend on their database of listeners for financial support, they probably have the most up-to-date, active database of any media.

The Heart of Christian Radio

As a savvy marketer, you know that "engagement is the new reach." That is, just reaching customers through advertising is not enough. You need to establish significant connections with them. We are bombarded with more than 3,000 advertising messages a day, so just hitting us with another spot won't cut it. When it comes to engagement, Christian radio has the upper hand. Here's why:

- *Christians connect at a deeper level with their radio stations.* Professionals in the Christian radio business often speak of their work as a "ministry." They consider themselves an important partner to the church and other religious organizations. Listeners respond with their trust and loyalty. They listen because they believe the content will help them grow in their faith. They might also listen to a local classic rock station for entertainment, but they listen to Christian radio as if their faith depended on it. It goes back to what you learned in Chapter 3—Christians care deeply about their relationship with God and see Christian radio as a vital "lifeline" to faith.

- *Christians support their radio financially.* The majority of Christian radio stations are listener supported—they depend on donations from their listeners (much like National Public Radio, without their taxpayer support). In effect, this gives Christian radio a treasured place in the hearts of its listeners. Listeners love their stations so much they actually pay to listen to them.

- *Christian radio is less cluttered with advertising.* Typically, a secular radio station will run 16 to 20 commercial minutes per hour; Christian radio will run 3 to 4. That means your ad gets more attention, giving you a greater opportunity to engage the listener. If you're one of 20 ads in a given hour, you have to scream and talk fast and hope you're being heard. But if you're one of only four spots in an hour, you can deliver your message knowing you have the full attention of the listeners.

All this to say, Christian radio stations develop an intimate, emotional connection with their listeners. If you hang out with Christian radio people, you will hear the term "changed lives" a lot, and they can tell you countless stories to explain what they mean. Like the station in Seattle that heard from a woman who claimed the station saved her life. Despondent over the direction of her life, she woke up one morning and decided to commit suicide. She couldn't swim and thought that jumping in a nearby river would be the easiest way to go. She hiked to a remote bank where she planned to end her life, only to come upon a man holding one of those small transistor radios up to his ear. He engaged her in conversation, and when she told him why she was there, he held the radio up to her and said, "Here, this is for you." The music and encouraging lyrics of the song were so powerful that she felt a new will to live and eventually began attending a church and turning over a new leaf.

Stations share these stories with their listeners all the time, not to market their station or solicit donations. This is why they are in business. This is what Christian radio is all about. Many stations ask listeners to call in or e-mail with any special requests for prayer. The Christian radio network EMF Broadcasting has 28 people who work full time calling listeners, not to solicit donations but to ask them if they would like station employees to pray for them. Then they write down those requests and take them to an onsite chapel where four times during each day, employees stop by to pray for those requests.

If this seems a little weird to you, think of when you had a miserable day or got some really bad news. Wouldn't you like to know someone cared about you? Wouldn't you be loyal to anyone who reached out to you when you were down? That's how most listeners view Christian radio, and if you can find ways to partner with Christian radio, that loyalty will transfer to your business as well.

How to Market through Christian Radio

Before you buy a second of airtime on Christian radio, do your homework. Think of it as a church and do what you learned to do in Chapter 5. Even if you normally use an agency to make your media purchases, get to know the station, its people, and its mission. Spend time on the station's web site, and you will soon discover what's important to the station and its listeners, what they're passionate about. If they sponsor a community event—which is fairly common for Christian radio—attend it. Begin thinking creatively of how your product or service can connect with the station. Contact the station and ask for an appointment with the station manager. Ask her what her dreams and visions are for the station; what she would do with an additional $2 million (not that you'll spend that much)—her answer will reveal her goals. Then try to find ways to help her with those dreams.

How can your product or service fit into a win-win solution for the station? Remember, your emphasis should always be on serving, not selling. Explain your product or your service, but always end with "How can we help you?" If you can find a way to legitimately help the station, you may get more than an on-air campaign. It could lead to fully integrated partnerships that deliver big results.

Since the majority of Christian radio stations are listener supported, you'll need to know exactly what you can and cannot do. Generally, as we stated earlier, you can't include a call to action in your message, but each station has its ways to deal with government regulations, and all of them will gladly explain them to you. Usually, you will be offered an opportunity to underwrite a program—basically an opportunity to gain exposure. Some businesses, having worked primarily with public radio, do not place much value on underwriting, but remember, we're talking about Christian radio. Your brief mention on National Public Radio may not generate much business, but when the folks who listen to Christian radio in your town hear your spot, they will, in a sense, hear the station saying, "We approve of this business." You don't get that from any other media. And as a result, the listeners will begin to think of you as part of the family. This isn't dishonest or misleading, because when you support their station, you are supporting something they believe in.

If you advertise at all, you probably use an ad agency to create and buy your print, radio, and other media, which makes sense. But not every advertising agency is familiar with Christian radio. Mike Reed, executive pastor of Northwood Church near Dallas, who also works with Advocace Media, an agency specializing in connecting national advertisers with listener-supported Christian radio, cautions potential advertisers to look for agencies that can demonstrate successful experience working with Christian stations. "You need to find people who really understand this market—who live and breathe it—and work closely with them," Reed advises. "Don't assume you can write an effective ad or underwriting message for the Christian market because you put something together that's really great for another station. As little as one word may keep it from working in Christian radio. You have one chance to make an impression, and if you offend the market, it's hard to get them back."

How do you find such agencies? Consult the reference section in the back of this book or visit www.faithbasedmarketing.com for a listing of agencies. You can also ask the radio station which agencies give them the best ads. Ask agencies to show you their work with Christian radio. Shop around until you find an agency with a consistent and successful record of working with Christian radio. If you cannot find an agency in your area that has worked with Christian radio, Reed suggests working with a local pastor or regular listener to Christian radio. "Find your own personal 'consultant' and at least run your copy past them, explaining that you want to run the ad on Christian radio and want to make sure it communicates effectively with Christians."

If you decide to underwrite a program—and we recommend you do—work closely with the advertising salesperson to come up with a creative connection that will enhance the effect of your message. For example, if you own a nice restaurant and the station runs a teaching program on marriage enrichment, that would be a great time slot for your message: "Marriage Alive is being underwritten today by The Birchwood Inn, a great place for couples to enjoy a candlelight dinner." If you have a product or service for young people, the salesperson can help you find a time slot when they know teenagers are listening. The more you think "serve," the more ways you'll find to connect with the station and its listeners.

By law, listener-supported stations won't let you place a call to action in your ads, but don't let that bother you. After describing the delicious taste of Tony's Pizza, the suggestion that listeners go get one is implied. Plus, you are building awareness. What you must do, however, is direct the listener to your web site. With noncommercial radio, you can't tell the listener to buy your product, but you can give your web site address and use it to provide additional information and even the specific call to action you couldn't give on the air.

Think of your spot as a fully endorsed advertisement for your business, regardless of what your product or service is, and the goal is to get listeners to learn more about your business on your web site. Then make sure you are ready for these new customers. Immediately after you run your spot, create a presence on your web site exclusively for these new customers by making a "special offer for listeners of WXYZ." Those listeners will click on it immediately, and your regular web site patrons will go there out of curiosity anyway, increasing your overall sales with this offer to Christians.

ADVERTISING CONTENT AND CHRISTIAN RADIO

Some businesses have never tried to market through Christian radio because they think they need to have a "Christian" product in order to be successful. But according to Paul Martin, cofounder and president of Advocace Media, Christian stations are open to a broad range of products and services. "Think family friendly and children," Martin advises. "Appeal to children, and you'll get the parents." Martin also points out that the Christian radio audience has a higher proportion of single-income families with stay-at-home moms, which opens up the product range considerably: "Basically, anything for the home is fair game for sponsoring Christian radio," Martin says. Think what that stay-at-home mom needs to run the household, and you'll have a pretty good idea what works in Christian radio.

Anything off limits? Unlike secular radio, Christian radio draws the line at some products and services. The station serves as a gatekeeper for the listener, knows exactly what the listener is passionate about, and also knows what offends the listener. Christians enjoy sex as much as anyone, but they don't like to hear advertising with sexual or suggestive content. "A good rule of thumb is to avoid anything that would elicit an embarrassing question from the 10-year-old in the backseat of the mini-van," Martin cautions. So much for your special offer on Viagra—save it for the classic rock station.

Martin also says Christian radio stations do not like to showcase people (spokespersons) who live ungodly lifestyles. For example, if a nationally known spokesperson is involved in an intimate, live-in relationship with someone he's not married to, Christian radio would not use that person in a promotion because their listeners believe in traditional family values. Again, think family and children.

Because so many parents listen to Christian radio, new media products and services are especially welcome. Parents know their kids have strong interests in these areas. Video games are big, but a Christian radio station would most likely not accept a promotion of an extremely violent video game. Teaching and educational media are especially welcome.

If you would like to see the actual criteria many Christian radio stations use to filter content, you'll find it in the Bible. But just to show you we're not trying to turn you into a Bible thumper, here it is: "whatever is true, whatever is noble, whatever is right, whatever is pure, whatever is lovely, whatever is admirable..." (Philippians 4:8) If you can attach any of those descriptions to your product or service, you'll be welcome at any Christian radio station.

Almost as important as your product is how you structure the message. Your goal is to clearly describe your product or service in a way that connects powerfully with the Christian audience. An agency with experience in Christian radio can help you here, but if none are available, make sure you run your ad by someone who fully understands the church and listens regularly to Christian radio.

Note to ad agencies: You may not be a Christian ad agency, but chances are some members of your staff are believers. Ask which of your employees go to church and use them as consultants to ad campaigns on Christian media. You may be thinking, "I can't ask my people about their religious affiliation." You can't ask that question during the interview process, but you can ask it once they're employees.

How to Advertise When You Can't Advertise

Christian radio is often the "social life director" of a city's Christian community. Where individual churches could never afford to bring in a well-known author or popular Christian music group, Christian radio stations frequently sponsor events that bring these people to town. These are popular, heavily attended events that also get a lot of advance publicity. You can serve the station and the entire Christian community in your area by cosponsoring the event with the station. In exchange for your sponsorship, your name/logo will appear on every poster, banner ad, and so on that advertises the event. Every time the station promotes the event on air, listeners will hear the name of your business. And at the event itself you can promote your business in a number of ways: free product samples, coupons, brochures, bottled water with your company name on the bottle, and so on.

Another way to advertise on noncommercial stations is to provide content. Begin by asking yourself, "What expertise do I have that may be helpful to this station's listeners?" And don't think you have to provide religious content. Remember, Christians are like anyone else; they need information about their finances, their health, their homes, and so on. So if you own a landscape business, perhaps you could work with the program director of the Christian radio station to develop a call-in show, where listeners can ask you questions about getting rid of dandelions. The station gets free programming, your business gets great exposure, and most important, listeners become even bigger fans of their Christian station.

Many stations look for short, 90-second programs to drop in between regular programs. In fact, we know of one commercial station that worked with a business client to develop such a program and then sold advertising for it. Not sure you could generate the right kind of content for even six or seven 90-minute programs? Start by recalling the kinds of questions your customers ask you. In addition to selling a product or service, you probably dispense a lot of free information, and with a little creativity, you could turn that into content for a slot on Christian radio.

Turning Your Business into Content for Christian Radio

One way to gain exposure through Christian radio is to offer your expertise for free programming. Regardless of your business, you probably have information that would be helpful to a number of people. Here's a small list to show how business could offer content:

Businesses	Content
Restaurant/food service	Cooking/nutrition tips
Auto parts/service	Auto maintenance
Insurance	Home and car safety
Counseling/psychologist	Parenting/marriage/relationships
Physician/dentist	Personal health/dental care
Bookstore	Daily book review
Law firm	Legal advice/wills/probate
Real estate	Tips for buying/selling property
Investment firm	Money tips
Clothing store	Fashion tips
Hardware	Home maintenance and repair
Sporting goods	Hunting/fishing advice
Health club	Fitness tips
Beauty salon	Hair care/grooming/skin care

Listener-supported stations are unique in the broadcasting world. Because they rely on their listeners for financial support, they keep a database of the people who have donated in the past. As a result, Christian radio stations are more than radio stations. They often have multiple ways to reach the audience they serve. When planning your campaign, ask what else you can do beyond on-air announcements. You might be able to build a fully integrated campaign that includes on-air announcements and a direct mail campaign. Use the on-air announcements to reach the driest tinder. Follow up with direct mail to give them an experience or equip them to spread your message among their friends. This is how you can leverage Christian radio to start word of mouth that is far reaching.

Finally, Christian radio stations often run contests to keep their readers engaged, and this is a great opportunity for businesses to advertise, even on noncommercial stations: "We've got one free night for two at the Riverside Resort for the fifth caller, thanks to the generosity of Don and Mary Jones, owners of the Riverside Resort, truly a world-class hotel with a great restaurant and a friendly staff that will treat you like royalty."

Okay, so you're the marketing director for a residential construction company and you can't convince your boss to let you give away a $350,000 custom home on Christian radio? The product your company makes doesn't have to be the gift for a station's contest. For a lot of businesses that would be impractical. Even if you donated a box of candy or a dozen roses, your business will still get exposure. But take a creative look at your business to see if the gift itself reinforces your brand. For example, that construction company could give away a custom built doghouse or a "home repair expert for a day"—both subtle messages to promote the brand. If you can't come up with any creative ideas, print up a supply of T-shirts, coffee mugs, and other useful items with your logo on it and offer them to the station for their contest awards. What you're really doing is telling the station you're on their side—you want to help them increase listener engagement. It's just another way to serve through Christian radio that will ultimately lead to more sales.

CASE STUDY: REACHING AN ENTIRE CITY

How do you make sure every person in a major city knows about an upcoming event? That was the challenge put to Beth Cathey of Renegade Idea Group by the Billy Graham Evangelistic Association. The aging evangelist, Billy Graham, was to hold his last mission in the Dallas-Ft. Worth metroplex, and his organization actually

(Continued)

told Cathey they didn't want anyone living in the area in the two months leading up to the crusade to say they *hadn't* heard about the event.

Cathey and her crew rolled up their sleeves and put together a multimedia blitz that included:

- *Radio:* Christian radio (both commercial and noncommercial), secular radio, contemporary hit radio (to reach the teens), and a total market buy of traffic and weather sponsorships on all radio formats in the Dallas-Ft. Worth area the two weeks prior to the event.
- *Television:* Placements on network TV affiliates locally during the morning local and national news programs, daytime placement during key nationally syndicated programs such as Oprah with rotators for additional frequency, and evening releases during key PAX TV programs.
- *Newspaper:* Included major papers such as the *Dallas Morning News* and *Ft. Worth Star-Telegram,* as well as suburban newspapers within a certain radius of Texas Stadium (where the event took place), local Christian newspapers, and local Spanish publications.
- *Magazines:* Regional publications such as *D Magazine* and *Fort Worth, Texas,* as well as local family publications and surrounding community magazines.
- *Cinema advertising:* Movie screen ads placed in select theaters across the metroplex with the highest teen audiences, advertising the Next Generation Concert, which was a special feature of the crusade.
- *Outdoor:* Billboards, bulletins, and mobile truck ads, both in English as well as Spanish (in highly Spanish-populated areas of the metroplex); also placed *Billboards by the Day* the four days leading up to the event to remind people of the date and time.

Admittedly, this was a major effort to reach a faith-based audience, but its success demonstrates that it's possible to reach large numbers of Christians in a metropolitan area. According to the sponsoring organization, this was the largest audience to date for a Billy Graham mission.

CHAPTER NINE

PRINT STRATEGIES

As you've no doubt learned by now, the Christian community is a community of subcultures. Christians have their own radio stations, favorite musicians, authors, and preachers. They also have their own newspapers, magazines, and newsletters, and if you include print in your overall marketing strategy for Christians, you need to know the landscape. Here's a quick tour from the ground up.

THE LOCAL CHURCH OR PARISH

Every local church or parish in the United States has at least one regular print vehicle to communicate with its members: the Sunday bulletin. Not only is it a great source for you to use to gather information about a church, but also, in some cases you can use it to communicate to members of the church, albeit with a few caveats. For the most part, Protestant church bulletins do not accept paid advertising and generally do not allow promotional messages for area businesses. However, if you assist the church in some manner, they will gladly give you credit in the bulletin. ("The paint used to paint our Sunday School rooms was donated by Meadowbrook Paint & Supply.") Or if you provide a service to the church, it will be advertised several times in advance of the event. ("Sign up for the Personal Finance class, a 12-week adult education elective taught by Stephen Landorff of Landorff Financial Services.") If you're offering a discount on a product that is tied to an official church program, you may be able to place an insert in the bulletin with a coupon and product description (e.g., a bookstore offering a discount on a book that the church has decided to study together). This applies to Catholic churches as well, but in general, they also sell advertising space for area businesses.

Church bulletins may not sound very glamorous when it comes to your print strategy, but every Sunday they go to everyone who attends church, and parishioners often take them home, put them on the counter next to the family calendar, and refer to them often throughout the week. If you can find a legitimate way to highlight your business in the church bulletin, it will get noticed.

In addition to the regular Sunday bulletin, most churches publish some form of newsletter. Currently, most still publish and mail a printed version, though the trend is toward online to reduce costs. Still, the newsletter is another way to communicate directly with parishioners. Contact the editor (often the church secretary) for deadlines and policies regarding submissions. Not to beat a dead horse, but the best way to gain a presence in a church's newsletter is to provide content that speaks to the needs of the church community—what they're passionate about. Churches are family friendly. So if you own a video store, why not offer to provide a free review of a family-friendly video for the church newsletter—better than a paid advertisement. Be creative. What expertise do you have that would help Christians be better parents, keep their cars running, plan vacations, upgrade their computers, stay in shape, decorate their homes, and so on? Overt attempts to sell will most likely be rejected by most church newsletters, but they are always open to copy that meets a need in their church.

Local churches are also often open to barter—trading your services for some exposure. For example, many small to medium-size churches struggle with the labor and cost of publishing a newsletter. If your business has a graphics or design department or an employee who knows her way around publishing software, why not offer to design, print, and mail the newsletter in exchange for an exclusive ad in each issue?

Finally, local churches also communicate with their members through bulletin boards, posters, brochures, web sites and special mailings, and you might be able to piggyback on those vehicles with the same tactics described previously.

CITYWIDE PRINT OPTIONS

Virtually every major city and many smaller ones distribute some form of Christian periodical—usually a weekly newspaper. The Christian Newspaper Association lists 48 member publications that reach an estimated 1.5 million households (www.christiannewsassoc.com). In addition, most of these newspapers also offer an online version, furthering their reach. Yet they still represent only a small percentage of the overall Christian newspaper scene because their membership does not include Catholic papers or the hundreds of independent Christian newspapers. Check your city's Yellow Pages to find the Christian newspapers in your city and add them to your print media strategy.

The denomination that has developed the largest and most effective use of print media is the Catholic Church. Nearly all of their 195 dioceses in the United States (regional clusters of churches) publish at least a monthly newspaper that goes into the homes of every Catholic in that area. Most accept advertising, which can deliver a higher than usual response rate than comparable newspapers because Catholics exhibit strong loyalty to their publications. Your ad in a Catholic diocesan newspaper in effect has the approval and support of their beloved church. These newspapers are also open to content, especially if you can find an angle that connects to the needs of the diocese. One Catholic newspaper editor told us about a lawyer who wanted to publicize his mediation service for couples considering a divorce. He was willing to pay for an ad, but the editor asked him to write an article instead.

Your print strategy for reaching the faith-based community should also consider the local newspaper. Many newspapers publish a weekly religion page—usually in the Saturday edition—and depend on advertising for support. However, save for a few notable exceptions, religion pages do not attract significant numbers of Christians. It's not the best way to target the faith-based community in your area. We don't want to add to their woes, but there are reasons why total print advertising dropped a whopping 9.4 percent in 2007: Daily newspaper readership is declining. You're better off getting your business in front of local Christians through church publications and Christian newspapers.

Finally, explore the print options offered by your local Christian radio station. Remember, because many Christian stations are supported by listener donations, most have robust listener databases and use them to stay in touch with their donor base in a variety of ways. Chances are your local Christian radio stations have several print media vehicles you might use to reach the station's listeners with your message.

NATIONAL CHRISTIAN PRINT MEDIA

When it comes to reaching a national audience of Christians, you have a lot of options, and like too much candy, that can be a problem. Where do you start?

On the Protestant side of things, two major publications stand out, though neither will deliver the largest audience: *Christianity Today*, representing the more conservative evangelical movement, and the *Christian Century*, representing the more liberal mainline churches. Both warrant your attention if you are planning a national print campaign to reach Christians. While neither is the largest national Christian magazine, they are the most influential within their constituencies.

Christianity Today is actually part of a very successful family of magazines under the corporate banner of Christianity Today, Inc., which includes a magazine for women (*Today's Christian Woman*), a magazine specifically for church leaders (*Leadership Journal*), a magazine for men (*Men of Integrity*), a magazine for book lovers (*Books & Culture*), a magazine for the operational side of managing a church (*Your Church*), plus three newsletters that are pretty self-explanatory: *Church Finance Today*, *Church Law and Tax Report*, and *Church Secretary Today*.

Christianity Today was started more than 70 years ago by the popular evangelist, Billy Graham, and has grown into one of the most successful and influential media for the evangelical Christian community. Each magazine is supported by paid subscription and advertising, and the company deploys a very knowledgeable and helpful group of sales reps who can assist you in determining how to get the most out of your advertising dollar. Each magazine also has an online component that is considered to be one of the best in the business in terms of interacting with the Christian community.

Most of the advertising in the flagship magazine, *Christianity Today*, is related to religious products: books, music, Christian colleges and seminaries, seminars and conventions, and so on. Unless you're in that business, you probably won't find a good match between your company and this magazine. However, if your company is capable of national distribution, and you produce a product or service that could be used in the physical plant or campus of a church, probably no other publication offers the reach and influence of *Your Church*. To refresh your memory on what churches buy, go back to the sidebar on page 24, "Churches Are Big Business," to recall how one midwestern church spends its $5.3 million annual budget. To reach a national audience of committed Christians, both *Today's Christian Woman* and *Men of Integrity* ought to be considered for your print strategy.

While including the Christianity Today, Inc. group of magazines in your national print strategy makes sense, it's just one player on a team of national periodicals serving the faith-based community. For example, the Evangelical Press Association (www.epassoc.org) lists 320 periodicals serving a combined audience of 22 million households. Most of these are national publications serving individual denominations or other religious organizations. The advantages of these magazines over a magazine such as *Christianity Today* is reader loyalty—they serve as the connective tissue for churches and members in that denomination or organization. Many of these magazines are organized around affinity groups. Here's just a sampling of those magazines and their constituent demographic:

Brio	Practical advice and spiritual guidance for young teen girls
Charisma	Charismatic Christians, a fast growing subset
Highway News	Christian truck drivers (we're serious!)
Journal of Christian Nursing	Christian nurses
Marketplace	Christians in business
MomSense	Mothers of preschoolers
Sports Spectrum	Christian sports fans
Teachers of Vision	Christians who teach in public schools
The Wittenberg Door	Christian humor and satire

As you can see, you can narrow your target effectively with Christian print media, and these are just a few representative samples from one segment of the Christian church.

The Catholic Press Association (www.catholicpress.org) represents hundreds of regional and national newspapers and magazines that should be an integral part of any national print campaign targeted to Christians. They make things easy for you with their Catholic Advertising Network's "One buy, one bill" program allowing you to place an ad in every diocesan newspaper and magazine. But there are dozens of other national Catholic magazines that are not a part of the Catholic Press Association, including large circulation magazines like *American Catholic, St. Anthony Messenger, Commonweal, America,* and *U.S. Catholic.*

How to Reach Christians through Print

That pretty much covers the landscape of Christian print media. It's a vast terrain that deserves closer study because when you use Christian print media, you are making a direct connection with people who place a high value on their church periodical. But because you have so many options and probably a finite marketing budget, you need to make some choices about how to advertise and promote in print media.

First, determine your overall marketing goals. Obviously, you market to sell more products, but each campaign should have a specific goal. Are you trying to introduce yourself to the faith community? Are you trying to sell a product, induce trial, or build a database? Are you targeting a national, regional, or local audience?

Our assumption is that if you bought this book, you probably have not yet tried, or been successful, at marketing to Christians, so let's look at how you can use print media to introduce yourself to your local faith-based community:

- *Establish a relationship.* Get to know the editor and advertising sales manager of the Christian publications in your community. Be up front with them, telling them you would like to do a better job of communicating about your company to people of faith. Ask them what their needs are editorially and if they would be open to accepting an occasional article or running a regular column that you would provide. Give them samples of your product or let them experience the service your company sells. One word of caution: In order to avoid a conflict of interest in their reporting, professional journalists will not accept gifts. But most people who publish church newsletters would appreciate seeing your products and learning about your services. Ask specifically about their policies regarding advertising; for those who accept advertising, get a rate card.
- *Find a way to serve.* Churches struggle as much or more than other business to maintain their financial health. Is there a legitimate way your business could help the church? Sometimes the best ad comes from the preacher saying to his congregation on a Sunday morning, "Don't you love the way the parking lot is clear of snow after last night's blizzard? A special thanks to Sagebrush Landscaping for plowing out our parking lot at no charge; give them a call if you need your driveway cleared." We say it often because it's the best way to increase your business among Christians: Serve, don't sell.

- *Know your brand.* Every message in your print advertising campaign should support and strengthen your brand. Do you know what your company's brand is? Can you state it in five words or less? Learn from the nation's leading brands that state their brand promise in a few words that always appear in their print advertising:

Chevrolet	"An American Revolution"
Citi	"Citi never sleeps"
Principal Financial Group	"Life happens. Be ready."
Microsoft	"Your potential. Our promise."
State Farm	"Like a good neighbor"

Every message from your company placed in print media needs to galvanize your brand in the minds of the reader.

- *Work with a knowledgeable agency.* If possible, even at the local level, find an ad agency with experience working in the faith based environment to relieve you of the detail and design work and also give you counsel on which publications fit your overall marketing strategy.
- *Test and track your print advertising.* Your goal is to determine which publications deliver the strongest results, and then shift your spending to advertise more in those productive media. One simple way to track your ads is to ask readers to bring the ad to your store for a discount. Ads can also be coded if you include a reply mechanism.
- *Let print drive online marketing.* You'd be amazed at how many print ads in local Christian media do not include the web site for the business doing the advertising. Big mistake. Consumers have gotten accustomed to checking out a new business or product on the web site. They may not respond directly to your ad in the local Christian magazine, but they will check your web site to learn more about you before deciding if they want to give you their business. Print a custom URL in each publication so you can track which placements are driving traffic.
- *Offer coupons and inserts.* Even if a church won't run a paid advertisement in their weekly bulletin, they may be open to a tasteful insert or coupon, especially if you can make a connection between your product or service and what's important to church members. For example, if you learn from your visit to the church's web site that the young people are planning a mission trip, think about how your business could help parents reward their teenagers for helping others.

If you own a music store, instead of trying to get a church to insert a coupon into the church bulletin, focus on the mission trip: "Mom and Dad! Reward your teenager for building a school in Mexico by giving them this special half-off coupon for any CD at Mickey's Sound Shack." Now you've shown that you support teenagers who go on mission projects, you want to help parents encourage those activities, and you'll probably get a lot of new foot traffic into your store—both from the kids and their parents.

LEARN THE LANGUAGE

Leslie Burbridge-Bates owns her own public relations firm, L.A.B. Media. One of her specialties is helping secular businesses obtain publicity in Christian media. In April 2008, her firm handled publicity for the DVD release of *Moondance Alexander* for Fox Home Entertainment. In addition to a robust online and broadcast campaign, she secured 49 reviews in major daily newspapers and Christian magazines. Here's what she has to say about working with Christian media:

> The Christian media is a very unique industry. You have to take time to build relationships and really get to know the people and the vision of the media you're dealing with. Unless you learn to "speak the language" or know the industry, it will be close to impossible to make much headway or traction in this market. You do not have to be a Christian to work successfully with Christian media, but you have to know and respect what they believe. Your vision, mission, and motivation as a business interacting with Christians must be pure and clear. It must be genuine and real or it will not be a success and the relationship will never be established with the industry. When you pitch a story or idea to a particular publication, make sure it has an angle that intersects with their unique focus and audience. If you do it right, the print media will be an invaluable asset to your overall campaign.

FREE PRINT ADVERTISING

We'd like you to think of the one or two businesses in your area that always seem to generate a lot of publicity and goodwill. Whatever business you have in mind, we can tell you why you thought of them. They're everywhere. They sponsor the big road race. They have the biggest float in the Fourth of July parade. At high school football games, cheerleaders throw free minifootballs with their logo (and web site) printed on them. They have the biggest booth at every festival and give away cool stuff. They make frequent and sizable donations to causes important to the community. Their fingerprints are on just about every community-wide event.

It's no accident that you thought of that company. It's the result of a carefully orchestrated plan to be the most visible business in your community. Of course they advertise on radio and local television and on the Internet and in the newspaper. But they also allocate a significant portion of the budget to creating goodwill.

Depending on your vision and your budget, you can increase your visibility in the Christian community by doing the same kinds of things. Individual churches and local organizations of churches are always looking for businesses to help them with festivals, outreach activities, and other community events. When businesses engage their communities this way, it's called public relations. While your *advertising* in print should be focused specifically on Christian print media, *publicity* works in your favor in any media. Forty-four percent of the people who read newspapers and magazines are Christians and will see stories about your business in their local media. Consumers generally put more trust in something they read or hear about in the news, so the challenge is to find the right angle that will attract media attention.

That's exactly what the innovative public relations (PR) agency Rogers & Cowan did when they were contracted by the people behind GodTube.com to help launch their new online social network. Rogers & Cowan is a forerunner in PR development with widespread experience in both faith-based and secular media. Through a carefully crafted and comprehensive plan focusing on the family-friendly nature of GodTube. com, they were able to secure stories about it in media such as *Newsweek*, *USA Today*, CNN, MSNBC, and Fox. Paid advertising in those media would have been prohibitive.

While entire books have been written about developing public relations programs in businesses, here are three easy steps to generating publicity within the faith-based community in your local print media:

- *Form a "team of three."* In almost every city or town, you will find a daily newspaper and some type of free weekly newspaper (basically a shopping guide with editorial). Your goal is to meet and develop a relationship with the business editor and features editor of the daily newspaper and the editor of the weekly newspaper. These are the people who (1) need to fill space on their pages and (2) make decisions about what gets covered in their papers. Meet them, learn what kinds of stories they like to publish, tell them about your business.

- *Partner with a local church.* Find a way to assist a local church with an important project. For ideas, see Chapter 6. This should be a legitimate effort to help a church do something that is important to them and not simply offer them your product at a discount. If they're collecting food and clothing to send to hurricane victims, and you own a trucking company, haul the supplies for free. We're talking major commitment.

- *Contact your team.* If you've performed a truly remarkable service for the church, that's news. The weekly will certainly pick up the story and probably give you a front-page presence. The daily will also find it hard to resist because it's truly news—something out of the ordinary and an antidote to the "businesses are greedy" theme they have to report on so much.

Depending on the size of your business, it might pay to have a person on your staff who looks for ways to generate positive publicity for your business in the faith-based community. This person should not only look for ways to involve your business in the local church scene, but should also work with his or her media contacts to generate publicity. While readers demonstrate a degree of resistance to advertising, they respond favorably to positive stories in newspapers and magazines.

While some people express skepticism about the viability of print media, we're bullish on it, especially in the faith-based community. Christians regard their church newsletters and magazines with devotion unseen in the general print media. By adding a print media strategy to your overall faith-based marketing program, you will literally enter the homes of millions of Christians.

CHAPTER TEN

ONLINE STRATEGIES

When it comes to technology, Christians have gotten a bum rap. Remember the cell phone mogul in Chapter 3 who thought Christians didn't use cell phones? For some reason, that image has stuck, which might keep you from exploiting a great opportunity to market to Christians: the Internet.

Christians have actually been at the forefront of technology, especially as it's related to communication. The printing press was invented because a minister wanted more people to have access to the Bible. The first remote radio broadcast was a church service: Calvary Episcopal Church in Pittsburgh in 1920. Christians love to share their faith with others, and if technology helps them do it better, they go for it. And that's just what they've done on the Internet.

I (Bob) first started helping churches and Christian organizations learn about the Internet 15 years ago. In Internet years, that's a couple of centuries. Back then, there was no World Wide Web for the masses. Browsers and search engines hadn't been invented yet. I worked for a company called the Christian Interactive Network, and we led a series of forums on CompuServ that featured various faith-based organizations. Remember CompuServ? When it came to Internet service providers, they were the big guys, well ahead of Prodigy and a new upstart called America Online (AOL). My job was to help religious organizations see into the future, understand what was about to happen, and then get ready by making all their content digital. In other words, we helped them get ready for the Internet.

Fast forward to today. The Internet has changed the way we live, watch, play, earn, learn, and absolutely the way we market. The way that consumers receive and process information has changed, courtesy of the World Wide Web. MySpace and YouTube create overnight sensations with material from the average Joe with a camera. The world has been flattened, and life has become ruled by immediacy. And everything that has happened in the world at large has happened in the church. Christians use the Internet with the same frequency and sophistication as non-Christians. Virtually every church in the United States has at least a web presence. Its members no longer form phone trees to stay in touch and pass along information; instead, they do it via e-mail, blogs, message boards, and Twitter (for examples, check out www.journeymetro.com, www.mosaic.org, www.fumcdal.org). If you miss a Sunday, you can download the pastor's sermon as a podcast and put your offering directly into the church's bank account online. If your pastor had a rough week and couldn't prepare a sermon, he could go online to any number of services and download a free sermon (one of the most popular of such sites is www.sermoncentral.com with over 300,000 unique visitors per month and yes, they accept advertising). If he recommends a book from the pulpit, not much has changed; recommendations of products by clergy produce a huge run on the product, only now most members order those books online. Like other consumers, they opt for additional information whenever they buy a new computer, camera, or washing machine. It's second nature now, as they have learned that online shopping is not only convenient but often offers better deals.

ARE THERE *TWO* WEBS?

The Internet is changing so rapidly that I hesitate to mention the newest development because it could be outdated by the time you buy this book. I'm referring to something known as Web 2.0.

What, exactly, *is* Web 2.0? According to Wikipedia.com:

> Web 2.0, a phrase coined by O'Reilly Media in 2004, refers to a perceived second-generation of Web-based communities and hosted services—such as social networking sites, wikis, and folksonomies—that facilitate collaboration and sharing between users.

The main difference between old Internet (Web 1.0) and the new Internet (Web 2.0) is that Web 1.0 was you looking at a computer monitor; Web 2.0 is the computer monitor looking—and talking—back.

The beauty of Web 2.0 is that it expands the scope of your marketing without expanding your cost or efforts. The networked nature of Web 2.0 means that when you seed it with content, interested people can more easily share it with others in their social network. Best of all, people don't share content indiscriminately. Instead, they share it with the people most likely to appreciate it so that even as your marketing reach expands, it remains precisely targeted.

Consider the following Web 2.0 superstars and the impact they may have for your business:

- *Facebook.com:* When it comes to social networking, Facebook rises above the growing crowd. It was developed as a slightly more mature alternative to MySpace, which was getting too crowded with teens and tweens. All demographics, from teens to grandparents, are getting on Facebook. As a rule of thumb for your marketing, if you're maintaining a MySpace profile, create a slightly different one on Facebook to test that marketplace as well. Try searching for Facebook groups with the terms, Church or Christian. You will find thousands of connected individuals. Join some groups and start interacting.

- *MySpace.com:* Like Facebook, this is a social networking site. Here, users can post profiles, connect with others, spread news and broadcast content like wildfire. Use it as a research tool, especially for younger demographics. Whether you use it to search for likes, interests, books your audience members might read, where they're located, what denomination they are, or simply by faith, MySpace provides a wealth of information for those who know how to use it.

- *Xianz.com:* The good news about MySpace is that it is user-generated; the drawback to MySpace is that it is user-generated. In other words, you could have the most wholesome how-to knitting site or uplifting "skateboard for spirituality site," and a few prankster posters could ruin all your good work by using ribald imagery or crass language in reply. Fortunately, Xianz.com presents an alternative to MySpace, with lots of the same features as MySpace but lots of faith-based extras for believers, such as discussions on Christian topics, previews of new Christian music, and resources for studying the Bible. This is another great resource for finding individuals who are passionate about their faith and may want to hear your message.

- *YouTube.com, and other video-sharing sites* (for a list, go to http://mashable.com/2007/06/27/video-toolbox/): You can hardly log on to the Internet these days without some major site promoting the latest viral video from one central source: YouTube.com. But look past the home boxing videos or dangerous stunts, and you'll quickly realize how this user-generated site holds vast potential for the faith-based marketer. In a typical month in 2008, 134 million people went online to watch an average of 81 videos for a total of 11 billion videos, according to comScore. The average online viewer watches 228 minutes of video per month. YouTube makes it easy to create a truly viral marketing event if you're creative and "tag" your video properly (see below). By uploading a clever video that featured a product or service your company offers and using some of the tactics we'll discus later in this chapter, you might create the Web's next *Star Wars* parody or lonelygirl15, which created an online buzz in 2006. (Greg and Bob have started a small venture called Sneezecast that specializes in the creation, posting, and tracking of clever viral videos. If you are interested in this, go to www.sneezecast.com.)

Churches are using YouTube to promote their church and to spread the word. Search YouTube Channels by "church" and you get thousands of results. Or try "Christian videos." With millions of visitors watching YouTube daily, and obviously a large portion of them being believers, a simple video of your business, service, or product uploaded to YouTube with the right search description (we'll talk about that later) could yield great results.

- *TubeMogul.com:* One tool that is very useful for video marketing is Tube Mogul (www.TubeMogul.com), a free service that provides a single point for deploying uploads to the top video-sharing sites and powerful analytics on who, what, and how videos are being viewed. In other words, you upload your video to Tube Mogul, and it is automatically placed on several video-sharing sites at the same time. What's more, you can track how frequently your video is viewed on all of those sites from a single TubeMogul dashboard.
- *Tangle.com:* A fresh, innovative social network that is family friendly, kid-safe, and shares the belief and faith of many of its users. It provides a way for those interested in faith to connect with others around the world. It has some helpful features, including links to more than 1,500 Christian organizations, and it accepts advertising.

Who knows what will happen to Web 2.0 by this book's publication date. Still, you can see that if you keep on top of Web 2.0—by participating in it—you will be that much closer to finding and using your own strategy to reach your ultimate target audience.

INTERNET FOR MASS MARKETING?

Before you begin your Internet marketing to the faith community, you need to understand this simple fact: The Internet is a brilliant direct marketing tool, but it is a terrible mass marketing tool.

It was not designed to attract attention but to facilitate relationships.

Think of how you use the Internet. You choose where you will go on the Internet, when you go there, and precisely what page you want to view. And you have an opportunity to respond. Instantly. In mass marketing, the advertiser controls your access to information. With Internet marketing, you control your own access to information.

If you think of the Internet as a direct marketing tool for reaching individuals rather than a mass marketing tool, you'll be a lot more successful engaging Christians. In fact, we believe it's your most effective marketing tool for reaching the faith-based community. It allows you to communicate directly with individuals, learn who they are, and what their interests are; you are able to build a relationship with them as you do this over and over, much like friends who hang out with each other and get to know each other so well they can finish each other's sentences. The Internet enables you to get almost that close to your customers.

CASE STUDY: INTERNET MARKETING AND THE AFRICAN AMERICAN CHURCH

Veda Brown learned how to market to the African America church the old-fashioned way. "I had e-mail addresses from the gospel chat room, message boards, and AOL profiles and invited members to a site I launched called 'The Black Gospel Chapel,'" Brown explained (in the early days of the Internet, this was legal, but today you cannot harvest e-mail addresses from public forums and send unsolicited email to them). At the time, she was a volunteer channel manager for NetNoir, which was a part of AOL. Her site became so popular that NetNoir hired her as a consultant. Six years later, the company was sold, leaving Brown holding a list of 80,000 names and an idea.

"A friend asked me to promote his ministry, so I sent e-mails from my AOL account, choosing 'BlackGospelPromo' as my screen name. Pretty soon, another friend called and asked how

(Continued)

much I would charge to promote his project on the Internet. I just pulled a number out of a hat, and before I knew it, I owned my own company."

Brown modestly credits God for her company's success, but she acknowledges that great design has become her trademark. "You have to invest in design to attract attention and generate a response," Brown advises. Specifically, she suggests that African American consumers respond better to creative, active design. "African Americans like more pizzazz, more boom, more bells and whistles. Some might say our messages are a little busy, but it works for us."

Her advice to would-be Internet marketers: regular and consistent campaigns of e-mail blasts. "You're not going to get a response by just sending one blast for a campaign." To launch one new artist, Brown sent two e-mails a month for several months. And when we say e-mails, they're not your typical messages but are loaded with features such as video clips, audio samples, and photos. She gives her list members an experience, and they respond. Learn more at www.blackgospelpromo.com

Getting started with your Internet Marketing Strategy

Your Site

Here's the good news *and* bad news about Internet marketing: Anyone with a computer and access to the Internet can do it. Because of its ability to enable marketers to access consumers through a variety of web sites, blogs, social networks, and the like, people who understand neither the Internet nor marketing are trying to use both to sell their products. You can create a lot of stuff and send it to a lot of people, but that's not necessarily good marketing. Word processing made writing a lot easier, too, which exponentially expanded the supply of bad writing.

Entire books have been written about Internet marketing, including my own e-book (Bob): *The Bulls Eye Effect.* (*www.thebullseyeeffect.com*) But the following basics will help you get started on an online marketing strategy.

First and foremost, build a really great web site. Every online marketing campaign, even the most cutting edge, begins with a web site. Great web sites understand the mind of the audience. What do you know about the faith-based community that informs how you develop your web site? Remember, the Internet is primarily used for research. When we do buy things or avail ourselves of a service, it is because we went to the web site looking for information. Don't make the site all about you; make it all about the user. How can they use it? What can you offer them? How can you make their lives easier? How can you help them with what's most important to them?

Too many web sites are crammed with unnecessary bells and whistles. We recommend the PBS Principle: keep it *Professional But Simple*. Go easy on the Flash (animated graphics and video); they'll watch it once and never again; after that, it just becomes a nuisance—just one more obstacle they have to overcome to get to the information you're working so hard to provide. Most people aren't as wowed by Flash as you are. Soon enough they'll find an easier site to navigate, and it will be twice as hard to lure them back as it was to attract them in the first place. Besides, all those extras slow people down. Rule of thumb: If it takes more than five seconds to load, most users will move on to another site.

Search Engine Optimization

The whole point of a web site in terms of marketing is getting as many people to visit it, spend time on it, and value it enough to add it to their list of favorites so they can return easily and often. People discover new web sites through search engines, and there are things you can do to gain more visibility from those search engines so that people find *your* web site first. It's called "search engine optimization," or SEO, and includes a number of tactics you can use to increase your web site's visibility. Variations on these SEO techniques can also optimize your site for faith-based audiences.

Basically, search engines use mathematical formulas known as algorithms, which we won't try to explain except to say it's a way to rank how and where a web site will show up when someone does a search. When someone is searching for information about real estate in Des Moines, and you own a real estate business in Des Moines, you would like your company to be at the top of the list in their search. SEO can help you do that, and here are some of the basic html code suggestions for optimizing your web site's ability to attract increased traffic from search engines.

Title tags

The title tag is the most important aspect of your web site SEO (a tag is a specific word or phrase used by the search engine to determine what's on the site and therefore how to rank it). The title tag is the brief description you see at the very top of your browser when you go to a web site. Every page on your web site should have a relevant title, meaning the keywords in the title should correspond to the content on that site.

Meta tags

The copy that describes your site will not necessarily influence the ranking of the site, but it's a good idea to include a clear and compelling description of your site because that's what will appear in the search results. Think of it as optimized sales copy. Of course, including some of your keywords in the description won't hurt.

Body text

The first sentence in the body text and the first words per sentence are the most important ones for advanced on-page SEO results. Also, placing the body text in bold denotes strong emphasis to the search engines. The copy should be readable, but written with SEO in mind, using words that are relevant to what your site offers.

Here are a few tips to make the most of your site tags.

After you have determined what words and phrases you want your site to rank high for in the search engines, search the term yourself and see which sites come up first in the organic listings. Go to those sites and study what they're doing, then copy appropriate elements yourself. Look at their title tags and metatags to discover what they're doing. For example, www.christianlyricsonline.com uses the phrase "Christian music lyrics" in its title tag. That phrase is the third most frequently searched, relative to the term "Christian Music."

How to find the meta and title tags in websites:

1. Navigate to the page of interest
2. From your browser's menu choose "view source" or "view page source." This command lets you view the html code for that web page.
3. In the first few lines of code you will see the term "title." The next phrase after the word title is the title tag.
4. Continue down a line or two and find the term "Meta name=" The words and phrases that follow this command are the meta

tags for that page. Meta tags are the data that search engines use to understand what's on a web page. Google and other search engines use the description copy in a meta tag to define your site and when to present it in search results. You should treat meta tags like sales copy. Whenever possible, use meta tags that align with the words and phrases consumers are using, and the easiest way to do that is to identify those phrases with tools like Google Insights. www.google.com/insights/search

For more information about SEO, go to http://www.faithbased marketing.com

PPC Search

One of the most common methods of internet marketing is the "pay-per-click campaign," or PPC. Google paid search (Google Adwords) is the fastest and easiest way to drive traffic to your site in a matter of minutes. The first and most important step is choosing the right search words or phrases. How can you find the most effective words? We cannot pinpoint a particular keyword/key phrase which can guarantee the desired traffic and conversion, but we can show you a step-by-step approach to keyword research that will lead you to the best keyword for your PPC campaign.

The questionnaire

Starting the keyword research for PPC campaign with a questionnaire at hand organizes your thought process and gives a clear picture on where to lay your focus. A questionnaire should be comprised of questions like:

- What are my products and services?
- Who is the target audience?
- What is the USP (Unique Selling Proposition) of my company?
- Who are my competitors?
- What are the competitors' keywords that deliver traffic?
- What are the words customers use to find my website?

The basic keyword list

The series of answers to the questionnaire helps in determine the basic words that best describe your product and services, or the words people use to land on your page. From the clutter of related words prepare a list of keywords that best suits your product/service.

The keyword research tool

The next crucial step is to test the keywords for performance. Keyword research tools provide lots of variations for each keyword entry that includes synonyms, plurals, and abbreviations, which could have otherwise escaped your attention. Here are just a few:

https://adwords.google.com/select/KeywordToolExternal

www.wordtracker.com

www.nichebot.com

The fine tuned list

With statistics at hand it becomes easier to rule out the nonperforming keywords. Keywords with very low traffic or no traffic should be eliminated. Highly competitive keywords would be difficult to bid for, since the cost might exceed your PPC advertising budget. Less competitive keywords with good traffic would be an ideal choice for those aiming for a reasonable budget.

There are online sources that will tell you what people are paying for various search words, who is using them, where they're driving traffic, and what your competitors are buying. http://www.keywordspy.com and http://www.spyfu.com.

Optimize: To maximize ROI from your online PPC campaign, take the following steps:

A. Add Google Analytics to your web site. It's free. Learn more and set up your account at http://www.google.com/analytics. Google Analytics will help you monitor and understand the traffic on your web site. You'll see who is linking to your site so you can improve your reciprocal linking strategy. You'll also discover which search terms are driving traffic and whether that traffic stays to shop or hits the back button.

B. Set a cap on your adwords spending. Google will let you spend as much money as you like, and it's possible to spend a lot fast. Fortunately, Google also lets you cap your spending. Set a reasonable cap and leave it in place while you optimize your campaign.

C. Decide what one action you want people to take when they visit your site. If you have e-commerce, then it may be to make a purchase. If you don't sell from your site, then you may want them to register for your e-newsletter. You can't optimize your campaign unless you know what it is you want people to do.

D. Study Google Analytics and Ad Words reports to see which of your key words and phrases are delivering traffic that takes the desired action. Keep the words that work and cut the ones that don't.

These steps help you to zero in on a list of keywords with a high possibility of traffic and conversion. The evolution of keyword research should be an ongoing process, which has to be improved with innovative thinking, observation, and experimentation. Your first PPC campaign may not be a huge success, but if you consistently fine tune your research you will ultimately achieve the desired results: more sales and traffic from your target niche.

Online Display Advertising

Another way to drive traffic is to use online advertising. There are hundreds of sites that focus on the faith community that have paid banner advertising available. Rates vary depending on the amount of traffic the site receives, available inventory, time of year, and so on. Online display advertising can be very effective when focused on the right audience with the right message. (If you are interested in having someone manage this process for you, please visit www.buzzplant.com)

With millions of web sites and blogs, how do you find ones where Christians visit and which ones sell advertising? One of the best ways is to log on to www.alexa.com, a site that provides all sorts of information about other web sites:

1. Click "top sites by category" on the right hand side of the Alexa home page.
2. Then click "society" from the sites by category list.
3. Next click "Sub-categories" and choose "Religion and spirituality."
4. Finally, click "Sub-categories" again and choose "Christianity." Browse the list of the most popular Christian sites. Click the link by each one to visit the site and learn whether they sell advertising.

Alexa can also help you determine which Christian web sites would be best for you to use for advertising. Here are some steps you can use to gather information about specific web sites:

1. Type in the name of the domain in the "Search" box at the top of the page. This only searches the files in Alexa.com and is not a regular search engine.

2. Click on the "Site Info" box when the web site information is pulled up and you can learn the web site speed, links to the site, number of reviews, and other pertinent information.

3. Search the "Traffic Detail" link below the "Explore This Site" icon at the top of the page. Under this link you can find the countries that view the web site, how many pages are viewed in the web site, and the general trend of traffic.

4. Click on "Related Links" to view the competition. From here you can also research the competition's site information.

5. Research the "Sites Linking In" icon to learn the major web sites that people are using to find the site.

6. Perform this research on Alexa.com at least every three months as audiences and competition change.

You can pay to advertise directly to Christians via the Internet, and in the final section of this book we list some of those services that can direct your Internet advertising to the appropriate groups of Christians.

Blogging and Linking

Identify Christian bloggers in your community or writing about your industry. Go to www.technorati.com and search phrases related to your product. Identify bloggers who routinely write on that topic.

Blogging is huge in the faith-based community, especially in the younger demographics (20- to 35-year-old). Get to know these people. Subscribe to several blogs via an RSS reader so you can easily check them on a regular basis. E-mail them. Be up front with them and tell them you want to serve the Christian community with your product or service. Some of the blogs accept advertising, but if your product serves a need of the blogger, offer to send a free sample. He or she might mention it on their blog, which is even better than an advertisement. One caution: Always ask permission before you send anything of a commercial or "selling" nature. Some Christian bloggers may initially be wary of letting their blog be used for commercial purposes, but if you practice the "serve don't sell" rule, you will have a greater chance of success. Most local newspapers have web sites that allow commenting after articles just like blogs do. Go to the articles on Christian topics and get involved in the conversation by leaving comments that mention your business.

Don't use this space to place thinly veiled ads. That's abusing it, and the community will cast you out. Instead, look for articles that naturally connect faith to your business and honestly engage in the discussion.

For example, if you own a recording studio, and you'd like to expand your business by producing CDs for area bands, then meet with a youth pastor from a local church and ask him about any blogs that Christian musicians frequent. He'll know. Then e-mail the blogger(s) and tell them what you're trying to do. Don't try to sell anything, but offer to guest host a few sessions on the topic of "How to Launch Your Own CD." Find ways to connect what your target audience is passionate about receiving with information or advice that speaks to that passion.

If you haven't already, create your own blog. Go to www.wordpress.com or www.blogspot.com and set up a free blog. The advantage of having a blog in addition to your site are:

- Easy to update with new content
- People can subscribe to it via RSS (Really Simple Syndication)
- Provides inbound links to your website
- By using tools like Technorati and other aggregator sites, your blog will become syndicated and linked to hundreds of other sites.

Submit your site to social bookmarking sites like www.digg.com, www.delicious.com, and www.stumbleupon.com. Be sure to tag your site with the same keywords you used in your meta tags.

BUILDING AND MANAGING A LIST

Now that you are driving targeted traffic to your site, make sure you have a way to collect their information. Provide a sign-up form on the top part of the front page that collects at minimum their name and e-mail address. This information can be saved in a database on the back end of your site.

Build a List of Opt-In Consumers

This is basically a group of people who have said to you, "Yes, I want to get information from you regularly about your product or service." It's the digital equivalent of "permission marketing," and you'll blow through a lot of money if you don't start here. The opt-in list is the foundation of your Internet marketing program; in PyroMarketing terms, you're gathering the driest tinder. Ideally, you will build it on your own, but if that's not possible you can rent lists from list companies such as *info*USA and EmailResults. How do you build your own opt-in list? The easiest way is to create a place on your web site, prominently displayed, inviting people to click if they want to receive periodic information from your company about its products. Then make sure every other communication vehicle (business cards, Yellow Pages listing, brochures, and other forms of advertising) drives customers to your web site. Response rates for opt-in e-mail can be anywhere from 15 to 30 percent or more, as opposed to 1 to 2 percent with traditional direct mail. So make this a priority!

Just make sure you don't turn your opt-in program into spam. Abide by SPAM rules, which are governed by the CAN-SPAM Act of 2003: every e-mail sent must (1) qualify as opt-in, (2) include your physical address in the e-mail, and (3) offer a way to opt out. You can learn more about these rules at the law's official web site: www.ftc.gov/bcp/edu/pubs/business/ecommerce/bus61.shtm.

You can also create an e-mail newsletter or send your list to a podcast dispensing helpful information to consumers. A podcast is simply an audio recording made available on the Internet. It's a lot easier than you think. iTunes provides a way for you to put podcasts online, and there are other online services that you can use to help you distribute your podcast. (www.podcastalley.com)For example, if you own a fitness center and you want to target your local faith-based community, then with a one-page e-mail newsletter or a three-minute podcast, you could pack in a lot of valuable health and fitness advice. E-mail it to the appropriate staff person at the churches you've researched and visited (senior pastor, sports director, women's ministry leader) and ask them to send it on to anyone in their church who might benefit from it. People who receive it can click the opt-in function, giving you permission to contact them using the e-mail address that pops up on your screen. As they share the podcast or newsletter with their friends, it grows virally and before you know it you have a substantial list of Christians who have said they want to hear from you. To jump-start your thinking about the kind of consumer information your business could provide, turn back to the sidebar, *Turning Your Business into Content for Christian Radio,* on page 108.

Gather as Much Information as Possible from List Members

It's one thing to have a substantial e-mail list, but the more information you obtain from these list members, the better you will be able to serve them. Getting information from people who opt to join your list is not difficult. Here are some suggestions:

- *Online surveys:* This is a great way for visitors to your web site to provide useful information in a stress-free and beneficial way. It helps when the survey is tied to both the user (them) and provider (you). For instance, if you're working out the kinks in those knitting handbooks, why not ask for a little (targeted) audience participation by asking a relevant question, such as, "Which stitch do you think is the easiest for a beginner?" and/or "What type of knitting needles do you prefer?" This could not only provide helpful data for you, but also give users of your site a way to feel involved and useful. www.surveymonkey.com is a very easy-to-use service for conducting surveys and collecting data.

- *Permission marketing:* The days of getting something for nothing are long gone. Today, Web visitors are almost as savvy about what we do as we are; they know that when they fill out a form or provide an e-mail address or phone number, it's for a specific reason. They are as careful about giving away this information as we are interested in receiving it; so providing incentives like a gift, special offer, or discounted product may help.

- *Contact forms:* These have long been a great way to elicit voluntary information from web site visitors, but the problem now becomes knowing just how much information to ask for. Ask for too much, and you turn users off. Don't ask for enough, and the exercise is futile. Make sure your webmaster tests various contact forms to find out which one works best—for you and the consumer. Begin by asking for the bare minimum and then, as you build the relationship, you'll earn the right to ask for more. Don't ask them to marry you on the first date. Just get permission for a second date. (www.formlogix.com provides a good solution with its free/affordable online form-building and database hosting service.)

- *Text messages:* Lately, companies have used text messaging via cell phones to elicit customer information. Experiment with several ways to have users text a certain number in exchange for either

information or a special discount, and utilize the incoming information to collect even more. Some good resources for this are www.text-
marks.com, www.broadtexter.com

Segment the Niche

One hundred and forty million people make for a pretty big niche. So
do the 5,000 people down the street at Redeemer Community Church.
So before you start building your opt-in list, decide which segments
within the niche you want to target. Remember, churches make this
easy for you because they are organized around various segments: children, teenagers, singles, married with small children, men, women,
senior citizens, and so on. Even if you think *everyone* in the faith-based
community would value your product or service, we still recommend
you narrow your target because the Internet works best when it is
focused as narrowly as possible. Experiment with one segment to begin
with and create a campaign that targets only that segment.

Behavioral targeting is another way to find Christians on the Internet.
Internet ads serving companies like Blue Lithium and Specific Media
have the ability to present ads to people based on their Internet activity during the previous 90 days. If someone visited Christian web sites
and read a religion article at the local paper's web site, they would be
marked as interested in Christianity and could be specifically targeted
with ads whenever they visited any site along the network—even if they
were just checking the weather. Making use of these networks is a perfect way for businesses wanting to reach Christian consumers on the
Internet. Traditional advertising places ads on particular sites hoping
the right consumers will pass by. It fishes the fishing hole. Behavioral
targeting presents ads to particular people no matter what site they're
on. It fishes the fish.

Behavioral targeting should be supplemented with retargeting,
which works like this. If a consumer visits a particular site, a retargeting pixel (cookie) is inserted on the consumer's computer. Then, when
they leave that site for others on the network, they are shown specific
ads. Retargeting complements your search engine campaign because it
enables you to convert interested consumers who specifically searched
for your products but did not immediately complete your desired
action.

Companies such as mine (Bob's) provide services for creating all
sorts of chatter on blogs, message boards, and forums about a product

or service, which in turn spreads virally because everyone who arrives at the site does so because of a shared interest in the topic (www.buzzblitz. net). It's all about communicating something that is worth telling others about—not selling something.

Obtain and Use Endorsements

There's an interesting human psychological phenomenon called "social proof" that is especially powerful on the Internet. It's why Amazon always includes reader reviews for the books it sells online. Social proof simply means people will respond better to a product if they know others like it. Social proof can be so powerful that if people hear that a movie has sold out, they will attend the next night thinking if that many people attended, it must be good. When my (Bob's) company was asked to handle digital marketing for Mel Gibson's *The Passion of the Christ,* we built our Internet campaign on literally thousands of endorsements we received from key pastors and church leaders who previewed the film. Christians look up to and deeply respect their leaders, so when we were able to e-mail Christians an endorsement for the film from their pastors, the response was almost guaranteed. In the faith-based community, social proof will be extremely important to you if you are unknown within that arena. So any endorsement from a recognized church leader or even just a well-known Christian in your community should appear in your Internet advertising.

CASE STUDY: TALES OF GLORY

Ground Force Network, a company that I (Bob) own, specializes in using online and offline marketing. A great example of how that works occurred when we were hired by a toy manufacturer, One2Believe, to help with the debut of their product line of faith-based toys, Tales of Glory, in Wal-Mart.

We executed a two-month campaign by recruiting 205 volunteer "field agents," to create awareness of the line within their spheres of influence. We then, created a branded web site for the campaign, and regularly e-mailed them to guide them in how

(Continued)

they could promote the line. Each of these field agents demonstrated the product to their friends, gave free Tales of Glory coloring book pages to parents of children in their churches, shared an online eCard featuring Tales of Glory toys, and used web banners on their personal web sites. The combined efforts of online and offline marketing in this campaign netted hundreds of actual customers going to their local Wal-Mart and purchasing at least one Tales of Glory toy.

A FINAL WORD ABOUT RELATIONSHIP BUILDING.

Always keep in mind the unique nature of the Internet. It was designed for communication in its purest form, building and maintaining relationships between two people. If you ask people why they check their e-mail or visit a web site, they seldom say, "to buy something." Instead, people use the Internet to stay in touch, learn something, discover something, or share their thoughts about something.

Using the Internet to market your product or service will be as successful as your efforts to build relationships with members of your opt-in list and those who enter your web site. For Christians, it may be even more important because of the relational nature of faith. Christianity is a communal religion—people "join" a church and often refer to each other as "brothers and sisters." You can build and nurture strong relationships with them by remembering these eight easy tips:

1. *Stay in regular contact.* It can take your target audience several impressions to get to know you, no matter how perfectly you deliver your message. Too little is as bad as too much, so plan and regulate the amount of contact you make so that it's your most effective, not your least. Once a week is the best. We even get e-mails daily. It all depends on the amount of relevant content you have to share. But a good rule of thumb is not more than once every 72 hours and not less than at least once per month. The Internet has created very short memories for most of us, and it's easy to be forgotten quickly and deleted if your message is not in front of people regularly.

2. *Promote with a purpose—theirs, not yours.* The way to build a relationship is through contact, but not just any contact; it must have a purpose, and it must be appropriate. In other words, if you

are creating a new product for preteen skateboard enthusiasts, don't send them a newsletter filled with articles on healthy aging. Frankly, don't send them a newsletter at all. Instead, send them a quick video clip of the week's hottest moves from the coolest skaters. Make it so they look forward to that weekly clip—and maybe even get inspired to send in one of their own. Now *that's* a Web 2.0 relationship!

3. *Update your database.* Sending to wrong, broken, or defunct e-mail addresses is costly and ineffective. Make sure your tech people are constantly updating your database to ensure the message you work so hard to compose actually makes it to your target audience. The investment in database management pays big rewards when it comes to effectively and efficiently hitting your target.

4. *Be creative.* No message is insignificant. Be it the subject line of an e-mail update or the banner on your new web page, take the time to be creative and capture interest. Remember, if *you* can't get enthused about knitting, skating, or whatever it is you do or sell, chances are your target audience can't either.

5. *Don't scrimp on content.* Content isn't king just because it flows off the tongue; content is king because it drives relationships. If you are sending out a weekly e-mail newsletter, read it first. Be honest: Is it lame? boring? redundant? sloppy? If so, why are you sending it? Make it something you'd like to read; make it interesting, snappy, and fresh so that people will actually open it and read it.

6. *Be consistent.* People are funny about this. If you tell them they will get their e-mail newsletter every Monday at 10:00 A.M., they expect it then. Weekly should mean weekly; monthly should mean monthly. You can create the most fascinating newsletter, the most topical quizzes, the most dead-on surveys, and the greatest copy in the world, but if people start looking forward to seeing it every Thursday after lunch—only to start finding it in their weekend junk mail or Tuesday at 7 A.M. when they're too busy to enjoy it—all that hard work will go to waste.

7. *Don't pander.* Forming a relationship is about building trust. You can't send out cookie-cutter e-mails or post blog entries that are rushed, lazy, and skimpy on content. Your audience is growing more sophisticated with each passing day; act accordingly and don't write, send, post, or upload something you wouldn't waste the time reading yourself.

8. *Enable new opt-ins.* Every piece you send to your list should have a link for new members to opt in. If you do your job right and give your list members a great experience with your message, they will send it to their friends. Most people have their own small list of close friends, family members, fellow Christians, and so on, and it isn't unusual for them to forward things they find interesting or helpful to everyone on their list.

These are just a few quick tips on how to build, foster, and maintain a relationship; improvise and add your own. When you communicate to your opt-in list, think of what you would say if one of the members was sitting across the table from you. That's the level of intimacy you can and should try to achieve.

A friend of ours, known as a "late adopter" when it comes to technology, who never fully bought in to the idea that an impersonal slice of technology—his computer and the Internet—could produce anything resembling a relationship. That is, until he discovered a web site that caters to something he's passionate about: sailing. He opted in to receive updates about new products, special events, even stories from other sailors. Now, he can't wait until those e-mails pop up in his inbox. "They know my specific interests and somehow send me all sorts of stuff that I just love reading," he exclaimed. "It's magic!"

Not really, but his story underscores how the Internet has won over the hearts and minds of people of every age from all walks of life.

If you're new to Internet marketing, start small. Target one segment in the Christian market and build your opt-in list. Even if you only begin with 15 to 20 e-mail addresses, begin communicating with your list regularly. Make sure you send them information that is helpful, interesting, and targeted to their needs. If you give them a compelling experience, they will forward your e-mail to their friends, and your list will grow exponentially.

Finally, Internet marketing works best as part of an integrated campaign alongside your print, radio, direct mail, and other strategies. At the very least, every communication with those other media should include your web address. We know of at least one business that uses direct mail to Christians as a way of recruiting new opt-ins for its list. Something as simple as handing out your business card at a Christian businessman's breakfast will produce new members for your list, and if you're going to appear as a guest expert on Christian radio, you can send out a blast to your list informing them of your appearance.

Remember, it's easy to think of Internet marketing as mass marketing because it can reach so many people so quickly. But you have to earn each click, and you do that best by realizing every communication in your Internet strategy is a conversation between you and one other person.

Since this isn't primarily a book about internet marketing, there are several topics we have not covered in this chapter. If you would like to learn more and go deeper your Internet strategy, please refer to www.faithbasedmarketing.com for additional resources.

CHAPTER ELEVEN

DIRECT MARKETING TO CHRISTIANS

As you learned in Chapter 3, Christians are no different from anyone else, and that's especially true when it comes to direct marketing. You may find this surprising, but they have mailboxes! They go to them every day and sort through the—okay, we'll use the term—*junk mail,* and something may catch their eye. Was it the offer for yet another credit card? Probably not. Was it the big flyer filled with coupons? Not this time.

This time, Joe Christian folded the simple card he retrieved from the five other direct mail pieces in his stack of mail, slipped it in his pocket, and smiled as he headed to his car and drove to the jewelry store with his 20-percent-off coupon. "How could they have possibly known tomorrow was my anniversary?" he thought, and chuckled as he imagined his wife's reaction when she unwrapped the necklace.

They didn't, but they knew more about Joe than he thinks. They know his age and his approximate income level. They know he's married. They know he's shopped at that jewelry store before. And they know where he lives. Pretty much all they need to know to gamble on him, which is what direct mail is all about—careful, thoughtful, measurable gambling. But unlike a trip to the casino, you will *always* win; it's just a question of how much.

Direct marketing is the most cost effective form of marketing and needs to become part of your arsenal for reaching Christians and Christian organizations with information about your product or service. In fact, using direct marketing to reach Christians is more of an investment than a gamble, especially when used as part of a campaign that uses print, online, and word-of-mouth. Using the database that you have built, you can reach large numbers of people for pennies, where reaching people in the general public costs dollars. More on that in a minute, but first the basics for anyone who has not yet tried direct marketing.

It's Not Junk

Direct marketing is just what it says: marketing directly to the customer, usually through bulk mailings. Enlisting the youth group to put flyers on windshields in the church parking lot is a form of direct marketing. And most of the principles of direct marketing are transferable to the use of e-mail in marketing. Direct marketing is most successful when you mail to specifically targeted lists as opposed to sending promotions to "resident." Success is measured in terms of response rates, with 3 to 5 percent returns considered successful in most cases. In this chapter we will go over the three main components of any direct marketing campaign: acquire a list, develop the creative, and make the offer. In addition to the list, direct marketing depends on two other components: the creative (how the package looks)and the offer (special pricing, discount, limited edition, and how it is presented).

While both of us have had some experience with direct marketing, we went to one of the gurus of direct marketing to help us with this chapter. Jim Hicks has fine-tuned his direct marketing skills over a career spanning two decades. In addition to working with life and health insurance companies, Jim has helped the United States Army find new recruits through various direct marketing campaigns. It's one thing to try to convince someone to sign up for life insurance, but we think it takes some real expertise to get young men and women to respond to an offer to get their heads shaved and crawl through swamps during basic training. Jim now consults with businesses on direct marketing, so feel free to contact him if you need a real pro to help you with your direct marketing (jehicksiii@yahoo.com).

The List

According to Jim, acquiring the right list is the most important component of any direct marketing campaign. "Fundamentally, your list is the foundation of your direct marketing," Jim explained. "Without a good list, you will be sending everything to the wrong people, which means all that money you spend on postage and creative will be wasted." You can get everything else perfect but send it to the wrong people and you will get a dismal response. So how do you obtain the right lists? According to Jim, there are two common ways to obtain a list of consumers for your direct marketing campaign: rent your list from one of the many reputable companies who have compiled and segmented lists, or extract your list from compiled files.

Renting lists is relatively easy. If you type "direct mail list rental" into your search engine, you will find pages and pages of listings for hundreds of companies who will rent you lists for your campaign. For example, one of the first lists that came up on our search was Zunch Worldwide, Inc. and sure enough, one of their 16 categories of lists was "religion." A good start. But since we've had experience working in faith-based marketing, we knew of another list rental company that specializes in faith-based lists, www.trimediaonline.com. When we went to their website, we found a sampling of their list categories.

- Churches by size
- Liturgical churches
- Black churches
- Asian churches
- Churches planning to rebuild
- Churches with day care centers
- Churches with counseling services
- Churches with female music ministers

We clicked on another tab on this list rental site and found lists for individual Christians segmented by age, gender, and even some behaviors (Christian computer users, families who home school).

If you shop around, you will find a segmented list that will meet your direct marketing needs. The average cost for renting most lists is between $40 and $60 per thousand names. One of the benefits of renting lists is reliability. Companies often guarantee deliverability, meaning they keep their lists updated. However, as with any media purchase, do some research. Some companies rent lists that are not maintained or not very reliable. Avoid companies that advertise excessively cheap rates because you usually get what you pay for. And consult with other businesses that have experience with direct mail.

Another way to develop your list is to extract names and addresses from compiled files, which are data collected on households by large companies such as Experian, InfoUSA, and Acxiom. Basically, these types of companies collect data through surveys and public records on the 175 million households in the United States. Typically, they will have anywhere from 150 to 250 "data elements" for each household—things like whether they rent or own their homes, how many children they have, what their income is, and so on. It's called a household file. They will allow you to select information from the various data elements to develop the list that you want to reach. For example, let's say you want to develop a list of consumers who would be most likely to purchase your product. You can ask for a consumer profile of everyone who has already purchased the product and develop a profile of that consumer, known as "profitable customers." Then you can develop a list of potential consumers who fit that profile. According to Jim, this is the best place to start when developing your lists. "Once you know what your 'sold' market looks like, you know who is most likely to buy your product or service based on the characteristics of those who have already bought it. Interestingly enough, these are called 'look-alikes' in the industry, and you can scour lists to find these look-alikes so that your own list has a better chance of being profitable."

This doesn't have to be a complex, sophisticated process. Jim worked with a nonprofit agency in his city who wanted to increase their donor base. He asked the agency board members to bring in the donor lists from any other nonprofit organization whose boards they served on, reasoning that people who give to nonprofit agencies are concerned about their communities and would be most likely to support other efforts to help their city. He then matched the names with Acxiom's lists to generate a new list for the agency to mail to.

Regardless of how you develop your list, you need a database for no other reason than having a place to keep your "house file." A house file is a file of those people who have either responded to your offer, names that you own that you want to mail to in the future, and your current customers. A house file has a couple of purposes. The main purpose is to prevent you from having to buy those names again. If you rent a list, you can only mail to the names on that list once. But if they respond to your offer, you "own" that name and can put it on your database and mail to them again at no rental fee. The house file also helps you with the "suppression" process—that is, if you purchase another list you can use your house list to compare and remove any names from the rented list that are on your household list. You do this because (1) you don't want to have that customer receive two offers from your company at the same time, and (2) you don't want to pay for mailing to one of your existing customers.

Jim also recommends that you have a system for tracking and testing your campaign. In other words, you may want to test pricing options or various creative packages. To do that, you need to assign a special code to the response vehicle. If it's a mail-in response card, you simply include the code on the card. If you offer a toll-free number for responding to your offer, you need to instruct the customer to mention the code when he or she calls your response center. When you receive the responses, make sure you capture and record the information in your database so you can determine what worked best. "Start simple with your testing and work your way forward as you gain more experience," Jim advises.

One final word on the use of your list. Make sure you have a fulfillment and follow up plan. The best way to get a response is to offer premiums (something of value) to anyone who responds. So if you promise to send the customer a free T-shirt if they fill out a card and mail it back to you, have a plan in place to ensure a quick response. As a general rule, if you use a vendor to fulfill your offers, you should never be satisfied with anything less than a response within 24 hours.

Also, know exactly what you want the premium to do. If you are just interested in getting a response, just about anything will work. But if you want to actually make a sale, you may need to test various premiums. For example, in one campaign for the Army, Jim offered two different premiums: a flashlight and a T-shirt, both with the Army logo. The flashlight produced twice as many responses as the T-shirt, but the T-shirt converted to enlistments better than the flashlight.

Once you have your list determined, the next step is to design the right creative package for your offer.

Creative

The graphics and design of your direct mail piece should say one thing: read me! Direct mail design is a science, not necessarily an art. The purpose of the design is to attract attention; to get the person who receives it to spend much time with it, reading it, and considering its offer. There are a variety of ways to do this, some subtle and others more direct, but when it comes to direct mail the two most common "packages" are the post card and the letter. Postcards are less expensive, and there is some research to suggest people are more likely to keep a postcard lying around, while they are more likely to toss a letter. On the other hand, postcards are limited by their size and lack of space to communicate your offer. Both, however, are used extensively and successfully. For our purposes, we will focus on the letter, and again our friend Jim Hicks shared generously from his extensive experience in creating effective direct mail campaigns.

Let's start with the envelope. The #10 envelope is the most common size used, but you have a couple of choices: an envelope with a window or one without. If you opt for a windowless envelope (some think it feels more personal and less like junk mail), you may run into problems matching the name and address on the envelope with the name and address on the letter—something printers call a blind match. Think of it this way: Your printer has a stack of 10,000 envelopes and another stack of 10,000 letters. If he makes a single mistake, a lot of your customers are going to be confused because they will receive a letter addressed to them on the envelope but someone else on the letter. This is not a huge problem in the industry because printers are pretty good at checking things during their press runs. Just something to consider.

Regardless of which envelope you use, it's your first impression—your first opportunity to communicate with your customer, and the most important message you want to communicate is "Open me now!" In the earlier days of direct mail, companies would put a tiny pencil or a coin inside the envelope on the notion that people were more likely to open a "lumpy" envelope to see what was inside. Now they use teasers: free gift inside; $50 coupon inside; free information. Incidentally, this is where the postcard has the advantage—the customer doesn't have to open anything to see the offer. Even the type of postage can influence whether or not the customer will open the envelope, with an actual postage stamp generally getting a better response than either a fake stamp or printed metered postage.

The next component of your creative package is some type of response vehicle, and the goal here is simplicity—making it as easy as possible for the customer to respond. The best way to do that is to give them as many choices as possible: a postage-free card or #9 envelope, highly visible web site address, or toll-free telephone number. Different people respond in different ways, so make sure you offer as many ways to respond as possible.

Depending on your budget, you may also want to include a brochure in your mailing. According to Jim, your brochure should be able to tell your story without using words. In fact, he asks to see the brochure before any text has been added, just to make sure the customer could determine the offer just from the graphics. Why? "Some people are more visually oriented and just don't pay attention to words," Jim explains.

Have you ever opened up a direct mail piece and had something fall out of it and onto the floor? That's called a "lift piece," perhaps because you have to bend over and lift it up after it falls to the floor. But it's especially designed as yet another way to motivate you to respond. Usually, it's a short note from the CEO or company president telling you what a great offer this is and asking you to respond. Short, to the point, yet often effective.

Then there's the "buddy card," which is a vehicle to enable your customer to become an evangelist for you and your product or service. Essentially, it's an abbreviated form of the offer that the customer can pass along to a friend. So in effect, when you use a buddy card you are theoretically reaching two households per mailing. Here's an insider's tip: Christians love to share with their friends. If they like what you're offering there is a very good chance they will share that with someone else, so always include a buddy card in your faith-based direct marketing campaigns. There's an interesting study by the Wharton business school and AT&T that found that people who know a current customer are three to five times more likely to become customers themselves than are people targeted by the best marketing techniques but who do not know a current customer. That's great news for people who market to Christians because Christians meet together at least once a week in church. Giving your direct mail recipients the tools to tell others about the product they purchase will provide greater returns on your campaigns.

Just a few practical tips before we move on to the offer:

- Always mail to yourself. This helps you learn how long it takes from the time the mail drops until the customer receives it. It also helps you experience what your customers are experiencing.
- Start collecting mail you get from other companies' direct marketing campaigns. It's good "quick and dirty" research on the various methods and best practices.
- Bulk mail is often delivered in the same time frame as first class mail. So if you are doing large mailings, think twice about paying extra for first class.

The Offer

The offer is the business end of your direct marketing campaign. It's really the whole reason why you have gone to the trouble of finding a list and creating an irresistible package. You want them to open the envelope so that when all is said and done, they respond. The offer is what they respond to.

In the early days of direct marketing, the four-page letter was standard. No longer. People just do not have that kind of time and will most likely toss something that appears to be too long and time consuming. Jim recommends trying to get your offer on one page, two at the most. If you have done a good job up to this point, you probably have a customer who is at least inclined to see what's in the envelope. Don't lose your momentum with a lot of reading material, and whatever it is that they read, make sure it is clear and compelling. Great copywriters do not try to sound like William Faulkner when they write to consumers. Here are just a few things to consider about how the offer is presented:

- Although direct mail is a form of mass marketing, write to an individual. Specifically, an individual who fits the profile of the customer you are trying to reach. Demonstrate that you know them (because from their profiles, you really do).
- State your offer early and repeat it at the end. If the customer doesn't know what you are offering by the time they finish reading the first paragraph, you've failed.
- Highlight the solutions your product or service delivers—how it meets a strongly felt need.
- Pieces that offer guarantees generally pull better than those that don't. ("100 percent satisfaction or your money back!")
- Create a sense of urgency without sounding desperate. Consider offering an incentive for a prompt response ("Act now and receive this bonus gift!")
- Make sure the recipient knows exactly how to respond. Give them as many options as possible. Make it sound easy to respond. And make sure every piece in the package has both your web site address and toll-free telephone number on it so that if they lose the response card but really wanted to accept your offer, they can still respond.
- Consider various graphic techniques to grab the reader's eye: highlighting or underlining key phrases or sentences; "handwritten" notes in the margin; bold or colored text.

TEST YOUR WAY IN, THEN KEEP TESTING

Successful direct mail relies on careful and consistent testing. For example, test small mailings to multiple lists to see which performs the best and then mail larger quantities to those lists. You should also test multiple creative designs, multiple offers, and different pricing options. The best performing offer is not necessarily the one that gets the best response. It's the one that nets the most profit. You want the right combination of price and response rate to net your company the greatest financial return.

Other factors to test: the tone, length, and style of the copy; timing (i.e., early in the month versus end of month); overall size or type of package (postcard versus envelope); and frequency. Only change one variable at a time, so you can easily tell which change altered the results. Keep detailed records of everything you do so that you know what works, what doesn't, and especially, who responded. In general, it has been found that people who buy through the mail often prefer this type of shopping and are likely to become repeat customers. Know who they are and go back to them frequently. One of the most common errors in direct mail is not mailing often enough.

At the same time, our friend Jim Hicks warns against testing too much within a given campaign. "As a general rule, two to ten tests per 100,000 mailings is fine. Any more than that and you will have problems."

Direct Marketing and Christians

As you consider developing a direct marketing component to your overall marketing strategy to Christians, we'd like you to consider two drivers that may enhance your results: timing and need. And here's where working with church people gives you an advantage. Remember in Chapter 5 that we showed you how to use the church information to learn more about them. Here's where you can put that to use in your direct marketing program.

First, timing. As you review the church's web site, you will notice occasional churchwide events or activities that may provide great opportunities for you to send a direct marketing piece to your list from that church. For example, most churches conduct some type of food or canned good drive around Thanksgiving. If you are in the food business, this would be a good time to send a two-for-one coupon—one for the customer and one to donate at church. This simple approach accomplishes three goals that should be important to you: (1) increased traffic and sales, (2) serving the church in a meaningful way, and (3) visibility and goodwill.

As you learn more about a church, you also discover their needs. If you learn from their web site that a church is engaged in a major capital campaign and your business is personal finance, send a direct mail piece to members offering expert investment advice to help them increase their donations to the church.

One word of caution: Unless you have church member contact information from an opt-in service, resist the temptation to build a list from other sources. For example, most churches publish photo directories that also include addresses and phone numbers. Usually they include a disclaimer requesting marketers not to use the directory for marketing purposes. Honor those requests, and if you are in doubt, ask the pastor's permission. The number-one complaint from churches that have partnered with marketers is lack of integrity. There are many legitimate ways to build a mailing list; don't jeopardize your reputation by "borrowing" a list.

One final note about direct marketing to the faith-based community: We normally think of direct marketing as a way to sell something, and that's its primary function. But access to a targeted list also presents helpful research opportunities. In addition to asking recipients to buy something, devote at least one direct mail program to asking for information. Give the recipient an opportunity to evaluate your business, your product, and your direct mail packages. Not only will you gain valuable information to help you improve your business, but you will also generate a lot of goodwill. Customers appreciate being asked for their opinions and advice.

CHAPTER TWELVE

REACHING PASTORS

WHAT WORKS AND WHAT DOESN'T WORK

"*A Baptist pastor, a Jewish Rabbi, and a Catholic priest were playing golf...*"

Ah, the clergy. Men of the cloth. Guys who work one day a week and spend the rest of the time fishing or on the golf course. Did you hear the one about the preacher whose sermons always had happy endings? Everyone was happy when his sermons ended!

Pastors love a good joke, but if you're trying to develop a relationship with them, don't tell the one about the happy endings and don't make jokes about them playing golf all week. Then again, they probably have a few preacher jokes a lot funnier than those. Some of the funniest jokes we've ever heard came from pastors. When you get to know them, you'll learn pastors are pretty normal, and yet anything but normal.

If a church were a football team, the pastor would be the head coach. These men and women are great motivators, compassionate listeners, competent managers, and innovative visionaries. If you want to market to the faith-based community, you'll be far more successful if you reach the pastor first.

WHO THEY ARE

The word "pastor" comes from the French word *pasteur*, which means shepherd. It's an appropriate term because a pastor tends to his congregation much like a shepherd cares for his sheep. This is why any effort to market to Christians has to include the pastor. He or she feels responsible for people in the church, often protective of them. Don't be discouraged or offended if you sense you are being scrutinized at first. You are. It's their job. Churches and religious organizations are often targeted by scammers and schemers. If you're not one, you'll be fine because they absolutely love anyone who has the best interests of the parishioners in mind.

We have used the awkward "he or she" pronouns to refer to pastors, but in reality most pastors—especially senior pastors—are men. In the more liberal mainline churches where you might expect to see more women pastors, only 5 percent of all senior pastors are women. In the evangelical wing of the church, that number would be much lower.

Almost all Protestant pastors are married. Catholic pastors, called priests, do not marry. Pastors aren't perfect: 13 percent of married pastors have been divorced and almost all of these are remarried.

Pastors are getting older. The average age of Protestant pastors was 44 in 1992 and is 48 in the most recent survey (2007). A common worry among Protestant and Catholic leaders is an impending shortage of clergy. As a businessperson, you might find this interesting: Some of the new pastors entering the ministry are former business leaders.

The typical pastor is highly trained and well educated, with at least a master's degree. Their training is usually done at a seminary—a graduate school primarily established to produce pastors and church leaders.

Pastors receive a special designation called "ordination," often given by a local church, a denomination, or other governing body. For pastors to be officially recognized by the government as clergy, they must receive this ordination.

Catholic pastors are called priests and addressed as "father," and they are not allowed to marry. If you greet a Protestant pastor for the first time, call him Reverend (last name), but don't be surprised if he invites you to call him by his first name.

Pastors measure success in many different ways, but one convenient measure is numerical growth. They want to see their churches grow, not just for numbers' sake but because they truly believe people's lives will be better if they know God and are part of a church. This is an important clue for marketers, because you also understand the desire to grow. You're trying to grow your business. The pastor is trying to grow his church. What can you do to help that will also help you? We'll come back to that, but right now we want you to let that soak into your brain for a while.

WHAT PASTORS DO

A pastor's most visible job is delivering a sermon. Here's where Catholics get lucky. For whatever reason, Catholic sermons seldom last more than 15 minutes. Protestant sermons can run up to 45 minutes, but pastors are getting better about that. Regardless of our immature carping about long sermons, this is a big deal for pastors. It's their one chance each week to do what they feel called to do: provide spiritual guidance for their people. As such, they take it seriously. It has been estimated that for each minute of a sermon, a pastor spends one hour in preparation. Between that and staff meetings and visiting members who are in the hospital and scolding the youth pastor for letting the teenagers build a halfpipe skateboard ramp in the parking lot and meeting with an older gentleman who thought the sermon was too liberal followed by a meeting with a younger woman who thought it was too conservative, pastors will be happy to meet you. In other words, don't just drop by the church and ask to see the pastor. He's as professional as any other business executive you meet with, so call ahead and make an appointment.

Pastors are generally on call 24/7. Not officially. They try to keep regular business hours like any other community leader, but when parents get that dreaded call in the middle of the night, one of the first people they call is their pastor. Pastors are present at all the significant stages of a person's life. They dedicate or baptize babies, marry couples who grew up in the church, attend members' golden wedding anniversaries, and officiate at members' funerals.

This may seem pretty basic, but we wanted you to see why the pastor is such an important person in the church. You won't get very far without his help. Sell him *only* your sincere desire to help. If he sees you as an ally, you'll have plenty of opportunities to sell your product or service. If he thinks you're swooping in to make a quick buck, game over.

HOW TO REACH THE PASTOR

If you want to work with a church, you need to gain the confidence of the pastor. Remember, Rick Warren served pastors through the www.pastors.com website for nearly a decade before inviting them to participate in the 40 Days of Purpose Campaign that popularized *The Purpose-Driven Life* book. You don't have to invest 10 years, but gaining their confidence means more than just getting an appointment and making a presentation. Because you do not attend his church regularly and are ultimately trying to sell stuff to the church or his congregation, he needs to know you have the best interests of his church in mind. Don't let this deter or intimidate you. Pastors are generally warm and outgoing, open-minded, and always willing to meet business leaders in the community.

To help you better understand the pastors you will meet, we sent a survey to 70,000 ministry leaders. We wanted to learn how they were influenced—what magazines they read, which podcasts they listen to, and the web sites they frequent. More important, we wanted to ask them directly about how you can grow your business through their churches. Here's what we learned.

The majority of pastors have never entered into a formal partnership with local businesses, but they appear open to it and even gave us advice on how businesses can work with churches. From our perspective, this means you have a wide-open opportunity to partner with churches. Seventy-six percent said they had never partnered with a business before, so you're not going to face a lot of competition.

We wanted to help you get a better idea of the types of partnerships churches have entered into with businesses, and here's a sampling from our survey:

- Local printing companies
- Costco
- Sam's Club
- Minor league ball park concessions company
- Chick-fil-A
- Local Nissan dealership
- Local contractor on a home makeover for someone in need
- Local travel agency for faith-based travel packages
- Local business's parking lot for a live Nativity at Christmas
- Local businesses provided trucks to deliver supplies after Hurricane Katrina

Even this partial list demonstrates the diversity of businesses that churches are willing to partner with. You could easily make a case for each of these businesses that working with a local church would be impossible. But someone at the business was able to connect the dots. According to Ron Forseth, vice president of business development for

Outreach (a full-service agency devoted to helping churches grow), churches that are serious about growing and having an impact on their communities are eager to partner with businesses if it will help them accomplish what's important to them. "Discover what the church is trying to do in their community, and then find ways to connect your business to that mission," Forseth explained.

Pastors of growing churches are dynamic leaders. Many of them have all the qualities of a CEO or small business owner. These are the pastors you need to start with in your community. They will be the ones most receptive to establishing a relationship with your business as long as you approach them professionally and are patient enough to truly understand what the pastor and church are all about.

When we asked pastors to name three things businesses *must always do* if they want to partner with a church, the majority of the answers had to do with honesty, integrity, and sincerity. Fully 90 percent of the answers mentioned this. But some of the other answers are worth noting:

- Promote family values
- Attach no strings to your partnership
- Be candid about any fears you have about working with the church
- Be consistent in contacting and communicating
- Care about community needs, especially the poor
- Provide credentials and references
- Market to the church community

These responses confirm what we know about pastors. They are more likely—even eager—to develop relationships with local businesses that respect the mission and values of the church. That doesn't mean you have to pretend to be a Christian—don't even try it because pastors have a sixth sense for fakes. But it does mean you did enough of your homework in Chapter 3 to know and respect what they believe, and that you spent enough time learning about the church so that you can speak intelligently about it with the pastor. If you were trying to reach a new client in the business community, wouldn't you do the same thing?

We also asked pastors to identify three things a business *must avoid* if it wants to partner with a church. Not surprisingly, the majority of them warned against unethical or dishonest business practices. If you haven't gotten it yet, this survey puts an exclamation mark on the fact that Christians and religious organizations want to work with businesses that have stellar reputations. But again, some of the other answers are worth noting:

- Pushy sales pitches
- Poor customer service
- Poor workmanship
- Involving other businesses in our collaboration without our approval
- Greed, manipulation
- Promoting political agendas

Bottom line: Be a decent marketer, and be open and honest with the pastor. If he trusts you, his congregation will.

HELPING CHURCHES GROW

Outreach is a business in Southern California dedicated to helping churches grow. Their tagline says it all: "Empowering Churches for Effective Outreach." VP Ron Forseth has been instrumental in a number of campaigns that have produced spectacular growth for the churches that have used them. He and his colleagues broker relationships between prominent secular businesses and local churches, often working with major motion picture studios to create a package of resources churches can use to tie in with a major release. Some of the movies they've worked with include *The Lion, the Witch, and the Wardrobe, The Passion of the Christ,* and *Fireproof.*

"Our goal is not to promote a movie, though what we do drives a lot of church people to theaters," Forseth explained. "We create materials that lead people through a series of experiences where they can see how the themes of the movie intersect with faith, particularly the gospel message. Resources include small group discussion guides, sermon outlines for the pastor, promotional materials, and so on. But the goal is to let the popularity of the movie and our materials get more people into the church, not simply the movie."

Forseth says any effort to market to the church has to be based first on what's good for the church. "We get approached all the time by studios wanting us to promote their movies to churches, but if we cannot find a legitimate connection to the church's

(Continued)

needs, we won't do it." Many movies have some sort of spiritual element. But most don't have a prevailing theme that is gospel related. "Churches don't want to be used for advertisers' ends; they want to engage a business because it benefits the church and advances the gospel."

Outreach works with hundreds of advertisers who want to reach the church. They have unprecedented access to pastors via three exclusive channels. Online: SermonCentral.com is the largest community of pastors on the Internet with more than a quarter million church leaders visiting each month; print: Outreach magazine reaches nearly all of the largest and fastest growing churches in the United States; face-to-face: They sponsor an annual National Outreach Conference where they interact with 2,000 pastors.

INFLUENCES ON PASTORS

Where do pastors go for information, instruction, and inspiration? We spoke with Tom Betts, who spent several years researching this for a major Christian publishing company. Many churches are organized around denominations, with a hierarchy and leadership structure that exerts influence over churches. They publish resources for pastors and their churches, offer training and other services to help them succeed, and perhaps most important, they facilitate a network allowing them to communicate and learn from each other. While Betts acknowledges that denominational influence has declined in recent years, pastors who are part of a denomination still consider it a source for information. If you were planning a national campaign to reach as many pastors as possible, you would be wise to build a database of denominational leaders. For example, the United Methodist Church has more than 18 thousand pastors. Let's assume you represent a national company that provides a service such as supplemental health care, retirement portfolio management, or identity theft security. One presentation to church executives at United Methodist headquarters in Nashville could put your business in front of 18 thousand customers, with the backing and endorsement of their denominational leaders.

How do you find these denominations? Go to www.electronicchurch. org and order the current edition of *The Yearbook of American and Canadian Churches*, which not only gives you contact information for every denomination in North America, but also membership statistics, total number of churches in each denomination, and a description of the denomination. You will also find resources at www.faithbasedmarketing.com.

Betts also acknowledged that many successful pastors look to two major Protestant "megachurches" for inspiration and practical advice: Willow Creek Community Church and Saddleback Church. If you want to really understand what's important to the larger Protestant churches in your area, become familiar with both. It's not an exaggeration to say that these two churches have influenced more churches in the United States than any denomination. If you walk into one of the larger, newer churches in your city, everything from the design of the building to the style of worship and music, to the use of media can most likely be traced back to one of these two churches.

Willow Creek, founded by senior pastor Bill Hybels, began in a theater and now spreads across 155 acres in Barrington, Illinois, a northwest Chicago suburb. In addition to the 20,000 people who attend services at the South Barrington campus, several thousand other Chicago area residents attend one of four satellite churches in the area. The church's success attracted so much attention from other churches that in 1992 they formed the Willow Creek Association, a loose-knit collection of churches from multiple denominations that purchase resources and training materials and attend one of several national conventions sponsored by the association each year. According to Betts, if you want to reach pastors of forward-thinking, dynamic churches, develop a relationship with the Willow Creek Association.

Before Rick Warren became one of the most successful authors in publishing history, he was a Baptist preacher trying to start a church in Southern California—not an easy assignment. Today, Saddleback Church welcomes 23,000 worshipers every Sunday, making it the largest church in California and the fourth largest church in the United States. To put all of this in perspective, Bill Hybels and Rick Warren are sort of like the Bill Gates and Warren Buffett of Protestant Christianity.

Where Hybels formed an association to help and influence U.S. pastors, Warren created a web site, www.pastors.com, an absolutely brilliant effort to assist and impact U.S. pastors. Its tagline says it all: "Where pastors hang out." Basically, everything he learned about building a dynamic church from scratch (Saddleback first met in a tent) is offered freely on this site. If a pastor had a rough week and it's Saturday night and he doesn't have a sermon for tomorrow? Download one for free at pastors.com. Need some ideas for getting people who don't like church to begin attending yours? Go to Saddleback's "Ministry Toolbox."

Thousands of pastors click on pastors.com every week, and nearly as many look to the Willow Creek Association for guidance. We're not suggesting you call them up and try to place a banner ad for your product on their web site. In fact, don't. However, if you want to get a better understanding of what pastors care about, what they are thinking, what books they read, and what large-church ministry is all about, hang out on pastors.com or go to www.willowcreek.com. Better yet, attend Willow Creek's annual Leadership Summit. Spending time with either organization will change the way you think about pastors and church and jump-start your thinking about how your business can serve the needs of both.

On the Catholic side of things, parish priests will certainly be open to learning how your business could serve the church and its members, but the hierarchical nature of the denomination could make it a little more difficult to approach them on the national level. The United States Conference of Catholic Bishops wields enormous influence over individual Catholic parishes and dioceses, but primarily on matters of official church teaching and policy. You can learn more about how this organization serves the Catholic Church by going to their web site: www.usccb.org. Two other web sites will help you learn more about what's going on in the Catholic Church—what's important to their clergy: www.catholicexchange.com reflects the more mainstream, traditional church while www.bustedhalo.com features trends among younger, more progressive Catholics.

If you're interested in reaching Catholic priests, we recommend you begin at the local parish or diocese level. A diocese is basically a cluster of Catholic churches in a geographical area, led by a bishop. The bishop is the person you would need to contact if you wanted to develop a relationship with local Catholic priests in your area.

What Pastors Read

Another way to reach pastors is to understand their media habits. We mention this to dispel any notion that pastors isolate themselves in the ivory tower of theology and doctrine. Today's effective pastor tries to stay current with cultural trends and is more likely to read a business book than a theological text. They are especially interested in books about leadership, management—even marketing—because they want to be more effective leaders of their flocks. Walk into a pastor's office and you could easily see Malcolm Gladwell's *Blink* next to the Bible on the pastor's desk.

When it comes to magazines and periodicals, here again you might be surprised. We asked pastors which magazines they read, and not surprisingly they mentioned *Christianity Today* (see Chapter 9)—77.7 percent of the pastors we surveyed told us they read it. *Discipleship Journal* and *Relevant* were second and third respectively. If you are considering a national print strategy to reach pastors, those magazines should be on your list, but we also recommend you go to a Christian bookstore and buy copies to see what interests pastors.

But when we asked them what magazines they read aside from religious ones, their answers were puzzling at first. The highest percentage of pastors told us they read entertainment magazines, with financial magazines coming in a close second. But actually, this is consistent with what we know about successful pastors. They want to be in tune with popular culture so that they can communicate effectively with people inside and outside their church. And they are responsible for keeping their ministries financially healthy in today's turbulent economy.

Eighty-six percent of the pastors told us they listen to Christian radio, which suggests that you need to find a Christian radio station on your dial and listen to it occasionally. And of course, if you want to reach pastors, you should consider advertising or underwriting on a Christian radio station.

What we also found interesting is the number of pastors who have a personal profile on a social networking site: 42.4 percent, with Facebook apparently the network of choice for pastors (75.9 percent) and MySpace a distant second (37 percent). At the very least, you should try searching these two sites to see if the pastor you want to reach is in the network.

It's All about Relationships

As a marketer, you know the importance of relationships in your business. You don't attempt to develop relationships in order to exploit someone. You develop relationships because it allows you to serve your client better. A major complaint among many pastors is that too often a business appears to be in a hurry to make a quick buck. They know, as do we, that at the end of the day you want to make a sale, close a deal, and deposit a check, and you don't need to make any apologies for that with pastors.

But if you take the time to listen to a pastor, hear his heart for the church, and approach him as an ally who wants to find ways to help him serve his people, you will not just make a sale but earn a loyal customer.

So here's your assignment. Spend some time on the web sites mentioned in this chapter. Locate copies of some of the magazines listed in the sidebar "Christian Magazines Pastors Read." Select just one church in your community that you would like to reach as a marketer. Visit the church and do the homework we suggested in Chapter 5. Then call the church and make an appointment with the senior pastor. It could be the beginning of a long and productive relationship with that church, and it might even give you a new friend.

CHRISTIAN MAGAZINES PASTORS READ

Based on our survey of pastors, here are the most frequently mentioned Christian magazines that they read:

Christianity Today

Discipleship Journal

Relevant

Charisma

Leadership Journal

Outreach

Rev

Preaching Today

World

Today's Christian Woman

WHAT NEXT?

The next and final chapter is really written for pastors. You're certainly welcome to read it. If you want to dig into the next section, that's fine by us. It's the most comprehensive collection of resources for marketing to Christians that we know of, and there's even more at www.faithbasedmarketing.com.

CHAPTER THIRTEEN

HOW TO MARKET YOUR CHURCH

We're going to switch things around in this chapter, and here's why. We know that the majority of people who read this book are marketers who want to learn how to reach Christians and Christian organizations, and everything up to this point has been designed to help you do that. But we also know that many pastors and church leaders are reading this book because dynamic church leaders spend a lot of their time promoting—their faith, their mission and vision, and their church or organization. Some of the best marketers we know are pastors.

So now, we'd like to speak directly to pastors and church leaders about marketing their organization. We hope this chapter will still be helpful to all the marketers who have stuck with us so far, but if it doesn't make sense, go ahead and skip to the next section that contains a treasure trove of sources to help you market to the faith-based community. But before you leave, at least visit the blog www.churchmarketingsucks.com.

DO WE REALLY NEED TO MARKET JESUS?

Here's our assumption. You are a pastor or church leader, and you bought this book for two reasons. Initially, you wanted to see if we're trying to sell out the church. Serve it up to greedy marketers, giving them trade secrets to help them rip off your unsuspecting parishioners. We hope you were pleasantly surprised to discover that we're on your side. That we represented you and your church fairly and helped the business community respect it. If marketers use what they have learned in this book, you're going to win as much as they do, and we love it when that happens.

The other reason you bought this book is because you hoped to learn some things about marketing. If you're like most pastors we know, you want to see your church grow—not to satisfy a denominational bigwig who's breathing down your neck or win a prize for being the fastest growing church in the United States. You want your church to grow because you really do believe people are better off when they know Jesus and are fully integrated into His church. In other words, you want your church to grow for all the right reasons, and you thought you could learn something useful to help you accomplish that.

That is why we added this chapter—to speak directly to you about marketing your church, so let's start with a complaint we often hear from church folk: Jesus doesn't need a marketing plan. In a way, that's true. He already has one, and it's pretty clearly stated in the Gospels. More on that later. But we'd like to address a sentiment that we hear a lot, especially about fast-growing, *seeker-friendly* churches, and that's the notion that churches shouldn't rely on "secular" marketing techniques to get people to go to church. As you might guess, we disagree. In fact, whether churches believe they are doing it or not, they are marketing every day, so we probably need to explain what we mean by marketing as it relates to the church: knowing your message, connecting it with people you want to hear that message, and building a movement around it.

In essence, everything you do as a church communicates a message, though maybe not the message you want to communicate. On one hand, when I pull into your parking lot on Sunday morning and it's empty, that tells me you must be selling something no one wants. If the paint is peeling on your building, and the grass hasn't been mowed, and the flower bed is weed strewn, it tells me you don't have a lot of respect for a building that you want me to believe is God's house. If you hand me a bulletin with misspellings, invite me to sing songs I can't understand played on instruments that remind me of a funeral home, and then scream at me for 45 minutes, you're giving me a very clear message: You're not welcome here. We're sure this doesn't describe your church, but it does describe some churches.

On the other hand, if your parking lot is so crowded that you have attendants in orange vests directing traffic, we get the impression that we stumbled into the parking lot at Lambeau Field, not First Presbyterian. When you have friendly greeters welcoming us at the front door and offering to answer our questions or directing us to an inviting booth where someone hands us a cup of coffee and a colorful brochure, we get the idea that this is a happening place. When we are directed to the auditorium where we hear lively music and see people swaying to the beat or raising their hands or just singing their little hearts out, it's infectious. We want to get in there and join in. And if you speak to us in language we understand and relate ancient truths to the lives we live every day, you begin to capture our hearts.

Yes, Jesus had a marketing plan: Go and make disciples. You can't do that successfully by sending messages that say, "Stay away." But when your message is "We're glad you're here—stick around and it might change your life," you will be bursting at the seams with new disciples.

So, as long as you're marketing your church anyway, why not do it right?

Marketing Sucks

To help you enhance your church marketing, we decided to go to a man who studies church marketing and wants to see it improved. Brad Abare is the founder of the Center for Church Communication (www.cfcclabs.org), a great resource for anyone interested in learning how to market his or her church more effectively. But that's not why we contacted Brad. We just had to interview this guy because of the name of his blog: www.churchmarketingsucks.com. That's right: church marketing sucks! We also loved his blog's stated mission: "to frustrate, educate, and motivate the church to communicate, with uncompromising clarity, the truth of Jesus Christ."

Brad's a funny guy, but also a really smart one. We know it because he realized that a lot of nice Christian people hate the word sucks and therefore would never go to his blog to learn about church marketing. So he created another blog with identical information and called it www.churchmarketingstinks. As they say in the food business, it's all in the presentation. Brad tells us he actually gets a lot more traffic at the stinks site than the sucks site.

Might be a good idea to pay attention to Brad:

> Marketing as a concept is morally neutral. It's neither good nor bad. For church people who don't like that word, I just tell them to substitute it with communication, because that's really what marketing is. If you have something that will meet people's needs as the church does, shouldn't you try to communicate it in the most effective ways possible?

We asked Brad, who coaches churches all over the United States about how to become better marketers, what advice he would give to a pastor who wanted to market his church more effectively, and his initial answer surprised us:

> Every church marketing campaign should begin with this question: "Who are we?" Not who you want to be, but who are you as a church? What are you passionate about? If the church is like a person, what gets you going in the morning? It's the DNA question, and we're living in a culture where it's easy to forget who we are. Too many times, churches are more interested in being "the church on the cover" rather than "the church on the corner." The church on the cover tries to get everyone excited, attract a lot of attention, make it on the front page of the newspaper, while the church on the corner says, "God has us here for a reason, and we want to know what that is."

Brad works with organizations and churches all over the United States to help them answer that simple, foundational question. He walks them through a process of discovery using four words: role, relationships, responsibility, and results. We call it the "blankety-blank" exercise from churchmarketingsucks, and it works like this. Fill in the blanks with the words or phrases that best describe your church:

> "We are a   (role) , serving   (relationships) , doing   (responsibility) , to accomplish   (results) ."

Once a church spends some time working through this exercise, they might come up with a statement like this:

> We are a group of people who share a common belief in Jesus Christ, serving our neighbors within a one-mile radius of our church, showing them through our actions that Jesus cares about them, so that they experience wholeness through our charity and their new life in Christ.

What Brad is describing is a basic foundation of good marketing. Whether you represent a law firm or a church, your first task in creating a marketing program is to determine what's true about your product. The next step is even more important—make it true throughout your church. It's one thing for you as a pastor or even for your staff or board of elders to know who you are. It's quite another to make sure everyone in your parish knows who they are as a church because the people of your church—the lives being lived out in the community—are the most influential marketers of your church. Most people who begin attending a church for the first time report that it was their association with another person—not a newspaper ad or a slick brochure, but another person—that led them to try church.

Maybe when you baptize a new believer you should give him or her the title of marketing associate. Okay, bad idea, but it makes a point. The best strategy to market your church to your community is your people. We'll be the first to admit we're not theologians, but we find it interesting that the Great Commission didn't command believers to "go and make converts," but to "go and make disciples." A disciple is a follower, so the task of every one of your church members is to live the kind of life that makes others want to follow them. To represent their church so well that people want to follow them to the front door.

Once you have figured out who you are as a church, and the congregation is aligned with that identity, then as the leader you need to establish specific objectives that enable you to stay true to who you are—to execute your mission. And you should do this in small increments. For example, this year we are going to adopt five families in our neighborhood, provide tutoring for their children, make sure they have access to health care, get them involved in a Bible study, and so on. That would be just one of your objectives to keep you focused on your mission, and when you are finished, everyone in the church will have a clear picture of who they are and how they are going to live out their identity as a church.

It's at this point, according to Brad, that what we think of as marketing kicks in. How do we communicate to others who we are? When you look at marketing as a way to communicate who you are, you may not need a direct mail campaign or an expensive brochure. A lot of churches launch elaborate marketing campaigns that just aren't appropriate for executing their mission. Marketing for you might mean waiting on a playground after school to tell kids about the skateboard park the church built to give kids something to do until their parents get home. It might mean calling businesses near your church to let them know you're sponsoring a fund-raiser and inviting them to contribute prizes.

"Sometimes churches hide behind their fancy marketing tactics because we see that's what everyone else does; because that's how Wal-Mart and Target get people into their stores," Brad explained. "They've got a different product, a different message. Churches need to focus on their own unique message and market accordingly."

One of the common themes we have tried to impress on marketers who want to work with the church is that marketing is all about relationships. The church ought to know this better than anyone. Jesus didn't hand out coupons for discount healings—he reached out to the beggar alongside the road. He turned and spoke to a woman who brushed his garment when passing him. He didn't advertise a seminar for rich people or cheats—he met face-to-face with a rich young ruler and had dinner with a tax collector. That doesn't mean you should never advertise your church on Christian radio or try to drive traffic to your web site. But without the human touch—people who have been transformed by what they found in your church inviting others to find the same thing—you could be wasting a lot of money on marketing.

APPROPRIATE MARKETING VEHICLES

Having said all that, we still believe it's important for churches to create strategies for spreading their message and develop tools to spread it. One of the biggest divisions of Outreach, the agency that helps churches market themselves in their communities, is one that provides them with everything from banners to bulletins. In fact, their web site lists 30 different categories of marketing products you can order to get the word out about your church.

Regardless of the type or types of vehicles you use, do it right or don't do it at all. In Chapter 1 we tried to eradicate some of the stereotypes about Christians, and one of those is that Christians are unsophisticated. Nothing supports that more than sending out cheesy-looking promotional material to your neighbors. If you don't have a professional designer and a competent copywriter on your staff, farm out the creation of all your promotional material to an ad agency (or contact Outreach). Every marketing message you deliver to your constituency competes with thousands of messages they receive every day sent by professionals who know how to attract the right kind of attention. We believe yours should rise to the top, compelling the person who gets it to look at it first and set the others aside. The following general guidelines are pretty basic, so consider them the *minimum* standard for every communication piece carrying the name of your church.

- *Is the message clear?* If someone unfamiliar with your church gets your e-mail, will they know what you're saying? Are you using "insider language?" Will they have had to be in church last Sunday to know what you're talking about?
- *Is there a call to action?* Why go to the expense and effort of creating a piece if it doesn't result in action? In other words, don't just announce an event—promote it: "Join us!" "Come early for a good seat," "Tell five of your friends about it," and so on.

- *Has it been proofread?* Sending a marketing message with misspellings or typos sends the wrong message about your church. We know you're always under tight deadlines, but slow down and let a professional proofreader go over your material. This is becoming an increasing problem in e-mail blasts.
- *Is your church's contact information included?* If nothing else, every marketing vehicle should include your church's web site. You'd be surprised how many church ads we see in newspapers that don't include the address. We believe God leads our steps, but we still need to find your church if we want to attend.
- *Does it pass the cringe test?* This is a tough one because it's subjective, but a lot of marketing material from churches makes us cringe. That's why we recommend churches either hire professionals to create their marketing vehicles or at least hire a consultant to spend some time training the people in your church who create print and online marketing materials.

EVENTS AS MARKETING

One of the best ways to market your church in your community is to sponsor events that people enjoy. This gives you an opportunity to showcase your church, in the best sense of that word, in a nonthreatening manner. As you know, getting someone to come to church for the first time on a Sunday morning is still a challenge. Getting them to attend a free concert is a lot easier.

We did some anecdotal research among some pastor friends of ours, and here are the types of events that seem to work well in marketing a church:

- Seasonal festivals (Fourth of July, Fall, and so on)
- Concerts (both at the church and in popular venues like a band shell in the park, coffee houses, and so on)
- Drama and musicals (several churches perform a holiday musical for several days prior to Christmas, and the majority who attend are not regular churchgoers)
- Participation in parades and other civic events (for years, College Church of Wheaton's float won "best of parade" in the Independence Day parade)
- Professional development events (some churches sponsor events for businessmen with nationally know business leaders as speakers)

- Free services (free oil changes or minor repairs, especially for single moms)
- "Fifth Quarter" Friday night events for teenagers following football games
- Day care (often a self-supporting business that turns customers into members)
- Sporting events (10K, softball tournaments, golf outings)

Each of these types of events requires careful planning and promotion for them to be successful. For example, know who your target audience members are, how to reach those customers, how to engage customers who attend, and use a follow-up strategy after the event. Several pastors we talked to have begun joining with other churches in their town to sponsor events. What a great concept—cooperation! Sadly, people outside the church often see us fighting with each other, so events like this ought to draw a lot of interest.

Events don't have to be huge undertakings. You know how difficult it is to recruit enough volunteers to sponsor those types of event. So think "segmented marketing" when it comes to events. Let the church become *the* place to be for smaller groups during the week. One church transformed their tired (and poorly attended) Wednesday night service into a buffet of options that included a quilting class, a chess club, gourmet cooking classes, home repair workshops, and so on. They promoted it like crazy in their town and people showed up who had never set foot in a church to learn how to repair drywall!

How to Advertise Your Church

Mike Reed's background in marketing serves him well as executive pastor of Northwood Church in Dallas, Texas. Northwood is currently growing at around 18 percent a year, and the growth comes primarily from people who have never attended church. Here's how Northwood advertises its church:

Web site: According to Mike, 85 to 90 percent of the non-churched will go to your web site before they consider setting foot in your church. "Every other form of advertising needs to highlight your church's web site because that's where they will go to get their questions answered and decide if your church is right for them."

Signage: After a recommendation from a friend, the second most important factor to a person attending a church is signage. "Sounds simple, but we changed all our signage to make it more inviting and compelling. Most church signs are for the benefit of those who already attend. We wanted our signage to be for those who might be shopping for a church. It changes the way you think about signage."

Targeted mailings: Northwood conducts seven direct mail campaigns annually targeted to the needs of the surrounding communities. "We create a four-week sermon series geared to things like improving your marriage or becoming a better parent because we are in an area where families are important." Knowing that men generally attend church once a year at Easter, he advertised a sermon series called "Man Up!" beginning Easter Sunday. "It was the highest attended sermon series ever," Mike said.

Good News

Journalists will tell you the easiest news to report is good news. People love to hear it. Amid all the bad news, a little light shines pretty brightly. Sometimes we in the church have to remind ourselves that we carry the Good News. The best news. It's news that transforms lives, heals brokenness, and lifts people out of despair.

Your church may not need a slick marketing program, but it needs to share the Good News. It starts with knowing who you are and spreads through every member. We hope this book will help marketers understand the church for what it is—a family of ordinary people who love God and want their lives to reflect that. We hope they do their homework and try to find ways to help you accomplish what's important to you and your church. But we also hope when they meet you, when they hang out on your web site and rub shoulders with your people, they will see some pretty good marketing as well.

PART III

KEY RESOURCES FOR CHRISTIAN MARKETERS

In the first two sections of this book you discovered the size and opportunity presented by the Christian market. You studied who Christians are and what they believe. You learned to serve rather than sell. And you read about specific tactics for reaching Christians through print, broadcast, online, and even word-of-mouth.

It's time to put what you've learned into practice. The final portion of the book is a reference section that will help you connect to the Christian power niche from various angles. It's loaded with contacts for public relations and marketing firms, Christian media and music festivals, faith-based retailers, distributors, and trade associations. You'll find listings for the largest and most innovative churches in the United States and a collection of ministries and organizations. But that's just the beginning.

There are many more important contacts than could ever fit in this book, and that's why we built the Faith-Based Marketing website. Your purchase of this book entitles you to a free 90 day subscription to www.faithbasedmarketing.com, where you'll find a database with thousands of up-to-date records for faith-based organizations of all kinds along with bonus content like podcasts, video, and articles. It even has social networking functionality so you can meet Christian ministry leaders and forge partnerships online. Log onto the site with this book by your side, and follow the instructions online to unlock all the additional resources.

Spend some time with the reference section and the web site identifying those organizations important to your plans, then reach out, make contact, and begin building relationships using the advice from this book.

If you'd like professional help with your faith-based marketing from consulting to fully executed plans, we are here to help. Please contact us at:

Bob Hutchins
BuzzPlant
709 West Main
Franklin, TN 37064
(615) 550-2305
E-mail: info@buzzplant.com
www.buzzplant.com

Greg Stielstra
PyroMarketing
909 Miranda Place
Franklin, TN 37067
(615) 812-3821
E-mail: pyromarketing@bellsouth.net
www.pyromarketing.com

Marketing Firms

Advocace/Dallas (Corporate Offices)
265 Parkway Boulevard, Suite 210
Coppell, TX 75019
(972) 304-1100
Fax: (972) 692-8655
www.advocace.com

Advocace/Chicago
18-5 East Dundee Road, Suite 204
Barrington, IL 60010
(847) 756-2921
Fax: (847) 842-0195
www.advocace.com

C. Grant and Company
207 Reber Street
Wheaton, IL 60187
E-mail: jymette@cgrantandcompany.com
www.cgrantandcompany.com

Ground Force Network
E-mail: joinus@groundforcenetwork.com
www.groundforcenetwork.com

Motive Marketing
1303 Oakgrove Place, Suite 100
Westlake Village, CA 91362
(805) 778-1930
E-mail: info@moviemarketing.biz
http://moviemarketing.biz

Propeller Consulting
436 Main Street, Suite 204
Franklin, TN 37064
(615) 599-9392
E-mail: info@propellerconsulting.net
www.propellerconsulting.net

Salem Music Network
Music Programming
402 BNA Drive, Suite 400
Nashville, TN 37217
(615) 367-2210
Fax: (615) 367-0758
www.salemmusicnetwork.com

Salem Radio Network
New/Existing Affiliation, Barter Agreement,
Contracts, Commercial Clearance,
Technical Support
6400 N. Beltline Road, Suite 210
Irving, TX 75063
(972) 831-1920
Fax: (972) 831-8626
www.srnradio.com

Salem Radio Representatives
New/Existing Sales (Spot Time)
6400 N. Beltline Road, Suite 220
Irving, TX 75063
(972) 402-8800
Fax: (972) 402-8200
www.srnradio.com

Generator, LLC
4670 Everal Lane
Franklin, TN 37064
(615) 790-7300
E-mail: mike@generatornetwork.com
www.generatornetwork.com

Public Relations Firms

A Larry Ross Communications
4300 Marsh Ridge Road, Suite 114
Carrollton, TX 75010
(972) 267-1111
www.alarryross.com

B&B Media Group
109 South Main
Corsicana, TX 75110
(800) 927-0517
www.tbbmedia.com

Dechant-Hughes & Associates
1440 N. Kingsbury Street
Chicago, IL 60622
(312) 280-8126
www.dechanthughes.com

The DeMoss Group
3235 Satellite Boulevard, Suite 555
Duluth, GA 30096
(770) 813-0000
www.demossgroup.com

L.A.B. Media
215 Ward Circle, Suite 200
Brentwood, TN 37027
(615) 321-6400
www.labmediaonline.com

McCain and Company
1318 Riverwood Drive
Nashville, TN 37216
(615) 262-1727
www.mccainpr.com

McClure/Muntsinger Public Relations
PO Box 804
Franklin, TN 37065-0804
(615) 595-8321
www.mmpublicrelations.com

Rogers & Cowan
8687 Melrose Ave., 7th Floor
Los Angeles, CA 90069
(310) 854-8100
Fax: (310) 854-8107
www.rogersandcowan.com

FILM AND VIDEO PRODUCTION

abOmb
Adam Stielstra
477 Sudden Valley
Bellingham, WA 98229
616-635-9525
E-mail: adam@goabomb.com
www.goabomb.com

Franklin Films
317 Main Street
Suite 212
Franklin, TN 37064
615-599-0950
E-mail: info@franklinfilms.com

Sam Hill Entertainment
Steven Feldman
615-430-5002
E-mail: Steven@samhill.tv

SneezeCast: Viral Video
709 West Main Street
Franklin, TN 37067
E-mail: info@sneezecast.com
www.sneezecast.com

Music Festivals

Each year more than 22 million people attend a live Christian music event, according to Bob Thompson, the president of the Christian Festival Association, a newly formed coalition of 25 of the nation's largest Christian music festivals. Sponsorship opportunities abound. Together, these events send out more than 2.5 million pieces of direct mail and over 4 million e-blasts, to say nothing of the sponsorship opportunities at and around the events. The typical lineup included the following. Learn more at each event's web site or from the CFA web site at www.christianfestivals.org.

Event Name	Location	Dates	Web site
AgapeFest	Greenville, IL	May 1–2	http://www.agapefest.com/
Alive Festival	Canal Fulton, OH	June 16–20	http://www.alive.org/
Atlanta Fest presented by Chick-fil-A	Atlanta, GA	June 18–20	http://www.atlantafest.com/
Collide Festival	Bells, TX	June 11–13	http://www.collidefestival.com/
Cornerstone	Bushnell, IL	June 29–July 4	http://www.cornerstonefestival.com/
Creation NE	Mt. Union, PA	June 24–27	http://www.creationfest.com/
Creation NW	George, WA	July 22–25	http://www.creationfest.com/
Crossover Festival	Lake of the Ozarks, MO	June 11–13	http://www.crossoverfestival.org/
Hills Alive	Rapid City, SD	July 18–19	http://www.hillsalive.com/
Ichthus	Wilmore, KY	June 10–13	http://www.ichthusfestival.org/
Kingdom Bound	Buffalo, NY	August 2–5	http://www.kingdombound.org/
King's Fest	Doswell, VA	July 9–11	http://www.premierfestivals.com/
LifeLight Festival	Sioux Falls, SD	August 28–30	http://www.lifelight.org/
Lifest	Oshkosh, WI	July 8–12	http://www.lifest.com/
Purple Door Festival	Lewisberry, PA	August 14–15	http://www.purpledoor.com/
Rock the Coast	Muskegon, MI	May 16–17	http://www.unitychristianevents.com/

Event Name	Location	Dates	Web site
Rock the Desert	Midland, TX	August 7–8	http://www.rockthedesert.com/
Rock the Light	Kansas City, MO	August 28–29	http://www.rockthelight.com/
Sonshine Fest	Willmar, MN	July 16–18	http://www.sonshinefestival.com/
Soulfest	Gilford, NH	July 29–Aug. 1	http://www.thesoulfest.com/
Spirit West Coast	Del Mar, CA	May 22–24	http://www.spiritwestcoast.com/
Spirit West Coast	Monterey, CA	July 29–Aug. 1	http://www.spiritwestcoast.com/
SpiritSong	Cincinnati, OH	July 9–11	http://www.premierfestivals.com/
Unity Festival	Muskegon, MI	August 6–8	http://www.unitychristianevents.com/
Winterfest	Lynchburg, VA	Dec. 30–Jan. 1	http://www.libertywinterfest.com/

CHURCHES

For a gigantic database of churches large and small, across the country and right next door, visit www.faithbasedmarketing.com

Impressive size, spectacular growth, and outside-the-pew thinking characterize churches doing things right. In this section, you'll find information on the largest, fastest-growing, and most-innovative churches in America. These lists were compiled from surveys administered by Outreach, Inc. in partnership with LifeWay Research. Outreach, Inc. conducts this survey annually and publishes the results in a special edition of Outreach magazine called "The Outreach 100." Contact them with your partnership ideas, apply the advice from this book, and explore what's possible by working together.

Most Innovative Churches

Church	Location	Web site	Pastor
LifeChurch.tv	Edmond, OK	http://www.lifechurch.tv/	Craig Groeschel
Mars Hill Church	Seattle, WA	http://www.marshillchurch.org/	Mark Driscoll
Granger Community Church	Granger, IN	http://www.gccwired.com/	Mark Beeson
Flamingo Road Church	Cooper City, FL	http://www.flamingoroad.org/	Troy Gramling
Seacoast Church	Mt. Pleasant, SC	http://www.seacoast.org/	Greg Surratt
Saddleback Church	Lake Forest, CA	http://www.saddleback.com/	Rick Warren
Mosaic Church	Los Angeles, CA	http://www.mosaic.org/	Erwin McManus
Fellowship Church	Grapevine, TX	http://www.fellowshipchurch.com/	Ed Young Jr.
North Point Community Church	Alpharetta, GA	http://www.northpoint.org/	Andy Stanley
Willow Creek Community Church	South Barrington, IL	http://www.willowcreek.org/	Bill Hybels

National Community Church	Washington, DC	http://www.theaterchurch.com/	Mark Batterson
NewSpring Community Church	Anderson, SC	http://www.newspring.cc	Perry Noble
Community Christian Church	Naperville, IL	http://www.communitychristian.org/	Dave Ferguson
Elevation Church	Charlotte, NC	http://www.elevationchurch.org/	Steven Furtick
Healing Place Church	Baton Rouge	http://www.healingplacechurch.org/	Dino Rizzo
North Coast Church	Vista, CA	http://northcoastchurch.com/	Larry Osborne
NorthWood Church	Keller, TX	http://northwoodchurch.org/	Bob Roberts
NewSong Church	Irvine, CA	http://newsong.net/	Dave Gibbons
New Hope Christian Fellowship	Honolulu, HI	http://enewhope.org/	Wayne Cordeiro
Redeemer Presbyterian Church	New York, NY	http://redeemer.com/	Tim Keller
Crossover Church	Tampa, FL	http://crossoverchurch.org/	Tommy Kyllonen
Perimeter Church	Duluth, GA	http://perimeter.org/	Randy Pope
Mars Hill	Grandville, MI	http://marshill.org/	Rob Bell
The Orchard Church Community	Aurora, IL	http://orchardvalleyonline.com/	Scott Hodge
The Sanctuary Covenant Church	Minneapolis, MN	http://sanctuarycovenant.org/	Efrem Smith

100 Fastest Growing Churches in the United States

Rank	Church	City	State
1	Church of The Highlands	Birmingham	AL
2	Elevation Church	Charlotte	NC
3	Triumph Church	Detroit	MI
4	Fellowship NorthWest Arkansas	Rogers	AR
5	The Rock Church	San Diego	CA
6	Destiny Metropolitan Worship Church	Atlanta	GA
7	Flatirons Community Church	Lafayette	CO
8	New Hope Christian Fellowship	Honolulu	HI
9	Reid Temple AME Church	Glenn Dale	MD
10	Mission Eben-Ezer	Carson	CA
11	The Austin Stone Community Church	Austin	TX
12	The Living Word Bible Church	Mesa	AZ
13	McLean Bible Church	McLean	VA
14	The Greater Travelers Rest Baptist Church	Decatur	GA
15	Harvest Bible Chapel	Rolling Meadows	IL
16	12 Stone Church	Lawrenceville	GA

Rank	Church	City	State
17	Greater Grace Temple	Detroit	MI
18	Lifepoint	Tampa	FL
19	New Direction Christian Church	Memphis	TN
20	Griffin First Assembly	Griffin	GA
21	Potter's House Christian Fellowship	Jacksonville	FL
22	The Church Without Walls	Houston	TX
23	The Village Church	Flower Mound	TX
24	Community Bible Church	San Antonio	TX
25	Crossroads	Cincinnati	OH
26	North Point Church	Springfield	MO
27	Hickory Grove Baptist Church	Charlotte	NC
28	The Rock Church & World Outreach Center	San Bernadino	CA
29	Gateway Church	SouthLake	TX
30	Eagle Brook Church	Hugo	MN
31	Abundant Living Faith Center	El Paso	TX
32	Cornerstone Christian Fellowship	Chandler	AZ
33	Cascade Hills Church	Columbus	GA
34	Brentwood Baptist Church	Houston	TX
35	Heartland Community Church	Rockford	IL
36	Newlife	Silverdale	WA
37	Lutheran Church of Hope	West Des Moines	IA
38	Hope Presbyterian Church	Cordova	TN
39	Seacoast Church	Mount Pleasant	SC
40	Bethany Baptist Church	Lindenwold	NJ
41	North Point Community Church	Alpharetta	GA
42	Faith Reformed Church	Dyer	IN
43	Central Christian Church of the East Valley	Mesa	AZ
44	Quest Community Church	Lexington	KY
45	Family Christian Center Church	Munster	IN
46	Rock Bridge Community Church	Dalton	GA
47	Church Of The Resurrection	Leawood	KS
48	Grace Community Church	Cranberry Township	PA
49	Church On the Eastern Shore	Fairhope	AL
50	Parklawn Assembly Of God	Milwaukee	WI
51	Christ Fellowship	Miami	FL
52	New Vision Baptist Church	Murfreesboro	TN
53	Fairhaven Church	Dayton	OH
54	Friends Church	Yorba Linda	CA
55	Bay Area Fellowship	Corpus Christi	TX
56	Sun Valley Community Church	Gilbert	AZ
57	Christian Faith Fellowship Family Church	Middletown	NY
58	Angelus Temple	Los Angeles	CA
59	Southland Christian Church	Lexington	KY
60	First Baptist Church–Hammond	Hammond	IN
61	Celebration Covenant Church	Frisco	TX
62	CedarCreek Church	Perrysburg	OH
63	Free Chapel Worship Center	Gainesville	GA
64	Kensington Community Church	Troy	MI
65	Calvary Temple Worship Center	Modesto	CA
66	Timberline Church	Fort Collins	CO
67	Northland, A Church Distributed	Longwood	FL
68	Bethel Baptist Institutional Church	Jacksonville	FL
69	Iglesia Cristiana Segadores de Vida	Hollywood	FL

70	Heights Church	Prescott	AZ
71	EastLake Church	Chula Vista	CA
72	Lake Pointe Church	Rockwall	TX
73	Calvary Chapel	Albuquerque	NM
74	First Baptist Church–Jacksonville	Jacksonville	FL
75	Parkview Christian Church	Orland Park	IL
76	James River Assembly	Ozark	MO
77	Summit Christian Center	San Antonio	TX
78	Community Bible Church	Stockbridge	GA
79	Sunrise Church	Rialto	CA
80	Crossroads Christian	Grand Prairie	TX
81	The Chapel at CrossPoint	Getzville	NY
82	Brookwood Community Church	Simpsonville	SC
83	Bethany World Prayer Center	Baker	LA
84	The Sanctuary at Kingdom Square	Capital Heights	MD
85	Voices of Faith Ministries	Stone Mountain	GA
86	Northside Christian Church	New Albany	IN
87	Westover Hills Assembly of God	San Antonio	TX
88	West Ridge Church	Dallas	GA
89	NewPointe Community Church	Dover	OH
90	Saint Stephen Church	Louisville	KY
91	Faith Fellowship Ministries World Outreach Center	Sayreville	NJ
92	The Grove Community Church	Riverside	CA
93	Mount Zion Baptist Church	Nashville	TN
94	Shepherd of The Hills Church	Porter Ranch	CA
95	Bell Shoals Baptist Church	Brandon	FL
96	Scottsdale Bible Church	Scottsdale	AZ
97	Grace Community Church	Sun Valley	CA
98	Vineyard Community Church	Cincinnati	OH
99	Lancaster County Bible Church	Manheim	PA
100	Trinity Chapel Church of God	Powder Springs	GA

100 Largest Churches in the United States

Attendance	Rank	Church	City	State
43,500	1	Lakewood Church	Houston	TX
23,659	2	Second Baptist Church	Houston	TX
22,557	3	North Point Community Church	Alpharetta	GA
22,500	4	Willow Creek Community Church	South Barrington	IL
20,823	5	LifeChurch.tv	Edmond	OK
20,000	6	West Angeles Cathedral	Los Angeles	CA
19,913	7	Fellowship Church	Grapevine	TX
19,414	8	Saddleback Church	Lake Forest	CA
18,000	9	Calvary Chapel Fort Lauderdale	Fort Lauderdale	FL
17,000	10	The Potters House	Dallas	TX
16,380	11	Woodlands Church	The Woodlands	TX
16,264	12	Southeast Christian Church	Louisville	KY
16,000	13	Hopewell Missionary Baptist	Norcross	GA
15,000	14	New Birth Missionary Baptist	Lithonia	GA
14,762	15	NorthRidge Church	Plymouth	MI

Attendance	Rank	Church	City	State
14,500	16	New Hope Christian Fellowship	Honolulu	HI
14,450	17	Prestonwood Baptist Church	Plano	TX
13,699	18	McLean Bible Church	McLean	VA
13,678	19	First Baptist Church Hammond	Hammond	IN
13,500	20	Calvary Chapel	Albuquerque	NM
13,500	21	New Light Christian Center Church	Houston	TX
13,010	22	Central Christian Church	Henderson	NV
13,000	23	Thomas Road Baptist Church	Lynchburg	VA
12,535	24	Christ's Church of The Valley	Peoria	AZ
12,339	25	Christ Fellowship	Palm Beach Gardens	FL
12,120	26	Community Bible Church	San Antonio	TX
12,000	27	Calvary Chapel Golden Springs	Diamond Bar	CA
12,000	28	Harvest Christian Fellowship	Riverside	CA
11,752	29	Fountain of Praise	Houston	TX
11,500	30	Free Chapel Worship Center	Gainesville	GA
11,133	31	Lake Pointe Church	Rockwall	TX
10,988	32	Harvest Bible Chapel	Rolling Meadows	IL
10,878	33	The Rock Church	San Diego	CA
10,800	34	Valley Bible Fellowship	Bakersfield	CA
10,600	35	Family Christian Center Church	Munster	IN
10,556	36	Crossroads	Cincinnati	OH
10,484	37	Kensington Community Church	Troy	MI
10,334	38	Eagle Brook Church	Hugo	MN
10,170	39	Gateway Church	SouthLake	TX
10,052	40	Bayside Covenant Church	Roseville	CA
10,035	41	St Matthews Baptist Church	Williamstown	NJ
10,000	42	Faith Community Church	West Covina	CA
10,000	43	Faith Landmarks Ministries	Richmond	VA
10,000	44	First African Methodist Episcopal Church	Los Angeles	CA
10,000	45	Heritage Christian Center	Denver	CO
10,000	46	Mount Zion Baptist Church	Nashville	TN
10,000	47	World Changers Church International	College Park	GA
9,600	48	Calvary Chapel South Bay	Gardena	CA
9,500	49	Abundant Living Faith Center	El Paso	TX
9,500	50	Calvary Chapel of Costa Mesa	Santa Ana	CA
9,358	51	Southland Christian Church	Lexington	KY
9,232	52	Seacoast Church	Mount Pleasant	SC
9,200	53	Faith Fellowship Ministries World Outreach Center	Sayreville	NJ
9,137	54	Salem Baptist Church	Chicago	IL
9,000	55	Christian Cultural Center	Brooklyn	NY
9,000	56	Christian Faith Center	Federal Way	WA
9,000	57	Church Of The Resurrection	Leawood	KS
9,000	58	Mariners Church	Irvine	CA
9,000	59	Redemption World Outreach Center	Greenville	SC
9,000	60	Saint Stephen Church	Louisville	KY
9,000	61	The Rock Church & World Outreach Center	San Bernadino	CA
8,792	62	Northland, A Church Distributed	Longwood	FL
8,750	63	Sa-Rang Community Church	Anaheim	CA
8,500	64	Calvary Chapel Chino Valley	Chino	CA

8,406	65	CornerStone Church	San Antonio	TX
8,400	66	Real Life Ministries	Post Falls	ID
8,272	67	Angelus Temple	Los Angeles	CA
8,258	68	Grace Community Church	Sun Valley	CA
8,250	69	The Church Without Walls	Houston	TX
8,200	70	St. John Baptist Church	Grand Prairie	TX
8,168	71	Church of The Highlands	Birmingham	AL
8,100	72	Bethel Baptist Institutional Church	Jacksonville	FL
8,005	73	Flamingo Road Baptist Church	Cooper City	FL
8,000	74	Bethany World Prayer Center	Baker	LA
8,000	75	Calvary Chapel Melbourne	West Melbourne	FL
8,000	76	Calvary Chapel of Philadelphia	Philadelphia	PA
8,000	77	Covenant Church	Carrollton	TX
8,000	78	Fellowship NorthWest Arkansas	Rogers	AR
8,000	79	New Life Church	Colorado Springs	CO
8,000	80	Times Square Church	New York	NY
7,900	81	Hickory Grove Baptist Church	Charlotte	NC
7,726	82	NewSpring Church	Anderson	SC
7,716	83	James River Assembly	Ozark	MO
7,652	84	Lancaster County Bible Church	Manheim	PA
7,500	85	Church of The Redeemed of The Lord	Baltimore	MD
7,500	86	Hope Presbyterian Church	Cordova	TN
7,500	87	Inspiring Body of Christ Church	Dallas	TX
7,500	88	Reid Temple AME Church	Glenn Dale	MD
7,500	89	The Greater Allen A.M.E Cathedral of New York	Jamaica	NY
7,500	90	The Living Word Bible Church	Mesa	AZ
7,425	91	Central Christian Church of the East Valley	Mesa	AZ
7,400	92	Shepherd of The Hills Church	Porter Ranch	CA
7,335	93	Calvary Temple Worship Center	Modesto	CA
7,200	94	Flatirons Community Church	Lafayette	CO
7,069	95	Iglesia Cristiana Segadores de Vida	Hollywood	FL
7,015	96	Celebration Church	Jacksonville	FL
7,000	97	Antioch Missionary Baptist Church	Miami	FL
7,000	98	Calvary Chapel Downey	Downey	CA
7,000	99	Elmbrook Church	Brookfield	WI
7,000	100	First Baptist Church–Jacksonville	Jacksonville	FL
7,000	101	First Baptist Church Orlando	Orlando	FL
7,000	102	Maranatha Chapel	San Diego	CA
7,000	103	The Chapel	Akron	OH

RADIO

Christian radio is a powerful ally in your faith-based marketing efforts, providing a tacit endorsement of every product promoted on its airwaves. Here are lists of Christian music stations by format that report airplay to charting organizations. Explore a larger list, including preaching, teaching, and talk stations at www.faithbasedmarketing.com.

Inspirational Christian Radio

Call Letters	Market	Group Owner	Address	City	State	Zip Code	Web site
American Family Radio (Soft AC/IN)	Network	American Family Association	PO Box 3206	Tupelo	MS	38803	www.afr.net
Family Life Communications	Network		7355 N Oracle	Tucson	AZ	85704	www.myflr.org
KLVV-FM	Ponca City, OK	Love Station	PO Box 14	Ponca City	OK	74602	www.mypraisefm.com
KCBI-FM	Dallas-Ft. Worth, TX	Criswell Center	411 Ryan Plaza Dr.	Arlington	TX	76011	www.kcbi.org
KNLB-FM	Phoenix, AZ	New Life Christian School	510 N Acoma Blvd.	Lake Havasu City	AZ	86403	www.knlb.com
WCDR-FM	Dayton, OH	Cedarville University	PO Box 601	Cedarville	OH	45314-0601	www.thepath.fm
WSMR-FM	Sarasota-Bradenton, FL	Northwestern College Radio Network	240 N Washington Blvd. Ste. 500	Sarasota	FL	34236	www.lifefm891.org
KYCC-FM	Stockton, CA	Your Christian Companion Network	9019 N West Ln.	Stockton	CA	95210-1401	www.kycc.org
WAGO-FM	Greenville-New Bern-Jacksonville, NC	Pathway Christian Academy	PO Box 1895	Goldsboro	NC	27533	www.gomixradio.org
WHCB-FM	Johnson City-Kingsport-Bristol, TN-VA	Appalachian Educational	340 Martin Luther King Jr. Blvd.	Bristol	TN	37620	www.whcbradio.org
WNFR-FM	Flint, MI	Ross Bible Church	2865 Maywood Dr.	Port Huron	MI	48060	www.wnradio.com
WGSL-FM	Rockford, IL	Christian Life Center School	PO Box 2730	Rockford	IL	61132	www.radio91.com
WCRH-FM	Hagerstown-Chambersburg-Waynesboro, MD-PA	Cedar Ridge Ministries	PO Box 439	Williamsport	MD	21795	www.wcrh.org
KAMB-FM	Merced, CA	Central Valley Broadcasting	90 E 16th St.	Merced	CA	95340	www.celebrationradio.com
WLJN-FM	Traverse City-Petoskey, MI	Good News Media	1101 Cass St.	Traverse City	MI	49685	www.wljn.com
WOLW-FM	Traverse City-Petoskey, MI	Northern Christian Radio	PO Box 695	Gaylord	MI	49734	
KCFB-FM	St. Cloud, MN	Minnesota Christian Broadcasters	PO Box 409	Pequot Lakes	MN	56472	www.mcbiradio.org
WHCF-FM	Bangor, ME	Bangor Baptist Church	PO Box 5000	Bangor	ME	4402	www.whcffm.com
KLMP-FM	Rapid City, SD	Bethesda Christian Broadcasting	1853 Fountain Plaza Dr.	Rapid City	SD	57702	www.klmp.com
KCRN-FM	San Angelo, TX	Criswell Center	PO Box 32	San Angelo	TX	76902	

Rock Christian Radio

	Stations				Management			Contact Info		
Call Letters	Market	Format	Rank	AQH (00)	Group Owner	Address	City	State	Zip Code	Web site
Effect Radio	Network	C-Rock				4002 N 3300 E	Twin Falls	ID	83301	www.effectradio.com
Firexcape	Satellite	C-Rock				635 Haywood Rd.	Greenville	SC	29607	www.fxradio.org
SIST-ST	Satellite	C-Rock			Sirius Satellite Radio	1221 Ave. of the Americas 37th Fl.	New York	NY	10020	www.sirius.com
The Sound Of Light	Satellite	C-Rock				PO Box 2031	Spring Hill	TN	37174	www.soundoflight.com
WCWP-FM	Brookville, NY	C-Rock			Long Island University Public Radio	720 Northern Blvd.	Brookville	NY	11548	www.liu.edu/cwis/cwp/radio/wcwp
Whip Of Cords	Satellite	C-Rock			Glunt, Harold	PO Box 110226	Nashville	TN	37222	www.whipofcords.com
WHRZ-FM	Spartanburg, SC	C-Rock			First Baptist Church Spartanburg	250 E Main St.	Spartanburg	SC	29306	www.thez.com
KVRK-FM	Dallas-Ft. Worth, TX	C-Rock	5	19	Research Educational Foundation	11061 Shady Trail	Dallas	TX	75229	www.kvrk.com
WMKL-FM	Miami-Ft. Lauderdale-Hollywood, FL	C-Rock	12	0	Call Communications	PO Box 561832	Miami	FL	33256	www.callfm.com
WBVM-FM	Tampa-St. Petersburg-Clearwater, FL	C-Rock	19	40	St. Petersbug Diocese Bishop	PO Box 18081	Tampa	FL	33679	www.spiritfm905.com
KCLC-FM	St. Louis, MO	C-Rock	20	8	Lindenwood College	209 S Kings Hwy.	St. Charles	MO	63301-1695	www.891thewood.com
WUFM-FM	Columbus, OH	C-Rock	37	10	Spirit Communications	116 County Line Rd. W	Westerville	OH	43082	www.radiou.com

Call	Market	Format	#		Owner	Address	City	State	Zip	Website
WJLZ-FM	Norfolk-Virginia Beach-Newport News, VA	C-Rock	41	1	Virginia Beach Broadcasting	3500 Virginia Beach Blvd. Ste. 201	Virginia Beach	VA	23452	www.currentfm.com
WBFJ-FM	Greensboro-Winston Salem-High Point, NC	C-Rock	45	12	Word of Life Broadcasting	1249 Trade St.	Winston-Salem	NC	27101	www.wbfj.fm
WITR-FM	Rochester, NY	C-Rock	54	3	Rochester Institute of Tech.	998 Beaver Creek Rd.	Webster	NY	14580-9600	www.witr.rit.edu
KLYT-FM	Albuquerque, NM	C-Rock	69	13	Connection Communications Assn.	4001 Osuna Rd. NE	Albuquerque	NM	87109	www.m88.org
WJIS-FM	Sarasota-Bradenton, FL	C-Rock	73	26	Radio Training Network	6469 Parkland Dr.	Sarasota	FL	34243	www.lightforceradio.com
WYSZ-FM	Toledo, OH	C-Rock	88	7	Side by Side	5105 Glendale Ave. Ste. C	Toledo	OH	43614	www.yeshome.com
WJTL-FM	Lancaster, PA	C-Rock	113	22	Creative Ministries	PO Box 1614	Lancaster	PA	17608	www.wjtl.com
WVOF-FM	Bridgeport, CT	C-Rock	122	0	Fairfield University	112 Olde Towne Way Unit 3	Myrtle Beach	SC	29588	www.wvof.org
WSNL-AM	Flint, MI	C-Rock	127	1	Christian Broadcasting System	292 King George III Dr.	Flint	MI	48507	
WPRJ-FM	Saginaw-Bay City-Midland, MI	C-Rock	132	1	Come Together	PO Box 236	Coleman	MI	48618	www.1017thefuse.com
KIBZ-FM	Lincoln, NE	C-Rock	174	17	Three Eagles	3800 Cornhusker Hwy.	Lincoln	NE	68504	www.kibz.com
WORQ-FM	Green Bay, WI	C-Rock	187	4	Lakeshore Communications	1075 Brookwood Ste. 2C	Green Bay	WI	54304	www.q90fm.com
WCVK-FM	Bowling Green, KY	C-Rock	207	4	Bowling Green Community Broadcasting	1407 Scottsville Rd.	Bowling Green	KY	42104	www.christianfamilyradio.com
WDML-FM	Marion-Carbondale, IL	C-Rock	241	1	Volunteer Broadcasting	2485 E. Grand Rd.	Woodlawn	IL	62898	

Contemporary Hit Christian Radio

Stations					Management			Contact Info		
Call Letters	Market	Format	Rank	AQH (00)	Group Owner	Address	City	State	Zip Code	Web site
KADI-FM	Springfield, MO	C-CHR	140	11	Vision Communications Inc (MO)	5431 W Sunshine	Brookline Station	MO	65619-9433	www.kadi.com
KAFC-FM	Anchorage, AK	C-CHR	171	3	Christian Broadcasting Inc.	2709 Boniface Pkwy.	Anchorage	AK	99504	
KDUV-FM	Visalia-Tulare-Hanford, CA	C-CHR	100	15	Community Educational	130 N Kelsey Ste. H-1	Visalia	CA	93291	www.kduvfm.com
KJTH-FM	Ponca City, OK	C-CHR			Love Station	PO Box 14	Ponca City	OK	74602	www.thehousefm.com
KLFF-FM	San Luis Obispo, CA	C-CHR	172	3	Logos	PO Box 1561	San Luis Obispo	CA	93406	www.klife.org
KLYT-FM	Albuquerque, NM	C-CHR	69	13	Connection Communications Assn.	4001 Osuna Rd. NE	Albuquerque	NM	87109	www.m88.org
KNMI-FM	Farmington, NM	C-CHR				2103 W Main	Farmington	NM	87401	www.verticalradio.org
KTPT-FM	Rapid City, SD	C-CHR	279	1	Bethesda Christian Broadcasting	1853 Fountain Plaza Dr.	Rapid City	SD	57702	www.979thepoint.com
KXWA-FM	Denver-Boulder, CO	C-CHR	22	26	WAY-FM Media Group	1707 N Main St. Ste. 302	Longmont	CO	80501	www.wayfm.com
AIR-1	Network	C-CHR			Educational Media Foundation	5700 W Oaks Blvd.	Rocklin	CA	95765	www.air1.com
WAYK-FM	Kalamazoo, MI	C-CHR	188	5	Cornerstone University	1159 E Beltline Ave. NE	Grand Rapids	MI	49525-5805	www.way.fm
WAYM-FM	Nashville, TN	C-CHR	44	24	WAY-FM Media Group	1012 McEwen Dr.	Franklin	TN	37067	http://waym.wayfm.com
WBVM-FM	Tampa-St. Petersburg-Clearwater, FL	C-CHR	19	40	St. Petersburg Diocese Bishop	PO Box 18081	Tampa	FL	33679	www.spiritfm905.com

Call Sign	Market	Format			Licensee	Address	City	State	ZIP	Website
WBYO-FM	Sellersville, PA	C-CHR			Four Rivers Community	PO Box 186	Sellersville	PA	18960	www.wordfm.org
WCLQ-FM	Wausau-Stevens Point, WI	C-CHR	170	4	Christian Life Communications	4111 Schofield Ave. Ste. 10	Schofield	WI	54476	www.89q.org
WHJT-FM	Jackson, MS	C-CHR	120	8	Mississippi College	PO Box 4048	Clinton	MS	39058	www.star93fm.com
WHMX-FM	Bangor, ME	C-CHR	220	5	Bangor Baptist Church	PO Box 5000	Bangor	ME	04402-5000	www.solutionfm.com
WHRZ-FM	Spartanburg, SC	C-CHR			First Baptist Church Spartanburg	250 E Main St.	Spartanburg	SC	29306	www.thez.com
WJLZ-FM	Norfolk-Virginia Beach-Newport News, VA	C-CHR	41	1	Virginia Beach Broadcasting	3500 Virginia Beach Blvd. Ste. 201	Virginia Beach	VA	23452	www.currentfm.com
WJRF-FM	Duluth-Superior, MN-WI	C-CHR	206	2	Refuge Media Group	4604 Airpark Blvd.	Duluth	MN	55811	www.refugeradio.com
WLCQ-FM	Springfield, MA	C-CHR	86		Lighthouse Christian Center	522 Springfield St.	Feeding Hills	MA	1030	www.theq997.com
WNAZ-FM	Nashville, TN	C-CHR	44	4	Trevecca Nazarene University	333 Murfreesboro Rd.	Nashville	TN	37210	www.wnaz.com
WONU-FM	Chicago, IL	C-CHR	3	5	Olivet Nazarene University	1 University Ave.	Bourbonnais	IL	60914	http://shine.fm
WORQ-FM	Green Bay, WI	C-CHR	187	4	Lakeshore Communications	1075 Brookwood Ste. 2C	Green Bay	WI	54304	www.q90fm.com
WPRJ-FM	Saginaw-Bay City-Midland, MI	C-CHR	132	1	Come Together	PO Box 236	Coleman	MI	48618	www.1017thefuse.com
WSCF-FM	Ft. Pierce-Stuart, FL	C-CHR	96	8	Central Educational	6767 20th St.	Vero Beach	FL	32966	www.christianfm.com
WYLV-FM	Knoxville, TN	C-CHR	71	22	Foothills	1621 E Magnolia Ave.	Knoxville	TN	37917	www.love89.org
WYSZ-FM	Toledo, OH	C-CHR	88	7	Side by Side	5105 Glendale Ave. Ste. C	Toledo	OH	43614	www.yeshome.com

Adult Contemporary Christian Radio

	Stations				Management		Contact Info			
Call Letters	Market	Format	Rank	AQH (00)	Group Owner	Address	City	State	ZipCode	Web site
Family Life Ministries	Network	C-AC				PO Box 506	Bath	NY	14810	www.fln.org
KGTS-FM	College Place, WA	C-AC			Walla Walla College	204 S College Ave.	College Place	WA	99324	www.plr.org
KJIL-FM	Meade, KS	C-AC			Great Plains Christian Radio	PO Box 991	Meade	KS	67864	www.kjil991.com
New Life Media	Network	C-AC				PO Box 111	Morris	IL	60450	www.newlifemedia.org
SIST-ST	Satellite	C-AC			Sirius Satellite Radio	1221 Ave. of the Americas 37th Fl.	New York	NY	10020	www.sirius.com
XMES-ST	Satellite	C-AC			XM Satellite	1500 Eckington Pl. NE	Washington	DC	20002	www.xmradio.com
KFSH-FM	Los Angeles, CA	C-AC	2	119	Salem	701 N Brand Blvd. Ste. 550	Glendale	CA	91203	www.kfsh.com
KLTY-FM	Dallas-Ft. Worth, TX	C-AC	5	203	Salem	6400 N Beltline Rd. Ste. 120	Irving	TX	75063	www.klty.com
KSBJ-FM	Houston-Galveston, TX	C-AC	6	225	KSBJ Educational Foundation	PO Box 187	Humble	TX	77347	www.ksbj.org
WFSH-FM	Atlanta, GA	C-AC	8	157	Salem	2970 Peachtree Rd. NW Ste. 700	Atlanta	GA	30305	
WVFJ-FM	Atlanta, GA	C-AC	8	31	Provident Broadcasting Co.	120 Peachtree East S/C	Peachtree City	GA	30269	www.j933.com
WGTS-FM	Washington, DC	C-AC	9	102	Columbia Union College	7600 Flower Ave.	Takoma Park	MD	20912	www.wgts919.com
WMUZ-FM	Detroit, MI	C-AC	11	69	Crawford	12300 Radio Pl.	Detroit	MI	48228	www.wmuz.com
KCMS-FM	Seattle-Tacoma, WA	C-AC	14	142	Crista Ministries	19303 Fremont Ave. North	Seattle	WA	98133	www.spirit1053.com

Call Sign	Market	Format			Owner	Address	City	State	ZIP	Website
KTIS-FM	Minneapolis-St. Paul, MN	C-AC	16	188	Northwestern College Radio Network	3003 Snelling Ave. N	St. Paul	MN	55113-1598	www.ktis.fm
WLPJ-FM	Tampa-St. Petersburg-Clearwater, FL	C-AC	19	39	Radio Training Network	6469 Parkland Dr.	Sarasota	FL	34243-4091	www.thejoyfm.com
KHZR-FM	St. Louis, MO	C-AC	20	8	Four Him Enterprises	13358 Manchester Rd. Ste. 100	St. Louis	MO	63131	
WRBS-FM	Baltimore, MD	C-AC	21	63	Peter & John Radio	3600 Georgetown Rd.	Baltimore	MD	21227	www.wrbs.com
KFIS-FM	Portland, OR	C-AC	23	77	Salem	6400 SE Lake Rd. Ste. 350	Portland	OR	97222	www.1041thefish.com
WRCM-FM	Charlotte-Gastonia-Rock Hill, NC-SC	C-AC	25	54	Columbia Bible College	PO Box 17069	Charlotte	NC	28227	www.newlife919.com
KSGN-FM	Riverside-San Bernardino, CA	C-AC	26	46	KSGN	2048 Orange Tree Ln.	Redlands	CA	92374	www.ksgn.com
KKFS-FM	Sacramento, CA	C-AC	27	39	Salem	1425 River Park Dr. Ste. 520	Sacramento	CA	95815	www.1039thefish.com
WFHM-FM	Cleveland, OH	C-AC	28	71	Salem	4 Summit Park Dr. Ste. 150	Independence	OH	44131	www.955thefish.com
WAKW-FM	Cincinnati, OH	C-AC	29	52	Pillar of Fire	6275 Collegevue Pl.	Cincinnati	OH	45224	www.wakw.com
KLJC-FM	Kansas City, MO	C-AC	32	41	Calvary Bible College	15800 Calvary Rd.	Kansas City	MO	64147	www.calvary885.com
KSOS-FM	Las Vegas, NV	C-AC	33	35	Faith Communications	2201 S Sixth St.	Las Vegas	NV	89104-2962	www.sosradio.net
WPOZ-FM	Orlando, FL	C-AC	34	97	Central FL Educational	1065 Rainer Dr.	Altamonte Springs	FL	32714	www.zradio.org
K-LOVE	Network	C-AC			Educational Media Foundation	5700 West Oaks Blvd	Rocklin	CA	95765	www.klove.com
WCVO-FM	Columbus, OH	C-AC	37	67	Christian Voice of Central Ohio	881 E Johnstown Rd.	Columbus	OH	43230	www.1049theriver.com

(*Continued*)

Adult Contemporary Christian Radio (*Continued*)

	Stations				Management		Contact Info			
Call Letters	Market	Format	Rank	AQH (00)	Group Owner	Address	City	State	ZipCode	Website
KPEZ-FM	Austin, TX	C-AC	42	46	Clear Channel	3601 S Congress Ave. Bldg. F	Austin	TX	78704	www.theriver1023.com
WFFH-FM	Nashville, TN	C-AC	44	16	Salem	401 BNA Dr. Ste. 400	Nashville	TN	37217	www.94fmthefish.net
WBFJ-FM	Greensboro-Winston Salem-High Point, NC	C-AC	45	12	Word of Life Broadcasting	1249 Trade St.	Winston-Salem	NC	27101	www.wbfj.fm
WCRJ-FM	Jacksonville, FL	C-AC	47	8	Delmarva Educational Association	4190 Belfort Rd. Ste. 450	Jacksonville	FL	32216	www.ilovethepromise.com
WJIE-FM	Louisville, KY	C-AC	53	14	Evangel Schools	PO Box 197309	Louisville	KY	40219	www.wjie.org
WBSN-FM	New Orleans, LA	C-AC	55		Providence Edu. Foundation	3939 Gentilly Blvd.	New Orleans	LA	70126	www.lifesongs.com
WDJC-FM	Birmingham, AL	C-AC	57	49	Crawford	120 Summit Pkwy. Ste. 200	Birmingham	AL	35209	www.wdjconline.com
KVMV-FM	McAllen-Brownsville-Harlingen, TX	C-AC	58	37	World Radio	969 E Thomas Dr.	Pharr	TX	78577	www.kvmv.org
WLFJ-FM	Greenville-Spartanburg, SC	C-AC	59	47	Radio Training Network	2420 Wade Hampton Blvd.	Greenville	SC	29615	www.hisradio.com
KAIM-FM	Honolulu, HI	C-AC	64	20	Salem	1160 N King St. 2nd Fl.	Honolulu	HI	96817	www.thefishhawaii.com
KKCM-FM	Tulsa, OK	C-AC	65	15	Cox	7136 S Yale Ste. 500	Tulsa	OK	74136	www.spirit1023.com
KXOJ-FM	Tulsa, OK	C-AC	65	35	Stephens Media Group	2448 E 81st St. Ste. 5500	Tulsa	OK	74137	www.kxoj.com
WCSG-FM	Grand Rapids, MI	C-AC	67	47	Cornerstone University	1159 E Beltline Ave. NE	Grand Rapids	MI	49525	www.wcsg.org

Call	Market	Format	Rank	No.	Owner	Address	City	State	Zip	Website
WJQK-FM	Grand Rapids, MI	C-AC	67	18	Lanser	425 Centerstone Ste. 1	Zeeland	MI	49464	www.jq99.com
KGBI-FM	Omaha-Council Bluffs, NE	C-AC	72	19	Salem	11717 Burt St.	Omaha	NE	68154	www.kgbifm.com
WXHL-FM	Wilmington, DE	C-AC	75	3	Priority Radio	179 Stanton-Christiana Rd.	Newark	DE	19702	www.thereachfm.com
KKSP-FM	Little Rock, AR	C-AC	84	7	Crain Media Group	400 Hardin Rd. Ste. 150	Little Rock	AR	72211	www.spirit933.com
WMHK-FM	Columbia, SC	C-AC	90	32	Columbia Bible College	PO Box 3122	Columbia	SC	29230	www.wmhk.com
KNWI-FM	Des Moines, IA	C-AC	91	6	Northwestern College Radio Network	3737 Woodland Ave. Ste. 111	W. Des Moines	IA	50266	www.desmoines.fm
KBIQ-FM	Colorado Springs, CO	C-AC	95	35	Salem	7150 Campus Dr. Ste. 150	Colorado Springs	CO	80920	www.kbiqradio.com
WCQR-FM	Johnson City-Kingsport-Bristol, TN-VA	C-AC	101	19	Baker Family Stations	PO Box 8039	Gray	TN	37615	www.wcqr.org
KTSY-FM	Boise, ID	C-AC	102	19	Gem State Adventist Academy	16115 S Montana Ave.	Caldwell	ID	83607	www.895ktsy.org
WLAB-FM	Ft. Wayne, IN	C-AC	106	21	Indiana District Lutheran Church	8 Martin Luther Dr: 6600 N Clinton	Ft. Wayne	IN	46825	www.star883.org
WBDX-FM	Chattanooga, TN	C-AC	107	12	Partners for Christian Radio	PO Box 9396	Chattanooga	TN	37412	www.j103.com
WAFJ-FM	Augusta, GA	C-AC	110	18	Radio Training Network	102 LeCompte Ave.	N. Augusta	SC	29841	www.wafj.com
WJTL-FM	Lancaster, PA	C-AC	113	22	Creative Ministries	PO Box 1614	Lancaster	PA	17608	www.wjtl.com
WPAR-FM	Roanoke-Lynchburg, VA	C-AC	115	5	Baker Family Stations	20276A Timberlake Rd.	Lynchburg	VA	24502	www.spiritfm.com
WLGH-FM	Lansing-East Lansing, MI	C-AC	125	5	Superior Communications	PO Box 388	Williamson	MI	48895	www.smile.fm
WCLN-FM	Fayetteville, NC	C-AC	130	14	Christian Listening Network	996 Helen St.	Fayetteville	NC	28303	www.christian107.com

(Continued)

Adult Contemporary Christian Radio (*Continued*)

	Stations				Management		Contact Info				
Call Letters	Market	Format	Rank	AQH (00)	Group Owner	Address	City	State	ZipCode	Website	
KBNJ-FM	Corpus Christi, TX	C-AC	136	4	World Radio	PO Box 270968	Corpus Christi	TX	78427	www.kbnj.org	
KWND-FM	Springfield, MO	C-AC	140	22	Radio Training Network	2550 S Campbell Ave. Ste. 100	Springfield	MO	65807	www.thewindfm.com	
KVNE-FM	Tyler-Longview, TX	C-AC	145	10	Educational Radio Foundation of East Texas	2721 E Erwin	Tyler	TX	75708	www.kvne.com	
KGCB-FM	Flagstaff-Prescott, AZ	C-AC	147	14	Grand Canyon Broadcasters	3741 Karicio Ln.	Prescott	AZ	86303	www.kgcb.org	
KHPE-FM	Eugene-Springfield, OR	C-AC	148	2	Extra Mile Media Inc.	PO Box 278	Albany	OR	97321	www.hope1079.com	
KYTT-FM	Eugene-Springfield, OR	C-AC	148		Lighthouse Radio Group	580 Kingwood Ave.	Coos Bay	OR	97420	www.lighthouseradio.com	
WQFL-FM	Rockford, IL	C-AC	151	9	First Assembly of God	PO Box 2730	Rockford	IL	61132	www.101qfl.com	
WPER-FM	Fredericksburg, VA	C-AC	152	6	Baker Family Stations	6546 Lovers Ln.	Warrenton	VA	20186	www.positivehits.org	
WMIT-FM	Asheville, NC	C-AC	160	19	Blue Ridge Broadcasting	PO Box 159	Black Mountain	NC	28711	www.1069thelight.org	
WMSJ-FM	Portland, ME	C-AC	167	6	Downeast Christian Communications	PO Box 287	Freeport	ME	4032	www.positive.fm	
WCTL-FM	Erie, PA	C-AC	168	5	Inspiration Time	10912 Peach St.	Erie	PA	16441	www.wctl.org	
WGNV-FM	Wausau-Stevens Point, WI	C-AC	170	2	Evangel Ministries	PO Box 88	Milladore	WI	54454	www.christianfamilyradio.net	
KZKZ-FM	Ft. Smith, AR	C-AC	173	5	Family Communications	PO Box 6210	Ft. Smith	AR	72906	www.kzkzfm.com	
WFRN-FM	South Bend, IN	C-AC	179	4	Progressive Broadcast System	PO Box 307	Elkhart	IN	46515	http://wfrn.com/	

Call	Market	Format	Rank	#	Owner	Address	City	State	Zip	Website
WHPZ-FM	South Bend, IN	C-AC	179	4	LeSea	61300 S Ironwood	South Bend	IN	46614	www.pulsefm.com
American Family Radio (AC)	Tupelo, MS	C-AC	189	2	American Family Association	PO Box 3206	Tupelo	MS	38803	
WCVK-FM	Bowling Green, KY	C-AC	207	4	Bowling Green Community Broadcasting	1407 Scottsville Rd.	Bowling Green	KY	42104	www.christianfamilyradio.com
KKJM-FM	St. Cloud, MN	C-AC	218	5	St. Cloud Diocese	PO Box 547	Sauk Rapids	MN	56379	www.spirit929.com
KOBC-FM	Joplin, MO	C-AC	237	14	Educational Media Foundation	1111 N Main	Joplin	MO	64801	
WWIB-FM	Eau Claire, WI	C-AC	244	4	Stewards of Sound	2396 State Hwy. 53 Ste. 1	Chippewa Falls	WI	54729	www.wwib.com
KGNZ-FM	Abilene, TX	C-AC	247	4	Christian Broadcasting Co.	542 Butternut St.	Abilene	TX	79602	www.kgnz.com
KNWS-FM	Waterloo-Cedar Falls, IA	C-AC	250	10	Northwestern College Radio Network	4880 Texas St.	Waterloo	IA	50702	www.life1019.com
KNWS-FM	Waterloo-Cedar Falls, IA	C-AC	250	10	Northwestern College Radio Network	4880 Texas St.	Waterloo	IA	50702	www.life1019.com
KSWP-FM	Lufkin-Nacogdoches, TX	C-AC	254		Lufkin Educational	PO Box 151340	Lufkin	TX	75915	www.kswp.org
KCVO-FM	Columbia, MO	C-AC	255	0	Lake Area Educational Broadcasting Foundation	PO Box 800	Camdenton	MO	65020	www.spiritfm.org
KBMQ-FM	Monroe, LA	C-AC	258	7	Media Ministries	130 N Second St. Ste. C	Monroe	LA	71201	http://887fm.org
WGRC-FM	Williamsport, PA	C-AC	274	2	Salt & Light Media Ministries	101 Armory Blvd.	Lewisburg	PA	17837	
KSLT-FM	Rapid City, SD	C-AC	279	3	Bethesda Christian Broadcasting	1853 Fountain Plaza Dr.	Rapid City	SD	57702	www.kslt.com
WAYR-FM	Brunswick, GA	C-AC	299	3	Good Tidings Trust	1426 Newcastle St. Ste. 200	Brunswick	GA	31520	www.wayradio.org

Radio Programming Networks

Network	Web Address	Number of Stations/Affiliates
Air1	http://www.air1.com/	150
American Family Radio	http://www.afr.net/	100+
Bible Broadcasting Network	http://www.bbnradio.org/	135+
Bott Radio Network	http://www.bottradionetwork.com/	97
Calvary Satellite Network	http://www.csnradio.com/	400+
Children's Sonshine Radio	http://www.gospelcom.net/csn	
Christian Hit Radio Satellite Network	http://www.chrsn.com/	97
Christian Internet Radio Network	http://cirnet.com/	Web
EWTN–Global Catholic Network	http://www.ewtn.com	90+
Family Life Communications	http://www.flc.org/	16
Family Life Network	http://www.fln.org/	60+
Family Radio	http://www.familyradio.com/	
Informational Radio Network	http://www.inforadionet.com/	
Involved Christian Radio Network	http://www.icrn.com/	
K-LOVE Radio Network	http://www.klove.com/	150
Life Changing Radio	http://www.lifechangingradio.com/	7
Life Talk Radio	http://www.lifetalk.net/	66
Mars Hill Broadcasting	http://www.marshillnetwork.org/	19
Moody Broadcasting Network	http://www.moodyradio.org/	450+
PAR FM	http://www.parfm.com	7
Salem Communications Corporation	http://www.salem.cc/	75+
Salem Radio Network Top rated talk syndication	http://www.srnonline.com/	
SkyLight Satellite Network	http://www.nwc.edu/radio/skylight	60+
Sound of Life Network	http://soundoflife.org/radio/	
The CDR Radio Network	http://www.thepath.fm/	
Today's Christian Music	http://www.todayschristianmusic.com/	
USA Radio Network	http://www.usaradio.com/	
VCY America	http://www.vcyamerica.org/	

TRADE ASSOCIATIONS

CATHOLIC BOOK PUBLISHERS ASSOCATION

The Catholic Book Publishers Association facilitates the sharing of professional information, networking, cooperation, and friendship among those involved in Catholic book publishing in the United States and abroad.

Catholic Book Publishers Association
Terry Wessels, Executive Director
8404 Jamesport Drive
Rockford, IL 61108
(815) 332-3245
E-mail: info@cbpa.org
www.cbpa.org

CBA INTERNATIONAL

Formerly known as The Christian Bookseller's Association, CBA International, a Colorado Springs-based group, changed its name in 1996 to reflect a reality that books represented, at the time, only 35 percent of sales in Christian stores.

CBA publishes a monthly journal that carries news, new product information, and trade advertising. The publication, which changed its masthead to *Retailers+Resources* in 2007, accepts press releases on industry-related topics and distributes a frequent online news update via e-mail. The association also acts as a clearinghouse for information about the industry and hosts the International Christian Retail Show (typically held in July), in addition to training seminars and leadership symposia. A winter show in existence since 1994 was cancelled in 2007 and at press time details about a planned replacement were not available. There are various membership levels.

CBA International
Bill Anderson, President
PO Box 62000
Colorado Springs, CO 80962
(800) 252-1950
www.cbaonline.org

CHRISTIAN MUSIC TRADE ASSOCIATION

The Christian Music Trade Association (CMTA) exists to build community and cooperation among industry leadership in order to address mutual business issues and to maximize Christian music's sales and impact on culture.

CMTA
Gabriel Aviles, Director
1205 Division Street
Nashville, TN 37203
(615) 242-0303
www.cmta.com

CHRISTIAN TRADE ASSOCIATION INTERNATIONAL

Christian Trade Association International is a worldwide association of nations, companies, and individuals committed to fulfilling the Great Commission through the distribution of Christian resources.

Christian Trade Association International
Jim Powell, Executive Director
PO Box 62187
Colorado Springs, CO 80962
(719) 432-8428
www.ctaintl.org

EVANGELICAL CHRISTIAN PUBLISHERS ASSOCIATION

The Evangelical Christian Publishers Association (ECPA) is an international nonprofit trade organization comprised of nearly 250 member companies worldwide that are involved in the publishing and distribution of Christian literature.

Since ECPA was founded in 1974, the Christian publishing industry has experienced exponential growth with ECPA active in serving the industry and its members through cutting-edge technology, meaningful data, educational opportunities, and access to markets. ECPA sponsored events include: The Executive Leadership Summit, the CEO Symposium, ECPA Publishing University, Christian Book Expo, and more. See the complete list of their events and programs at www.ecpa.org.

ECPA
Mark Kuyper, President
9633 South 48th Street, #140
Phoenix, AZ 85044
(480) 966-3998
www.ecpa.org

EVANGELICAL PRESS ASSOCIATION

The Evangelical Press Association represents concerns of periodicals and writers working in the Christian market. It includes over 300 member magazines with contact and data card information.

Evangelical Press Association
Doug Trouten, Executive Director
PO Box 28129
Crystal, MN 55428
(763) 535-4793
E-mail: director@epassoc.org
www.epassoc.org

GOSPEL MUSIC ASSOCIATION

Founded in 1964, the Gospel Music Association (GMA) serves as the face and voice for the Christian/Gospel music community and is dedicated to exposing, promoting, and celebrating the gospel through music of all styles including pop, rock, praise & worship, black gospel, R&B, hip hop, southern gospel, country, and more.

The GMA community consists of 4,000 members, which includes agents, artists, church leaders, managers, promoters, radio personnel, record company executives, retailers, songwriters, and other industry visionaries.

The GMA produces the GMA Dove Awards, GMA Music Week, and the GMA Academy.

GMA
John Styll, President
1205 Division Street
Nashville, TN 37203
(615) 242-0303
www.gospelmusic.org

NATIONAL RELIGIOUS BROADCASTERS ASSOCIATION

The National Religious Broadcasters Association (NRB) is the preeminent association of Christian communicators working to keep the doors of electronic media open for the spread of the Gospel, which promotes standards of excellence, integrity, and accountability. NRB provides networking, educational, ministry, fellowship opportunities, and an annual convention for its 1400 members.

National Religious Broadcasters
Dr. Frank Wright, President/CEO
9510 Technology Drive
Manassas, VA 20110
(703) 330-7000
E-mail: info@nrb.org
www.nrb.org

SPANISH EVANGELICAL PUBLISHERS ASSOCIATION

The Spanish Evangelical Publishers Association (SEPA) represents publishing houses that publish material in Spanish. Membership is international.

SEPA
Tessie DeVore, Executive Director
Pablo Vera, Assistant to the Executive Director
1370 North West 88th Avenue
Miami, FL 33172
(305) 503-1195
E-mail: sepa@sepa.bmsi.com
(The association does not maintain a web site)

TRADE MEDIA

CHRISTIAN RETAILING

Christian Retailing magazine is an independent trade journal providing news, data, and opinion of concern to the Christian products industry. *Christian Retailing* is published every other week by Strang Communications of Lake Mary, Florida. Subscriptions are available by mail, and editors produce a regular electronic "headlines" edition.

Andy Butcher, Editor
600 Rinehart Road
Lake Mary, FL 32746
(407) 333-0600, x2860
www.christianretailing.com

CHURCH BOOKSTORE

Church Bookstore magazine is targeted specifically at the growing number of local churches that have established a retail store on their property. The magazine is published monthly by Strang Communications (see previous) and features articles of interest to church bookstore managers, as well as product advertising. They also publish the "Christian E-Tailing Newsletter," a twice-weekly update from *Christian Retailing* magazine.

Andy Butcher, Editor
600 Rinehart Road
Lake Mary, FL 32746
(407) 333-0600, x2860
www.thechurchbookstore.com

RETAILERS+RESOURCES

Retailers+Resources is the official publication of CBA. Subscriptions are available by mail; there is an online version available as well as a regular eNews edition distributed by request.

Kathleen Samuelson, Publications Director
PO Box 62000
Colorado Springs, CO 80962
(719) 265-9895
www.cbaonline.org

RETAILERS

Christian retailers fall into several different groups: chains, buying/marketing groups, franchises, and independents. Chains include Family Christian Stores, LifeWay, and Mardel, which own and operate their own retail outlets. Family Christian Stores is the largest. LifeWay, owned by the Southern Baptist denomination, is close behind with strength in the southeastern United States. Mardel, whose parent corporation also owns Hobby Lobby stores, is smaller but powerful, with stores in the Midwest and Texas.

Buying and marketing groups align independent stores to secure better pricing from suppliers and more powerful cooperative marketing. They include The Parable Group, Munce Marketing, Logos, and the Covenant Group. The only franchise operation is Lemstone. Christian Book Distributors is a successful direct, catalog, and Internet retailer. Bookschristian.com and its companion site musicchristian.com sell products exclusively online.

Association of Logos Bookstores
Becky Gorczyca
1675 E Main Street
Kent, OH 44240
(330) 677-8086
www.logosbookstores.com

Berean Christian Stores
Merchandise Submission Department
Bill Simmons, President
9415 Meridian Way
West Chester, OH 45069
(877) 484-2940
www.berean.com

BooksChristian.com
PO Box 1004
Franklin, TN 37065
(800) 840-8483
www.bookschristian.com

Christian Book Distributors
PO Box 7000
Peabody, MA 01961-7000
(800) 247-4784
www.christianbook.com

The Covenant Group
Chuck Wallington, President
PO Box 4009
Spartanburg, SC 29305
(864) 587-2637
www.covenantgroupstores.com

Family Christian Stores
5300 Patterson Avenue, SE
Grand Rapids, Michigan 49530
(616) 554-8700
www.familychristian.com/corporate

Lemstone Books/Insight Retail Group, LLC
Phil Darr, Vice President
209 E. Liberty Drive
Wheaton, IL 60187
(630) 682-1400
www.lemstone.net

LifeWay Christian Stores
Mark Scott, Vice President
One LifeWay Plaza
Nashville, TN 37234
(615) 251-2000
www.lifewaystores.com

Mardel Stores
7727 SW 44th Street
Oklahoma, OK 73179
(405) 745-1300
www.mardel.com

Munce Marketing
Bob Munce, President
415 Second Street
Indian Rocks Beach, FL 33785
(727) 596-7625
www.munce.com

The Parable Group
Steve Potratz, President
3563 Empleo Drive
San Luis Obispo, CA 93401
(805) 543-2644
www.parablegroup.com

DISTRIBUTORS

If you have a product that may sell well through Christian retail stores but lack a sales force large enough to call on the more than 2,000 Christian retail stores in the United States, then you may want to consider working with a distributor. Here is a list of Christian product distributors.

Anchor Distributors
1030 Hunt Valley Circle
New Kensington, PA 15068
(724) 334-7000
www.anchordistributors.com

Arbor (A division of Ingram Book Company)
One Ingram Boulevard
La Vergne, TN 37086
(615) 213-5000
www.springarbor.com

New Day Christian Distributors
PO Box 1363
Hendersonville, TN 37075
(615) 822-3633
www.newdaychristian.com

STL Distribution (formerly Appalachian Distributors)
PO Box 1573
Johnson, TN 37601
(800) 289-2772
www.stl-distribution.com

MAGAZINES

CHRISTIAN LIFESTYLE

Charisma
www.charismamag.org
Christian Single
www.christianitytoday.com/singles
Christianity Today
www.christianitytoday.com
Discipleship Journal
www.navpress.com/Magazines/
Focus on the Family
www.focusonthefamily.com/focusmagazine/
Guideposts
www.guideposts.org
Homecoming
www.HomecomingMagazine.com

HomeLife
www.lifeway.com/magazines/media
Lifeway
www.lifeway.com/magazines/media
Living with Teenagers
www.lifeway.com/magazines/media
Marriage Partnership
www.christianitytoday.com/marriage
ParentLife
www.lifeway.com/magazines/media
Today's Christian
www.christianitytoday.com/todayschristian

BOOKS AND LITERARY REVIEW

Books and Culture
www.christianitytoday.com/books
Christian Library Journal
www.christianlibraryj.org

Church and Synagogue Libraries
http://cslainfo.org/links.html

MUSIC

CCM Magazine
www.ccmmagazine.com
HM Magazine
www.hmmagazine.com

Paste
www.pastemagazine.com
The Worshiper
www.theworshipermagazine.com

GENDER SPECIFIC

Christian Women Today
www.christianwomentoday.com
New Man
www.newmanmag.com
Radiant Magazine
www.radiantmag.com

SpiritLed Woman
www.spiritledwoman.com
Today's Christian Woman
www.christianitytoday.com/tcw

TEENS/YOUNG ADULTS

Ignite Your Faith
www.christianitytoday.com/teens

Relevant Magazine
www.relevantmediagroup.com

CHURCH AND MINISTRY ISSUES

Leadership Journal
www.christianitytoday.com/leaders
Outreach Magazine
www.outreach.com
Preaching
www.preaching.com

Rev
www.revmagazine.com
Wireless Age
www.wirelessage.com

POLITICS AND CURRENT AFFAIRS

Citizen Magazine
www.citizenlink.org/citizenmag
Sojourners
www.sojo.net

World Magazine
www.worldmag.com

Parachurch and Ministry Organizations

There are more than 3,400 parachurch and ministry organizations operating in the United States. Explore the complete list at www.faithbasedmarketing.com.

Adoption

Bethany Christian Services
PO Box 294
Grand Rapids, MI 49501-0294
(616) 224-7610
Fax: (616) 224-7610
E-mail: info@bethany.org
www.bethany.org

Bethany Christian Services is a private child and family social service agency. Services provided in the Bethany offices which are located nationwide include pro-life pregnancy counseling, adoption, foster care, family counseling, family preservation.

Buckner International
600 N Pearl St Ste 2000
Dallas, TX 75201-2896
(214) 758-8000
Fax: (214) 758-8000
www.buckner.org

Based in Dallas, Texas, Buckner International is a diverse global ministry to orphans, at-risk children, families, and older adults. Our mission is to be a multi-service agency dedicated to the restoration and healing of individuals and the family.

Christian Family Care Agency
3603 N 7th Ave
Phoenix, AZ 85013-3638
(602) 234-1935
Fax: (602) 234-1935
E-mail: info@cfcare.org
www.cfcare.org

Christian Family Care Agency is a private, nonprofit agency, licensed by the Arizona Department of Economic Security for Foster Care and Adoption services and by the Department of Health Services for Counseling services.

Shaohannahs Hope
PO Box 647
Franklin, TN 37065-0647
(615) 550-5600
Fax: (615) 550-5600
E-mail: give@shaohannahshope.org
www.shaohannahshope.org

Shaohannahs Hope is a ministry created by recording artist Steven Curtis Chapman and his wife Mary Beth to care for orphans by engaging the church and helping Christian families reduce the financial barrier to adoption.

Alcohol and Drug Rehab

Atlanta Union Mission
PO Box 1807
Atlanta, GA 30301-1807
(404) 367-2244
Fax: (404) 367-2244
E-mail: info@myaum.org
www.aumcares.org

The Atlanta Union Mission is a non-denominational Christian ministry that brings Christ's healing power to any person in crisis through programs of rescue and recovery.

Rescue Mission Alliance
315 N A St
Oxnard, CA 93030-4901
(805) 487-1234
Fax: (805) 487-1234
E-mail: davec@erescuemission.com
www.erescuemission.com

The Rescue Mission Alliance is a Christian, faith-based, nonprofit organization that offers refuge, recovery, and restoration to the less fortunate in Southern California through emergency and long-term rehabilitation services.

Teen Challenge International, USA
PO Box 1015
Springfield, MO 65801-1015
(417) 862-6969
Fax: (417) 862-6969
E-mail: tcusa@teenchallengeusa.com
www.teenchallengeusa.com

Teen Challenge International, U.S.A. is a Christ centered, Bible based, discipleship program, reaching out to those with life controlling problems. The ministry focuses on evangelism and intensive discipleship.

Arts Ministries

Fellowship for the Performing Arts
1 High Street Ct
Morristown, NJ 07960-6861
(973) 984-3400
Fax: (973) 984-3400
E-mail: info@listenersbible.com
www.listenersbible.com

Each year, FPA works with theater companies, college fine art series, performing arts venues, churches, radio and television stations to present theatrical productions from the Bible.

Associations

ACSI
PO Box 65130
Colorado Springs, CO 80962-5130
(719) 528-6906
Fax: (719) 528-6906
www.acsi.org

ACSI (Acronym for Association of Christian Schools International) co-labors with over 5,000 member schools to provide services and teaching materials that enable Christian educators and schools worldwide to effectively prepare students for life.

Association for Christian Conferences, Teaching and Service
PO Box 27239
Denver, CO 80227-0239
(303) 985-8808
Fax: (303) 985-8808
E-mail: accts@accts.org
www.accts.org

The purpose of Association for Christian Conferences, Teaching and Service is to provide assistance to military Christians of all ranks worldwide in their efforts to evangelize, disciple, and develop strong fellowship groups.

Christian Leadership Alliance
635 Camino De Los Mares Ste 205
San Clemente, CA 92673-2804
(949) 487-0900
Fax: (949) 487-0900
E-mail: cma@cmaonline.org
www.christianleadershipalliance.com

The mission of Christian Leadership Alliance is to equip our member organizations with management information, leadership training, and strategic networking relationships so ministries are led and managed in God-honoring ways.

Christian Medical and Dental Associations
PO Box 7500
Bristol, TN 37621-7500
(423) 844-1000
Fax: (423) 844-1000
E-mail: main@cmdahome.org
www.cmdahome.org

The Christian Medical & Dental Associations (CMDA) was founded in 1931 and currently serves approximately 17,000 members.

Family Research Council
801 G St NW
Washington, DC 20001-3729
(202) 393-2100
Fax: (202) 393-2100
www.frc.org

Family Research Council provides educational materials to the general public concerning Judeo-Christian family values, as well as news of legislation and judicial developments affecting family life and values.

MOPS International
2370 S Trenton Way
Denver, CO 80231-7629
(303) 733-5353
Fax: (303) 733-5353
E-mail: info@mops.org
www.mops.org

MOPS International is an outreach ministry which includes radio, publishing, and regular church group meetings with instruction relating to womanhood, marriage, child rearing, and the home, from a Biblical perspective.

National Association of Evangelicals
PO Box 23269
Washington, DC 20026-3269
(202) 789-1011
Fax: (202) 789-1011
E-mail: info@nae.net
www.nae.net

The mission of the National Association of Evangelicals is to extend the kingdom of God through a fellowship of member denominations, churches, organizations, and individuals, speaking with a representative voice and serving the evangelical community.

National Religious Broadcasters
9510 Technology Dr
Manassas, VA 20110-4149
(703) 330-7000
Fax: (703) 330-7000
E-mail: info@nrb.org
www.nrb.org

NRB is an association of 1,600 organizations engaged in the production of religious programming for radio, television, cable, the internet, and the operation of these mediums.

Aviation Ministries

JAARS
PO Box 248
Waxhaw, NC 28173-0248
(704) 843-6000
Fax: (704) 843-6000
E-mail: info@jaars.org
www.jaars.org

JAARS is the center of training and support operation for Wycliffe Bible Translators. Our ministries include aviation (maintaining equipment and training personnel for fast, safe access to remote areas).

Mission Aviation Fellowship
PO Box 47
Nampa, ID 83653-0047
(208) 498-0800
Fax: (208) 498-0800
E-mail: maf-us@maf.org
www.MAF.org

Mission Aviation Fellowship is a team of specialists providing aviation and communications support for more than 500 Christian and humanitarian organizations around the world.

Mission Safety International
328 E Elk Ave Ste 1
Elizabethton, TN 37643-3351
(423) 542-8892
Fax: (423) 542-8892
E-mail: info@msisafety.org
www.msisafety.org

MSI is a nonprofit organization whose purpose is to contribute to the effective propagation of the Gospel of Jesus Christ by assisting missionary/Christian oriented aviation organizations in aviation safety and security issues.

Pacific Missionary Aviation
PO Box 3209
Hagatna, GU 96932-3209
(671) 646-6464
Fax: (671) 646-6464
E-mail: guam@pmapacific.org
www.pmapacific.org

The primary goal of Pacific Missionary Aviation/FMS is to make our Lord Jesus Christ known to the people of Micronesia and the Philippines by providing and initiating the development of spiritual and social economic programs.

Chaplain Ministries

Chaplaincy Ministries
7777 Forest Ln
Dallas, TX 75230-2505
(972) 566-7584
Fax: (972) 566-7584

Chaplaincy Ministries, Inc. was organized to provide pastoral care to health facilities that did not have a chaplaincy program. For more than 20 years we have strived to meet the growing spiritual and psychological needs of our medical community.

Community Chaplain Service
PO Box 117
Foxboro, MA 02035-0117
(508) 543-0322
Fax: (508) 543-0322
E-mail: commchap@verizon.net
www.chapservice.org

Community Chaplain Service is an evangelical faith home mission which engages and sends career and part-time missionary chaplains for ministry in nursing homes, with the two thrusts of evangelism and pastoral care.

Corporate Chaplains of America
2018 S Main St Ste 804
Wake Forest, NC 27587-5009
(919) 570-0700
Fax: (919) 570-0700
E-mail: info@chaplain.org
www.chaplain.org

Corporate Chaplains of America (CCA) provides genuine "Caring in the Workplace" through its workforce of "Certified Workplace Chaplains."

InStep International
41 Perimeter Ctr E Ste 510
Atlanta, GA 30346-1903
(678) 578-4444
Fax: (678) 578-4444
E-mail: instep.usa@mindspring.com
www.instep-usa.com

To lead people into a meaningful experience with God through personal mission, effective giving, and significant life work. We mobilize individuals and organizations to support and operate charitable and religious relief worldwide.

Child Sponsorship

Compassion International
PO Box 65000
Colorado Springs, CO 80962-5000
(719) 487-7000
Fax: (719) 487-7000
E-mail: ciinfo@us.ci.org
www.compassion.com

In response to the Great Commission, Compassion International exists as an advocate for children to release them from their spiritual, economic, social, and physical poverty and enable them to become responsible and fulfilled Christian adults.

Hope for the Hungry
PO Box 786
Belton, TX 76513-0786
(254) 939-0124
Fax: (254) 939-0124
E-mail: hope@hopeforthehungry.org
www.hopeforthehungry.org

Hope for the Hungry has as its goal to make a substantial contribution in "Sharing the Bread of Life with a Starving World." Meeting both the physical and spiritual needs in countries where its missionaries serve.

Hopegivers International
PO Box 8808
Columbus, GA 31908-8808
(866) 373-4673
Fax: (866) 373-4673
E-mail: info@hopegivers.org
www.hopegivers.org

Hopegivers International is a faith-based, not-for-profit humanitarian mission agency based in Columbus, Georgia. Organized in the United States in 1978, it exists to bring "Help for today and hope for eternity" by rescuing abandoned orphans and widows.

Mission of Mercy
PO Box 62600
Colorado Springs, CO 80962-2600
(719) 481-0400
Fax: (719) 481-0400
E-mail: mominfo@mofm.org
www.missionofmercy.org

Mission of Mercy is a Christian missions
organization that exists to see the children of
developing nations, who live in poverty, experience
transformation and wholeness through God's love.

World Harvest
301 E Foothill Blvd Ste 201
Arcadia, CA 91006-2551
(626) 359-8500
Fax: (626) 359-8500
E-mail: contact@worldharvest.cc
www.worldharvest.cc

World Harvest works with poor people in
transforming their lives mainly through
health care, food security, micro enterprise,
education, and awareness process.

Church Denominations

Advent Christian General Conference
of America
PO Box 690848
Charlotte, NC 28227-7015
(704) 545-6161
Fax: (704) 545-6161
E-mail: execdirect@acgc.org
www.adventchristian.org

The Advent Christian General Conference
exists to serve denominational churches
by providing resources and training
opportunities, maintaining legal entities
necessary to relate to governmental authorities.

Christian and Missionary Alliance, The
PO Box 35000
Colorado Springs, CO 80935-3500
(719) 599-5999
Fax: (719) 599-5999
E-mail: info@cmalliance.org
www.cmalliance.org

Our mission is to know Jesus Christ; exalt
Him as Savior, Sanctifier, Healer, and
Coming King; and complete His Great
Commission: Evangelizing and discipling
persons throughout the United States.

Church of the Nazarene General Board
17001 Prairie Star Pkwy
Lenexa, KS 66220-7900
(913) 577-0500
Fax: (913) 577-0500
E-mail: donorservices@nazarene.org
www.nazarene.org

For about 100 years, the Church of the
Nazarene has taken the message of
holiness to the world. Today, there are
nearly 1.6 million Nazarenes worldwide
with approximately 15,000 congregations
in over 150 world areas.

CI Apostolic Network
PO Box 9000
Santa Rosa Beach, FL 32459-9000

Colorado Baptist Convention
7393 S Alton Way
Centennial, CO 80112-2302
(303) 771-2480
Fax: (303) 771-2480
www.cbgc.org

Provide resources and services to assist
Colorado's Southern Baptist Churches in
fulfilling the Great Commission... saturating
Colorado with the Gospel and penetrating all
pockets of lostness in our state.

Conservative Congregational Christian
Conference
8941 Highway 5
Lake Elmo, MN 55042-8900
(651) 739-1474
Fax: (651) 739-1474
E-mail: dmjohnson@ccccusa.com
www.ccccusa.com

We are an evangelical, conservative,
congregational denomination that exists for
the purpose of promoting fellowship and
cooperative endeavor among congregational
churches of the historic biblical persuasion.

Evangelical Free Church of America, The
901 E 78th St
Minneapolis, MN 55420-1334
(952) 854-1300
Fax: (952) 854-1300
E-mail: adminfin@efca.org
www.efca.org

The mission of The Evangelical Free Church
of America is to glorify God by multiplying
healthy churches among all people. The
Evangelical Free Church of America is an
association of some 1,285 autonomous
churches united by a mutual commitment.

Evangelical Presbyterian Church
17197 N Laurel Park Dr Ste 567
Livonia, MI 48152-2680
(734) 742-2020
Fax: (734) 742-2020
E-mail: epchurch@epc.org
www.epc.org

The Evangelical Presbyterian Church
(EPC), established in 1981, is a conservative
denomination of eight presbyteries and
nearly 200 churches nationwide. Constituent
membership is 75,000.

Every Nation Churches
PO Box 1787
Brentwood, TN 37024-1787
(615) 371-8479
Fax: (615) 371-8479
E-mail: info@everynation.org
www.everynation.org

Every Nation Churches exists to preach the
Gospel, make disciples, advance the Kingdom
of God and establish Christ-centered, Spirit-
empowered, and socially responsbile churches
in every nation.

Free Methodist Church of North America
PO Box 535002
Indianapolis, IN 46253-5002
(317) 244-3660
Fax: (317) 244-3660
E-mail: fmcbishops@fmcna.org
www.fmcna.org

The Free Methodist Church of North America
is a holiness denomination with its World
Ministries Center located in Indianapolis,
Indiana.

Great Commission Churches
PO Box 29154
Columbus, OH 43229-0153
(740) 964-1002
Fax: (740) 964-1002
E-mail: info@gccweb.org
www.gccweb.org

Great Commission Churches is a fellowship of
churches and ministries devoted to Jesus Christ
and fulfilling the Great Commission. Presently,
there are over 180 churches and ministries as a
part of this association.

International Church of the Foursquare
Gospel
PO Box 26902
Los Angeles, CA 90026-0176
(213) 989-4234
Fax: (213) 989-4234
E-mail: comm@foursquare.org
www.foursquare.org

The vision of the International Church of the
Foursquare Gospel (ICFG) is to present Jesus
Christ, God's Son, to every person in every culture
and nation as the Savior; The Baptizer with the
Holy Christ, The Healer, the Soon-Coming King.

Midwest Baptist Conference
924 Busse Hwy
Park Ridge, IL 60068-2304
(847) 692-4125
Fax: (847) 692-4125
E-mail: mbc@midwestbap.org
www.midwestbap.org

The ministry of the Midwest Baptist Conference
is to serve as a catalyst for leadership in church
mobilization and church planting through
a variety of offerings made available to the
churches, pastors, seniors, and church planters.

Northwest Ministry Network, The
35131 SE Douglas St Ste 200
Snoqualmie, WA 98065-9233
(425) 888-4800
Fax: (425) 888-4800
E-mail: info@northwestministry.com
www.northwestministry.com

The Northwest Ministry Network exists to fulfill
the Great Commission by partnering with
and empowering church leaders to develop
healthy, growing Christians and churches; to
strengthen and network ministry teams.

Presbyterian Layman
PO Box 2210
Lenoir, NC 28645-2210
(828) 758-8716
Fax: (828) 758-8716
E-mail: laymanletters@layman.org
www.layman.org

The most important thrust of the Lay
Committee is its publication, the "Presbyterian
Layman," first published in 1968. With current
circulation of over 450,000, it is one of the
largest Protestant publications in the USA.

Salvation Army, The
PO Box 269
Alexandria, VA 22313-0269
(703) 684-5500
Fax: (703) 684-5500
E-mail: information@USN.salvationarmy.org
www.salvationarmyusa.org

The Salvation Army is an integral part of the
Christian Church, although distinctive in
government and practice. The Army's doctrines
follow the mainstream of Christian belief and its
articles of faith emphasize God's saving purposes.

Conflict Resolution

Advocates International
8001 Braddock Rd Ste 300
Springfield, VA 22151-2110
(703) 894-1084
Fax: (703) 894-1084
E-mail: info@advocatesinternational.org
www.advocatesinternational.org

Advocates International and its regional
networks are guided in their mission by Christ's
Good Samaritan parable. Working relationally,
professionally, and spiritually, they seek to
enable those committed to religious liberty and
human rights.

Peacemaker Ministries
PO Box 81130
Billings, MT 59108-1130
(406) 256-1583
Fax: (406) 256-1583
E-mail: mail@peacemaker.net
www.Peacemaker.net

The mission of Peacemaker Ministries is to
equip and assist Christians and their churches
to respond to conflict Biblically. We provide

conflict counseling, mediation, and arbitration
services to resolve church, ministry, and
business disputes.

Counseling

Barnabas International
PO Box 11211
Rockford, IL 61126-1211
(815) 395-1335
Fax: (815) 395-1335
E-mail: barnabas@barnabas.org
www.barnabas.org

The mission of Barnabas International is to
edify, enrich, encourage, and strengthen
servants in ministry. We creatively seek ways
to fulfill our charter through personal, small
group, and conference ministries.

Christian Counseling Center
1870 Leonard St NE
Grand Rapids, MI 49505-5650
(616) 956-1122
Fax: (616) 956-1122
E-mail: hope@cccwmich.org
www.cccwmich.org

The Christian Counseling Center has provided
professional Christian counseling in the West
Michigan area since 1941. Our mission is to
"provide affordable counseling, consultation
and educational services through professionals
committed to Christ."

Christian Financial Concepts
PO Box 100
Gainesville, GA 30503-0100
(770) 534-1000
Fax: (770) 534-1000
E-mail: questions@crown.org
www.crown.org

Please review the ministry description of the
parent organization for further details.

Crown Ministries
PO Box 100
Gainesville, GA 30503-0100
(770) 534-1000
Fax: (770) 534-1000
E-mail: questions@crown.org
www.crown.org

Please review the ministry description of the
parent organization for further details.

FamilyLife
5800 Ranch Drive
Little Rock, AR 72223
(501) 223-8663
Fax: (501) 223-8663
www.familylife.com

FamilyLife seeks to build strong families by
bringing Biblical principles to individuals and
couples, which they can apply in their lives and
pass on to the next generation.

Narramore Christian Foundation
PO Box 661900
Arcadia, CA 91066-1900
(626) 821-8400
Fax: (626) 821-8400
E-mail: ncf@ncfliving.org
www.ncfliving.org

The Narramore Christian Foundation (NCF)
is devoted to preventing and solving human
problems through a Christ-centered, Bible-
based training and counseling ministry.

United Marriage Encounter
PO Box 209
Muscatine, IA 52761-0069
(563) 264-8889
Fax: (563) 264-8889
E-mail: info@unitedmarriage.org
www.unitedmarriage.org

United Marriage Encounter is a non-
denominational Christian ministry to married
couples. We seek to help couples around the
world renew their marriages and build Christ-
centered homes.

Film Ministry

City on a Hill Productions
PO Box 436034
Louisville, KY 40253-6034
(502) 245-2425
Fax: (502) 245-2425
E-mail: contactus@cityonahillproductions.com
www.cityonahillproductions.com

City on a Hill exists to share the message
of the gospel, support the work of local
churches, challenge cultural perceptions of
Christianity, and bring the truth and character
of Christ to life through the art and craft of
filmmaking.

Deaf Video Communications of America
25W560 Geneva Rd Ste 10
Carol Stream, IL 60188-2231
(630) 221-0909
Fax: (630) 221-0909
E-mail: ruby@deafvideo.com
www.deafvideo.com

Deaf Video Communications (DVC) has
a video production studio dedicated to
working with pastors and missionaries for the
preparation and production of materials in
sign language and open caption for the deaf.

Gospel Communications International
PO Box 455
Muskegon, MI 49443-0455
(231) 773-3361
Fax: (231) 773-3361
E-mail: gci@gospelcommunications.org
www.gospelcommunications.org

Gospel Communications International exists
to proclaim the Gospel of Jesus Christ and
empower the body of Christ for ministry,
worldwide, through the effective use of media
resources and communication technologies.

JESUS Film Project, The
100 Lake Hart Dr
Orlando, FL 32832-0100
(407) 826-2300
Fax: (407) 826-2300
E-mail: info@jesusfilm.org
www.jesusfilm.org

The goal of The JESUS Film Project is to
reach every nation, tribe, people, and tongue
with the message of Jesus. Film teams travel
to remote places worldwide and hold public
viewings.

Marriage Today
8101 Royal Ridge Pkwy
Irving, TX 75063-2820
(972) 953-0500
Fax: (972) 953-0500
E-mail: ecfa@marriagetoday.org
www.marriagetoday.org

Marriage Today is a Texas nonprofit
corporation established in April 1994, to
produce, air, and distribute religious and
educational seminars, books, audiotapes,
videotapes, radio, and television programs.

Mars Hill Productions
4711 Lexington Blvd
Missouri City, TX 77459-2826
(281) 403-1463
Fax: (281) 403-1463
E-mail: doug@mars-hill.org
www.mars-hill.org

Mars Hill is a nonprofit ministry using media to draw people to Jesus Christ. Thousands of people view an award-winning Mars Hill film every week in schools, churches, camps, prisons, hospitals, and homes.

Strategic Resource Group
PO Box 1809
Easton, MD 21601-8936
(410) 820-6962
Fax: (410) 820-6962
E-mail: ronensminger@srginc.org
www.srginc.org

Strategic Resource Group (SRG) is a professional services firm specializing in international philathropic services for Christian donors who are seeking to improve both the stewardship and return of their Kindom investments.

Handicapped Ministries

CCFH Independent Living Program
PO Box 9869
Knoxville, TN 37940-0869
(865) 546-5921
Fax: (865) 546-5921
E-mail: RCC@ccfh.org
www.ccfh.org

The Independent Living Program is a supported living arrangement in the community with a Christ-centered approach to residential care for adults with a variety of developmental disabilities.

Free Wheelchair Mission
9341 Irvine Blvd
Irvine, CA 92618-1669
(949) 273-8470
Fax: (949) 273-8470
E-mail: involve@freewheelchairmission.org
www.freewheelchairmission.org

Free Wheelchair Mission (FWM) is a Christian based nonprofit organization that provides wheelchairs for the physically disabled poor in developing countries.

Inspiration Ministries
PO Box 948
Walworth, WI 53184-0948
(262) 275-6131
Fax: (262) 275-6131
E-mail: im@inspirationministries.org
www.inspirationministries.org

The mission of Inspiration Ministries is to encourage people with disabilities with the hope and joy found in Jesus by helping them meet their basic needs and realize their full potential in Christ.

Jewish Ministries

Ariel Ministries
PO Box 792507
San Antonio, TX 78279-2507
(210) 344-7707
Fax: (210) 344-7707
E-mail: homeoffice@ariel.org
www.ariel.org

Ariel Ministries exists to evangelize Jewish people and to disciple both Jewish and Gentile believers from a Jewish frame of reference.

Chosen People Ministries
241 E 51st St
New York, NY 10022-6502
(212) 223-2252
Fax: (212) 223-2252
E-mail: cpm@chosenpeople.com
www.chosenpeople.com

The purpose of Chosen People Ministries is to serve the Messiah in fulfilling the Great Commission with specific emphasis on the Jewish people.

Jewish Believers in Jesus
PO Box 79344
Charlotte, NC 28271-7063
(678) 528-5887
Fax: (678) 528-5887
E-mail: questions@jbij.com
www.jbij.org

The ministry of Jewish Believers in Jesus is fourfold. One, is to share with the Jewish community and also Gentiles that Jesus is our Jewish Messiah and the Messiah of the world.

Jews for Jesus
60 Haight St
San Francisco, CA 94102-5802
(415) 864-2600
Fax: (415) 864-2600
E-mail: jfj@jewsforjesus.org
www.jewsforjesus.org

Jews for Jesus is an outreach by Jewish Christian evangelists. Our methods vary from conventional missionary work like personal visitation and tract distribution to large display media ads proclaiming Christ in secular newspapers and magazines.

Messianic Vision
PO Box 1918
Brunswick, GA 31521-1500
(912) 265-2500
Fax: (912) 265-2500
E-mail: info@sidroth.org
www.sidroth.org

Messianic Vision is dedicated to reaching Jewish people with the Gospel. We broadcast on radio and television stations and distribute witnessing materials. Sid Roth, the President, also conducts evangelistic meetings.
Leadership Ministries

Leadership Ministries

Arrow Leadership International Ministries
PO Box 1243
Blaine, WA 98231
(877) 262-7769
Fax: (877) 262-7769
E-mail: info@arrowleadership.org
www.arrowleadership.org

Arrow Leadership International Ministries was founded to develop emerging young leaders across North America and around the world.

Christian Leadership Concepts
PO Box 3645
Brentwood, TN 37024-3645
(615) 370-5020
Fax: (615) 370-5020
E-mail: info@clchq.org
www.christianleadershipconcepts.org

The ministry of CLC is to equip Christian men to use their leadership abilities (under God's power) with Biblical principles to minister in their homes, businesses, churches and communities.

Leadership Network
2626 Cole Ave Ste 900
Dallas, TX 75204-1078
(214) 969-5950
Fax: (214) 969-5950
E-mail: customer.services@leadnet.org
www.leadnet.org

The Leadership Network is an evangelical ministry seeking to train church and parachurch leaders to better serve the Christian community.

Man in the Mirror
180 Wilshire Blvd
Casselberry, FL 32707-5352
(407) 472-2112
Fax: (407) 472-2112
E-mail: partners@maninthemirror.org
www.maninthemirror.org

Man in the Mirror exists to help leaders disciple men. Our vision is to help reach every man in America with a credible offer of Christ and the resources to grow.

Student Ministries
300 W Davis St Ste 530
Conroe, TX 77301-2573
(936) 756-2790
Fax: (936) 756-2790
E-mail: info@studentministriesinc.org
www.studentministriesinc.org

SMI seeks to empower ministers-in-training to gain practical experience while in seminary by contracting with them to perform ministry projects in their cultural setting.

Summit Ministries
PO Box 207
Manitou Springs, CO 80829-0207
(719) 685-9103
Fax: (719) 685-9103
E-mail: info@summit.org
www.summit.org

Summit Ministries is a nondenominational evangelical Christian training ministry for young adults. Our focus is primarily educational and is in the area of helping high school and college age students develop as Christians worldwide.

Wagner Leadership Institute
11005 State Highway 83
Colorado Springs, CO 80921-3602
(800) 683-9630
Fax: (800) 683-9630
E-mail: WLI@wagnerleadership.org

Wagner Leadership Institute trains and equips men and women for leadership positions in local churches and in trans-local ministries. Its goal is to equip leaders in the necessary skills for effective ministry.

YouthCompass International
4701 SW Admiral Way # 148
Seattle, WA 98116-2340
(206) 937-7070
Fax: (206) 937-7070
E-mail: info@youthcompass.org
www.youthcompass.org

YouthCompass International seeks to address the unique needs of mobile international high school and middle school students by providing caring adult role models who assist them in navigating life.

Legal Services

Alliance Defense Fund
15100 N 90th St
Scottsdale, AZ 85260-2901
(480) 444-0020
Fax: (480) 444-0020
E-mail: info@telladf.org
www.telladf.org

The Alliance Defense Fund is a legal alliance defending the right to hear and speak the Truth through Strategy, Training, Funding, and Litigation.

Christian Legal Society
8001 Braddock Rd Ste 300
Springfield, VA 22151-2110
(703) 642-1070
Fax: (703) 642-1070
E-mail: clshq@clsnet.org
www.clsnet.org

CLS is a national nondenominational Christian membership association of more than 4000 lawyers, judges, law professors, law students, and lay persons, located in all 50 states, who have signed CLS Statement of Faith.

International Justice Mission
PO Box 58147
Washington, DC 20037-8147
(703) 465-5495
Fax: (703) 465-5495
E-mail: contact@ijm.org
www.ijm.org

International Justice Mission is a human rights agency that secures justice for victims of slavery, sexual exploitation, and other forms of violent oppression.

Northern Churches Care
4210 Austin Bluffs Pkwy
Colorado Springs, CO 80918-2930
(719) 277-7470
Fax: (719) 277-7470
E-mail: jwilson@northernchurchescare.org
www.northernchurchescare.org

Northern Churches Care (NCC) is a collaboration of local churches that have come together to help provide emergency support for food, medical, and financial services such as rent, utilities, gas vouchers, bus tokens, and more to the needy.

Marriage and Family Ministries

American Family Living
PO Box 3400
Orange, CA 92857-0400
(714) 637-7900
Fax: (714) 637-7900
E-mail: afl1@pacbell.net
www.americanfamilyliving.org

American Family Living is a non-profit 501(c)3 organization that has a mission to "Renew and strengthen the foundation of the family through Judeo Christian values with tools to heal, grow and mature in love."

Focus on the Family
8605 Explorer Dr
Colorado Springs, CO 80920-1049
(719) 531-3400
Fax: (719) 531-3400
www.family.org

Focus on the Family is a nonprofit organization whose primary reason for existence is to spread the Gospel of Jesus Christ. We accomplish this objective by helping to preserve traditional values and the institution of the family.

Medical Ministries

American Leprosy Missions
1 Alm Way
Greenville, SC 29601-3060
(864) 271-7040
Fax: (864) 271-7040
E-mail: Amlep@leprosy.org
www.leprosy.org

To serve as a channel of the love of Christ to
persons with Hansens disease (leprosy) and to
those with disabilities, helping them to be healed
in body and spirit and to be restored to lives of
dignity and usefulness within their communities.

Center for Biblical Bioethics (CBB)
PO Box 3158
Grand Rapids, MI 49501-3158
(616) 257-6800
Fax: (616) 257-6800
E-mail: b4life@bfl.org
www.bfl.org

Please review the ministry description of the
parent organization for further details.

Christian Blind Mission International
450 E Park Ave
Greenville, SC 29601-2258
(864) 239-0065
Fax: (864) 239-0065
E-mail: info@cbmiusa.org
www.cbmiusa.org

Christian Blind Mission International is an
interdenominational, worldwide fellowship
of committed Christians dedicated to serving
the blind and handicapped in the developing
world, irrespective of nationality, race, sex, or
religion.

Global Health Outreach
PO Box 7500
Bristol, TN 37621-7500
(423) 844-1000
Fax: (423) 844-1000
E-mail: main@cmdahome.org
www.cmdahome.org

Global Health Outreach (GHO), an
international mission arm of the Christian
Medical and Dental Associations, with a
heart for evangelism, becomes a conduit for
the Gospel message by sharing the love and
compassion of Christ with those who are poor.

World Emergency Relief
PO Box 131570
Carlsbad, CA 92013-1570
(760) 930-8001
Fax: (760) 930-8001
E-mail: info@wer-us.org
www.worldemergencyrelief.org

World Emergency Relief delivers food,
medical, economic, and spiritual aid to meet
emotional, spiritual, economic, and physical
needs of orphans, refugees, disaster victims,
and developing countries and local church
support.

Men's Ministries

Bible Teaching Resources
PO Box 6611
Tyler, TX 75711-6611
(903) 939-1201
Fax: (903) 939-1201
E-mail: don@bibleteachingresources.org
www.bibleteachingresources.org

The mission of Bible Teaching Resources is
to glorify God through a teaching ministry
of national scale providing excellence in the
communication of Scripture in both sacred
and secular environments.

Gathering/USA, The
1220 E Concord St
Orlando, FL 32803-5453
(407) 422-9200
Fax: (407) 422-9200
E-mail: info@thegathering.org
www.thegathering.org

The Gathering/USA (also known as The
Gathering of Men) is a church-based
ministry of evangelism, discipleship, and
missions opportunities for men. The
mission is accomplished through city-wide
Outreach breakfasts using nationally known
communicators.

Ministry to Men Foundation
5712 Stage Rd
Memphis, TN 38134-4516
(901) 385-7740
Fax: (901) 385-7740
E-mail: ministrytomen@juno.com
www.ministrytomen.org

Ministry to Men is a nonprofit, interdenominational foundation with a commitment to the fundamental teaching of the Bible.

Promise Keepers
PO Box 11338
Denver, CO 80211-0338
(303) 964-7600
Fax: (303) 964-7600
E-mail: finance@pknet.org
www.promisekeepers.org

Promise Keepers is an exclusively religious nonprofit organization whose purpose is to ignite and unite men to be passionate followers of Jesus Christ through the effective communication of the Seven Promises of a Promise Keeper.

Military Outreach Ministries

Association for Christian Conferences, Teaching and Service
PO Box 27239
Denver, CO 80227-0239
(303) 985-8808
Fax: (303) 985-8808
E-mail: accts@accts.org
www.accts.org

The purpose of Association for Christian Conferences, Teaching and Service is to provide assistance to military Christians of all ranks worldwide.

Cadence International
PO Box 1268
Englewood, CO 80150-1268
(303) 762-1400
Fax: (303) 762-1400
E-mail: info@cadence.org
www.cadence.org

Cadence International is an evangelical, nondenominational ministry to the U.S. military community around the world.

Christian Military Fellowship
PO Box 1207
Englewood, CO 80150-1207
(303) 761-1959
Fax: (303) 761-1959
E-mail: admin@cmfhq.org
www.cmfhq.org

The Christian Military Fellowship (CMF) is a non-denominational fellowship of believers committed to Jesus Christ and to carrying out the Great Commission (Matthew 28:18-20) within the military society.

Military Community Youth Ministries
540 N Cascade Ave
Colorado Springs, CO 80903-3328
(719) 381-1831
Fax: (719) 381-1831
E-mail: mcym@mcym.org
www.mcym.org

MCYM is a cooperative venture combining the vision and skills of three U.S.-based Christian youth organizations: Youth for Christ, Young Life, and the National Federation Catholic Youth Ministry.

Officers Christian Fellowship of the U.S.A.
3784 S Inca St
Englewood, CO 80110-3405
(800) 424-1984
Fax: (800) 424-1984
E-mail: ocfdenver@ocfusa.org
www.ocfusa.org

The OCF is an organization of Christian military officers and former officers that provides a ministry to the military society at bases around the world, and to cadets and midshipmen at the service academies and ROTC schools.

Pregnancy

Care Net
44180 Riverside Pkwy Ste 200
Leesburg, VA 20176-8421
(703) 478-5661
Fax: (703) 478-5661
E-mail: info@care-net.org
www.care-net.org

Care Net is a Christian ministry assisting and promoting the evangelistic, pro-life work of pregnancy centers in North America.

International Christian Adoptions
41745 Rider Way # 2
Temecula, CA 92590-4826
(951) 695-3336
Fax: (951) 695-3336
E-mail: info@4achild.com
www.4achild.com

International Christian Adoptions believes in the sanctity of life in that all children born and unborn are valued and uniquely made. Our overriding mission is to offer children hope in the love and compassion of Jesus Christ. Hope for basic needs.

Life Choices
5575 Raleigh Lagrange Rd
Memphis, TN 38134-5724
(901) 388-1172
Fax: (901) 388-1172
E-mail: lchoices@bellsouth.net
www.lifechoicesmemphis.org

The ministry of Life Choices is a unique program designed to reach women and girls experiencing a crisis pregnancy with acts of mercy, compassion, and practical assistance.

New Life Family Services
1515 E 66th St
Minneapolis, MN 55423-2648
(612) 866-7643
Fax: (612) 866-7643
E-mail: info@nlfs.org
www.nlfs.org

NLFS is a Christian Social Service Agency dedicated to providing an atmosphere of support, hope, and compassion to those dealing with an unplanned pregnancy or other related issues.

Prison Ministry

Prison Fellowship Ministries
44180 Riverside Pkwy
Lansdowne, VA 20176-8421
(703) 478-0100
Fax: (703) 478-0100
E-mail: correspondence@pfm.org
www.prisonfellowship.org

Prison Fellowship Ministries is a non-profit organization founded by former Presidential Aide Charles W. Colson in 1976 to exhort and assist the Church in its ministry to prisoners, ex-prisoners, crime victims, and their families.

Public Policy

American Family Association
PO Box 2440
Tupelo, MS 38803-2440
(662) 844-5036
Fax: (662) 844-5036
E-mail: comments@afa.net
www.afa.net

American Family Association is a Christian organization promoting the Biblical ethic of decency as it relates to the family.

Concerned Women for America
1015 15th St NW Ste 1100
Washington, DC 20005-2619
(202) 488-7000
Fax: (202) 488-7000
E-mail: mail@cwfa.org
www.cwfa.org

The ministry of CWA is to educate our grass-roots constituents and Congress. This is done by training families on issues affecting them through the ministry of "Concerned Women Today," a daily radio program.

Family Research Council
801 G St NW
Washington, DC 20001-3729
(202) 393-2100
Fax: (202) 393-2100
www.frc.org

Family Research Council provides educational materials to the general public concerning Judeo-Christian family values, as well as news of legislation and judicial developments affecting family life and values.

Radio Ministries

Air 1 Radio Network
5700 West Oaks Blvd
Rocklin, CA 95765-3719
(916) 251-1600
Fax: (916) 251-1600
E-mail: datkinson@emfbroadcasting.com
www.air1.com

Please review the ministry description of the parent organization for further details.

Art of Family Living, The
PO Box 610350
Dallas, TX 75261-0350
(972) 745-7987
Fax: (972) 745-7987
E-mail: info@johnonline.org
www.johnonline.org

The Art of Family Living exists to present the light of the gospel to a dark world while also challenging believers to a greater commitment to Christ through the daily application of biblical truth.

Back to God Ministries International
6555 W College Dr
Palos Heights, IL 60463-1770
(708) 371-8700
Fax: (708) 371-8700
E-mail: info@btgh.org
www.btgh.org

The Back to God Ministries International is the radio and television ministry of the Christian Reformed Church. It produces radio programs in nine major world languages and television in four languages.

Back to the Bible
PO Box 82808
Lincoln, NE 68501-2808
(402) 464-7200
Fax: (402) 464-7200
E-mail: info@backtothebible.org
www.backtothebible.org

Back to the Bible is a worldwide service ministry whose purpose is to lead believers into spiritual maturity and active service for Christ in the local church and the world.

Coral Ridge Ministries Media
2831 W Cypress Creek Rd
Ft. Lauderdale, FL 33309
(954) 772-0404
Fax: (954) 772-0404
E-mail: letters@coralridge.org
www.coralridge.org

Started in 1974, Coral Ridge Ministries (CRM) is a television, radio, internet, and print outreach that touches the lives of millions, nationwide and overseas.

Cornerstone Broadcasting Corporation
4295 S Ridgewood Ave
Port Orange, FL 32127-4512
(386) 756-9000
Fax: (386) 756-9000
E-mail: wjlu@wjlu.org
www.wjlu.org

It is the goal of the Cornerstone Broadcasting Corporation to provide quality teaching programs and inspirational music to reach the lost, disciple the saved, and to strengthen, nurture, and unify the body of Christ.

Family Life Broadcasting System
PO Box 35300
Tucson, AZ 85740-5300
(520) 742-6976
Fax: (520) 742-6976
E-mail: correspondence@flc.org
www.flc.org

The total ministry of Family Life Broadcasting System is committed to reaching God's people.

Family Life Ministries
PO Box 506
Bath, NY 14810-0506
(607) 776-4151
Fax: (607) 776-4151
E-mail: mail@fln.org
www.fln.org

We provide activites and services for local churches to utilize, such as youth programs (sports, music, discipleship).

Focus on the Family
8605 Explorer Dr
Colorado Springs, CO 80920-1049
(719) 531-3400
Fax: (719) 531-3400
www.family.org

Focus on the Family is a nonprofit organization whose primary reason for existence is to spread the Gospel of Jesus Christ. We accomplish this objective by helping to preserve traditional values and the institution of the family.

K-LOVE Radio Network
5700 West Oaks Blvd
Rocklin, CA 95765-3719
(916) 251-1600
Fax: (916) 251-1600
E-mail: datkinson@emfbroadcasting.com
www.klove.com

Please review the ministry description of the parent organization for further details.

Trans World Radio
PO Box 8700
Cary, NC 27512-8700
(919) 460-3700
Fax: (919) 460-3700
E-mail: info@twr.org
www.twr.org

TWR is the world's most far-reaching Christian radio network. Programs in over 225 languages and dialects are aired from more than 2,000 outlets around the world, including 14 international broadcasting locations.

Words of Hope
PO Box 1706
Grand Rapids, MI 49501-1706
(616) 459-6181
Fax: (616) 459-6181
E-mail: woh@woh.org
www.woh.org

To proclaim Jesus Christ by radio and literature in the language of the world's peoples, seeking with our partners in ministry to win the uncommitted everywhere to faith in Christ, building up His Church to the glory of God.

Relief and Development

Blood:Water Mission
PO Box 60381
Nashville, TN 37206-0381
(615) 550-4296
Fax: (615) 550-4296
E-mail: bloodwater@bloodwatermission.com
www.bloodwatermission.com

Blood:Water Mission is a nonprofit organization whose mission is "to tangibly reduce the impact of the HIV/AIDS pandemic, to promote clean blood and clean water in Africa, and to build equitable, sustainable, and personal community links."

Food for the Hungry
1224 E Washington St
Phoenix, AZ 85034-1102
(480) 998-3100
Fax: (480) 998-3100
E-mail: hunger@fh.org
www.fh.org

Founded in 1971, Food for the Hungry is an international relief and development organization that answers God's call to walk with churches, leaders, and families in overcoming all forms of human poverty, physical and spiritual.

International Aid
17011 W. Hickory St
Spring Lake, MI 49456-9712
(616) 846-7490
Fax: (616) 846-7490
E-mail: ia@internationalaid.org
www.internationalaid.org

International Aid responds to the Great Commission by providing and supporting solutions in healthcare worldwide. Committed to serving the Church so it can serve others, International Aid works with and through local indigenous churches.

Mercy Ships
PO Box 2020
Lindale, TX 75771-2020
(903) 939-7000
Fax: (903) 939-7000
E-mail: info@mercyships.org
www.mercyships.org

Mercy Ships, a global charity, has operated a growing fleet of hospital ships in developing nations since 1978. Following the example of Jesus, Mercy Ships brings hope and healing to the poor, mobilizing people and resources worldwide.

World Vision U.S.
PO Box 9716
Federal Way, WA 98063-9716
(253) 815-1000
Fax: (253) 815-1000
E-mail: info@worldvision.org
www.worldvision.org

World Vision is a Christian relief and development organization dedicated to helping children and their communities worldwide reach their full potential by tackling the causes of poverty.

Rescue Missions

Door of Faith, The
6701 SW 9th St
Des Moines, IA 50315-6166
(515) 974-0545
Fax: (515) 974-0545
E-mail: info@hopeiowa.org
www.hopeiowa.org

Since 1969, the Door of Faith Mission has applied a tough love approach to helping homeless men find healing and hope. The Door's recovery program emphasizes accountability, sobriety, employment, and seeking God's help with their lives.

Food Service Department
2010 NW 1st Ave
Miami, FL 33127-4902
(305) 571-2241
Fax: (305) 571-2241
E-mail: info@caringplace.org
www.miamirescuemission.com

This department receives, stores, and controls inventory and distribution of donated and purchased food items and supplies as needed to sustain the ministry centers.

Haven of Rest Ministries
PO Box 547
Akron, OH 44309-0547
(330) 535-1563
Fax: (330) 535-1563
E-mail: hrm@havenofrest.org
www.havenofrest.org

Haven of Rest Ministries was founded in Akron, Ohio, in 1942, as a Christian social service organization providing emergency and residential care to the disadvantaged people of the community at large.

Lighthouse Women & Children's Mission
PO Box 5545
Oxnard, CA 93030
(805) 487-1234
Fax: (805) 487-1234
E-mail: jeffb@erescuemission.com
www.erescuemission.com

The Lighthouse Women and Children's Mission was established in 1998 to provide emergency and long-term rehabilitation services to homeless women and women with children in Ventura County.

Open Door Mission
2828 N 23rd St E
Omaha, NE 68110-2726
(402) 422-1111
Fax: (402) 422-1111
E-mail: odm@opendoormission.org
www.opendoormission.org

Open Door Mission provides basic needs and life-changing programs for homeless and needy men, women and families in an atmosphere reflecting the life and teaching of our Lord Jesus Christ.

Sunshine Ministries
PO Box 66880
Saint Louis, MO 63166-6880
(314) 231-8209
Fax: (314) 231-8209
E-mail: sunshine@sunshineministries.org
www.sunshineministries.org

Sunshine Ministries is committed to providing high-quality Christian social services to the poor and needy of St. Louis by offering healing from the past, help for the present, and hope for the future.

Union Mission Ministries
PO Box 112
Charleston, WV 25321-0112
(304) 925-0366
Fax: (304) 925-0366
E-mail: admin@wefeedpeople.com
www.wefeedpeople.com

Since 1911, Union Mission Ministries has been a ready, active hand of help to the needy of West Virginia. Our mission is "helping hurting people in Jesus name," and as such, we unabashedly share the gospel of Jesus Christ.

Sports Ministries

Fellowship of Christian Athletes
8701 Leeds Rd
Kansas City, MO 64129-1626
(816) 921-0909
Fax: (816) 921-0909
E-mail: fca@fca.org
www.fca.org

The Fellowship of Christian Athletes is a national organization which seeks to strengthen the moral, mental, and spiritual fiber of young men and women through implementation of its stated purpose.

Motor Racing Outreach
5555 Concord Pkwy S Ste 405
Concord, NC 28027-4622
(704) 455-3828
Fax: (704) 455-3828
E-mail: contactus@go2mro.com
www.go2mro.com

The mission of MRO is to lead the racing community and fans to personal faith in Christ-likeness, and to active involvement in a local church, through relationships that provide care in times of stress, by sharing knowledge of God's Word.

Sports World Ministries
1919 S Post Rd
Indianapolis, IN 46239-9429
(317) 862-7040
Fax: (317) 862-7040
E-mail: info@sportsworld.org
www.sportsworld.org

Sports World Ministries is sending professional athletes to share personal life experiences with students, helping them to recognize the consequences of their choices while challenging them with the Message of Hope.

Uncharted Waters
2501 W Colorado Ave Ste 204
Colorado Springs, CO 80904-3063
(719) 447-0311
Fax: (719) 447-0311
www.unchartedwaters.org

Uncharted Waters is an equipping ministry that enhances the vision of the Church by providing sports ministry resources for the effective communication of the gospel.

Upward Unlimited
198 White Star Pt
Spartanburg, SC 29301-5209
(864) 949-5700
Fax: (864) 949-5700
www.upward.org

Upward Unlimited, the leader in children's sports evangelism, desires to move beyond denominational and cultural barriers by partnering with churches across the United States to promote salvation, character, and self-esteem to every participant.

Urban Impact Foundation
801 Union Ave 4th Fl
Pittsburgh, PA 15212-5523
(412) 321-3811
Fax: (412) 321-3811
E-mail: info@urbanimpactpittsburgh.org
www.playballforkids.org

Urban Impact Foundation is a people-oriented nonprofit community development corporation committed to rebuilding the fabric of Pittsburgh's north side one person, one family, one block at a time through value-based programs.

Student Ministries

Fellowship of Christians in Universities and Schools (FOCUS)
PO Box 5106
Charlottesville, VA 22905-5106
(434) 245-6110
Fax: (434) 245-6110
E-mail: homeoffice@infocus.org
www.infocus.org

FOCUS was founded in 1961 as a nondenominational organization of alumni, teachers, administrators, parents, and friends of independent secondary schools for the purpose of conveying the traditional Christian message to students.

Student Mobilization
PO Box 567
Conway, AR 72033-0567
(501) 329-7676
Fax: (501) 329-7676
E-mail: stumo@stumo.org
www.stumo.org

The purpose of Student Mobilization is "to join God in raising up lifelong laborers for Christ from the college campuses of the world."

University Bible Fellowship
6558 N Artesian Ave
Chicago, IL 60645-5328
(773) 338-1155
Fax: (773) 338-1155
www.chicago.ubf.org

University Bible Fellowship (UBF) is an international, evangelical student organization dedicated to the task of campus evangelism. Our main work is helping students to study the Bible and live according to its teachings.

YouthFront
4715 Rainbow Blvd
Mission, KS 66205-1832
(913) 262-3900
Fax: (913) 262-3900
E-mail: lrunyan@youthfront.com
www.YouthFront.com

YouthFront, a Youth Ministry with a full-time staff of more than 40 employees. YouthFront works to bring youth into a growing relationship with Jesus Christ by creating environments where spiritual transformation occurs.

Television Ministries

ChangedLives.org
PO Box 100
Chattanooga, TN 37401-0100
(423) 875-0911
Fax: (423) 875-0911
E-mail: ben@changedlives.org
www.changedlives.org

For 33 years, ChangedLives.org produced a weekly, worldwide TV and radio program under the name of Changed Lives. It provided reprints of all messages, distributed Bibles and Christian books to listeners, and distributed video and audio cassettes.

Christian International Ministries Network
PO Box 9000
Santa Rosa Beach, FL 32459-9000
(850) 231-2600
Fax: (850) 231-2600
E-mail: cimn@cimn.net
www.christianinternational.org

Christian International Ministries Network provides ministers and training materials to help establish dynamic growing local churches building on the foundational ministries of the apostles and prophets.

Cornerstone TeleVision
1 Signal Hill Dr
Wall, PA 15148-1499
(412) 824-3930
Fax: (412) 824-3930
www.ctvn.org

Cornerstone TeleVision is called by God to serve and excel as a media ministry to bring glory to His name. In obedience to the Great Commission of Jesus Christ, this ministry seeks to provide entertaining means to evangelize and edify.

Encouraging Word, The
PO Box 2110
Spartanburg, SC 29304-2110
(864) 699-1762
Fax: (864) 699-1762
E-mail: info@tewonline.org
www.theencouragingword.org

The mission of the organization is to teach and preach the gospel of Jesus Christ by means of television, radio, and other media in such a way that people will come to know Jesus as their Lord and Savior.

Guidelines
PO Box G
Laguna Hills, CA 92654-8888
(949) 582-5001
Fax: (949) 582-5001
E-mail: guidelines@guidelines.org
www.guidelines.org

Guidelines is an international Christian ministry reaching into 100+ countries of the world. radio (broadcasting in 17 languages over 600+ stations), television and video production.

In Touch Ministries
3836 Dekalb Technology Pkwy
Atlanta, GA 30340-3604
(770) 451-1001
Fax: (770) 451-1001
www.intouch.org

In Touch Ministries is a broadcast ministry which primarily uses television and radio to present the teaching ministry of Dr. Charles F. Stanley. The broadcast ministry is supported by a discipling follow-up program which uses audio and video tape.

Jewish Voice Ministries International
PO Box 30990
Phoenix, AZ 85046-0990
(602) 971-8501
Fax: (602) 971-8501
E-mail: mail@jewishvoice.org
www.jewishvoice.org

Jewish Voice Ministries International is a worldwide outreach that shares the Good News of Yeshua, and encourages the Church to love, pray for, and reach out to the Jewish people.

Love Worth Finding Ministries
PO Box 38300
Germantown, TN 38183-0300
(901) 382-7900
Fax: (901) 382-7900
E-mail: minrel@lwf.org
www.lwf.org

Love Worth Finding Ministries is the radio and television ministry of Adrian Rogers, selling audio and video tapes of sermons.

Right From the Heart Ministries
1507 Johnson Ferry Rd Ste 100
Marietta, GA 30062-6438
(678) 388-1860
Fax: (678) 388-1860
E-mail: info@rfth.org
www.rfth.org

Right From The Heart Ministries of suburban Atlanta, Georgia, is a nonprofit corporation formed for the express purpose of reaching and discipling people for Jesus Christ through the use of media. Reaching is done through 60- second spots.

Studio 38
2880 Vision Ct
Aurora, IL 60506-8886
(312) 433-3838
Fax: (312) 433-3838
E-mail: administrator@TLN.com
www.TLN.com

Please review the ministry description of the parent organization for further details.

Teen Mania Ministries
PO Box 2000
Lindale, TX 75771-2000
(903) 324-8000
Fax: (903) 324-8000
E-mail: info@teenmania.org
www.teenmania.org

Teen Mania Ministrie's goal is to initiate, facilitate, and sustain a massive movement of young people from all over the world for strategic short and long-term mission endeavors.

Total Living International (TLN)
2880 Vision Ct
Aurora, IL 60506-8886
(630) 801-3838
Fax: (630) 801-3838
www.TLN.com

Total Living International (TLI) and combined affiliates provide Christian faith-based television programs through our broadcast and cable network, Christian faith-based DVDs, CDs, books, and instructional guides through our network.

Turning Point for God
10007 Riverford Rd
Lakeside, CA 92040-2772
(619) 258-3600
Fax: (619) 258-3600
E-mail: info@turningpointradio.org
www.TurningPointonline.org

Turning Point is dedicated to spreading the Gospel of Jesus Christ throughout the world to the greatest number of people by using the means of broadcasting.

Women's Ministries

Entrust
PO Box 25520
Colorado Springs, CO 80936-5520
(719) 622-1980
Fax: (719) 622-1980
E-mail: info@entrust4.org
www.entrust4.org

Entrust assists the church in responding to the global cry for servant leaders through accessible, transformational, and biblical training.

Good News
PO Box 150
Wilmore, KY 40390-0150
(859) 858-4661
Fax: (859) 858-4661
E-mail: info@goodnewsmag.org
www.goodnewsmag.org

Good News (formerly known as The Forum for Scriptural Christianity) is an evangelical organization committed to renewal within the United Methodist Church. We are a not-for-profit organization.

Women's Pregnancy Centers
Life Resource Center
2504 N Alvernon Way
Tucson, AZ 85712-2402
(520) 325-6041
Fax: (520) 325-6041
www.cpctucson.com

The Crisis Pregnancy Centers of Tucson is a Christian ministry, embodied by volunteers, which provides unconditional acceptance and assistance to women facing crisis pregnancies.

Proverbs 31 Ministries
616G Matthews Mint Hill Rd
Matthews, NC 28105-1760
(704) 849-2270
Fax: (704) 849-2270
E-mail: office@proverbs31.org
www.proverbs31.org

Dedicated to glorifying God by "Bringing God's Peace, Perspective, and Purpose to Today's Busy Woman," Proverbs 31 Ministries sheds light on God's distinctive design for women and the great responsibilities we have been given.

Pure Heart Ministries
PO Box 1024
Saint Peters, MO 63376-0018
(636) 679-6815
Fax: (636) 679-6815
E-mail: info@pureheartministries.org
www.pureheartministries.org

Sexual redemption ministry serving the Saint Louis bi-state region (most of Missouri and Southern Illinois). We provide Christian counseling and confidential pastoral care, various support groups for individuals and their affected family members.

Reconciliation Outreach Ministries
4311 Bryan St
Dallas, TX 75204-6738
(214) 545-6500
Fax: (214) 545-6500
E-mail: info@reconciliationoutreach.org
www.rodallas.org

Our vision is to establish and maintain a strong Christian community within the inner city. To provide a safe, loving environment for healing lives and restoring families and individuals to a productive lifestyle.

Setting Captives Free
PO Box 1527
Medina, OH 44258-1527
(330) 620-8448
Fax: (330) 620-8448
E-mail: webservant@settingcaptivesfree.com
www.settingcaptivesfree.com

Setting Captives Free exists to offer Christ-centered hope and freedom to those in the grip of sin through accountability to Bible-based truth resulting in the true enjoyment of life in and for the glory of God.

Women's Ministries International
PO Box 535002
Indianapolis, IN 46253-5002
(317) 244-3660
Fax: (317) 244-3660
E-mail: wmi@fmcna.org
wmi@fmcna.org

Women's ministry and outreach of denominations worldwide.

Youth Ministries

Acquire the Fire
PO Box 2000
Lindale, TX 75771-2000
(800) 329-3473
Fax: (800) 329-3473
E-mail: info@teenmania.org
www.acquirethefire.com

The Acquire the Fire department is responsible for the logistics and production of the ATF National Youth Convention tour.

Kids Around the World
2424 Charles St
Rockford, IL 61108-1602
(815) 229-8731
Fax: (815) 229-8731
E-mail: info@kidsaroundtheworld.com
www.kidsaroundtheworld.com

We travel to foreign countries to help rebuild hope within communities where natural disaster, war, or poverty has devastated homes and families.

Kids for the Kingdom
PO Box 85
Graton, CA 95444-0085
(707) 829-5504
Fax: (707) 829-5504
E-mail: kidsforthekingdom@earthlink.net
www.kidsforthekingdom.org

Kids for the Kingdom is organized to provide
support for Christian missionaries, nationals,
and organizations meeting the physical and
spiritual needs of children and people around
the world, especially third-world countries.

Kids Hope USA
100 Pine St Ste 280
Zeeland, MI 49464-2607
(616) 546-3580
Fax: (616) 546-3580
E-mail: info@kidshopeusa.org
www.kidshopeusa.org

Kids Hope USA (KHUSA) is a church-based
mentoring model that equips a church to build
a caring relationship with its neighborhood
public elementary school by providing faithful
mentors.

Kids With a Promise
132 Madison Ave
New York, NY 10016-7004
(212) 684-2800
Fax: (212) 684-2800
E-mail: tbrennan@chaonline.org
www.kidswithapromise.org

The Mont Lawn Summer Camp program
has operated continuously since 1894 to
allow inner city children a "mountain-top
experience." About 90 counselors provide
activities to help a child's physical, social,
spiritual, and intellectual growth.

Midwest Challenge
PO Box 7067
Minneapolis, MN 55407-0067
(612) 825-6871
Fax: (612) 825-6871
E-mail: mchallenge@qwest.net
www.midwestchallenge.org

Midwest Challenge is a Christ-centered
ministry which exists to help train, mentor,
and equip people to apply Biblical principles
in such a way as to overcome life-dominating
problems, particularly substance abuse and
other problematic lifestyles.

National Network of Youth Ministries, The
12335 World Trade Dr Ste 16
San Diego, CA 92128-3791
(858) 451-1111
Fax: (858) 451-1111
E-mail: info@nnym.org
www.youthworkers.net

The National Network of Youth Ministries is
a professional association for Christian youth
workers and youth ministries, representing
numerous cooperating organizations.

Pioneer Clubs
PO Box 788
Wheaton, IL 60189-0788
(630) 293-1600
Fax: (630) 293-1600
E-mail: info@pioneerclubs.org
www.pioneerclubs.org

Pioneers Clubs is a proven church-sponsored
midweek club program for today's kids,
preschool through middle school. Each
week this Christ-centered program integrates
spiritual and personal development to help
boys and girls build healthy relationships.

Ring of Champions
PO Box 761101
Dallas, TX 75376-1101
(972) 298-1101
Fax: (972) 298-1101
E-mail: info@lifechampions.org
www.lifechampions.org

Ring of Champtions (ROC) is outreach
to at-risk juveniles. The crime rate among
juveniles continues to skyrocket each year.
Eighty-five percent of incarcerated youths grew
up in a fatherless home.

Village Life
3630 N High St
Columbus, OH 43214-3652
(614) 848-4870
Fax: (614) 848-4870
E-mail: mtaylor@coyfc.org

Youth guidance intervention through in-home
family counseling.

YFC Online
3630 N High St
Columbus, OH 43214-3652
(614) 848-4870
Fax: (614) 848-4870
E-mail: ctalbert@coyfc.org

Spreading God's love and the message of
salvation via Internet chat rooms and e-mail.

Young Life
PO Box 520
Colorado Springs, CO 80901-0520
(719) 381-1800
Fax: (719) 381-1800
www.younglife.org

Young Life is a nonprofit, interdenominational
Christian organization, committed for over 50
years to ministry with adolescents both in the
United States and around the world. Ministry
starts when trained staff and volunteers
befriend teenagers.

Youth for Christ/USA
PO Box 4478
Englewood, CO 80155-4478
(303) 843-9000
Fax: (303) 843-9000
E-mail: info@yfc.net
www.yfc.org

The target of Youth for Christ is all lost youth,
wherever they are found, regardless of racial,
ethnic, or economic background. Our major
objective is responsible youth evangelism and
the discipleship of these young people into the
church.

·YouthFront
4715 Rainbow Blvd
Mission, KS 66205-1832
(913) 262-3900
Fax: (913) 262-3900
E-mail: 1runyan@youthfront.com
www.YouthFront.com

YouthFront is a Youth Ministry with a full-time
staff of more than 40 employees. YouthFront
works to bring youth into a growing relationship
with Jesus Christ by creating environments
where spiritual transformation occurs.

INDEX

Special Offer!

Your purchase of Faith-Based Marketing entitles you to a **FREE** 90-day subscription to the book's companion web site, www.faithbased marketing.com. It's the ultimate faith-based marketing resource. At the site you'll find:

- A gigantic database of churches, ministries, denominations, gate-keepers, Christian media, marketing agencies, PR firms, music festivals and more. Use it to identify and connect with faith-based marketing partners.
- Bonus content including podcasts, articles, newsletters, interviews, case studies, videos, survey results, white papers, and more.
- A complete social network connecting the business and faith communities. Create your profile and then connect with others.
- Discussion forums where you can share what you know and learn from others.
- The Faith-Based Marketing blog.

Go to www.FaithBasedMarketing.com and click on the link that says *Free 90 Day Trial*. Between this book and the website, you'll have everything you need to reach this 140 million person market.